Living in Wisdom

Living in Wisdom

A Path to Embodying
Your Authentic Self,
Embracing Grief, and
Developing Self-Mastery

DEVI BROWN

balance

NEW YORK BOSTON

Copyright © 2025 by Devi Brown, Inc.
Foreword copyright © 2025 by Charlamagne tha God

Cover design by Jim Datz
Cover copyright © 2025 by Hachette Book Group, Inc.

Hachette Book Group supports the right to free expression and the value of copyright. The purpose of copyright is to encourage writers and artists to produce the creative works that enrich our culture.

The scanning, uploading, and distribution of this book without permission is a theft of the author's intellectual property. If you would like permission to use material from the book (other than for review purposes), please contact permissions@hbgusa.com. Thank you for your support of the author's rights.

Balance
Hachette Book Group
1290 Avenue of the Americas
New York, NY 10104
GCP-Balance.com
@GCPBalance

First edition: April 2025

Balance is an imprint of Grand Central Publishing. The Balance name and logo are registered trademarks of Hachette Book Group, Inc.

The publisher is not responsible for websites (or their content) that are not owned by the publisher.

Balance books may be purchased in bulk for business, educational, or promotional use. For information, please contact your local bookseller or the Hachette Book Group Special Markets Department at special.markets@hbgusa.com.

Illustrations by Christina Towne

Library of Congress Cataloging-in-Publication Data

Names: Brown, Devi, author.
Title: Living in wisdom : a path to embodying your authentic self, embracing grief, and developing self-mastery / Devi Brown.
Description: First edition. | New York : Balance, 2025. | Includes index.
Identifiers: LCCN 2024048351 | ISBN 9781538768228 (hardcover) | ISBN 9781538768242 (ebook)
Subjects: LCSH: Self-actualization (Psychology) | Grief. | Self-help techniques. | Psychic trauma.
Classification: LCC BF637.S4 B813 2025 | DDC 158.1—dc23/eng/20241209
LC record available at https://lccn.loc.gov/2024048351

ISBNs: 9781538768228 (hardcover), 9781538768242 (ebook)

Printed in Canada

MRQ-T

1   2025

For Mei Haskell

I pray you are free

Contents

Foreword		ix
Welcome		xiii

Part I
Dancing with Grief and Joy

Chapter 1:	Pain as Purpose: Your Permission to Shatter	3
Chapter 2:	Moving from Awareness to Acceptance	10

Part II
Practices for Higher Consciousness

Chapter 3:	Devotion and the Path to Your Highest Self	29
Chapter 4:	Connecting with Your Practice	41
Chapter 5:	The Pillars of Practice	52
Chapter 6:	Meditation	57
Chapter 7:	Breathwork/Pranayama	69
Chapter 8:	Self-Inquiry/Journaling	78
Chapter 9:	Affirming Statements and Qualitative Words	84
Chapter 10:	Movement and Touch	97
Chapter 11:	Recapitulation	105

viii CONTENTS

Part III
The Path to Living in Wisdom

Chapter 12:	Grieve	111
Chapter 13:	Release and Find Intention	126
Chapter 14:	Retreat	146
Chapter 15:	Heal and Accept	167
Chapter 16:	Self-Care and Devotion	193
Chapter 17:	Set Boundaries, Live in Choice	219
Chapter 18:	Experience Joy	242
Chapter 19:	Self-Love as Divine Love	263
	Conclusion: Living in Wisdom	275
	Thank You	279
	Notes	283
	Index	285

Foreword

What is wisdom exactly? One of my daughters asked me something similar recently; her question was, "How does someone become wise?" I thought about answering with *age*, but that would be a lie, because there's plenty of foolish-ass older people out here. So my reply was "Experiences make you wise. Not just experiences but what you learn from those experiences." We have all heard the saying "Smart people learn from their own mistakes; wise people learn from the mistakes of others." That's just another way of saying we learn from experiences. The experiences don't have to be yours; the experiences can be so-called good or so-called bad, but it's imperative that we absolutely learn from any and all experiences. It has been said, "Life doesn't happen to you, it happens for you." Anything you experience firsthand or any experience you are privy to witness is an opportunity for you to learn and grow wise from. One of the most powerful teachers life gives us is grief. The process of coping with loss. You have experienced it on some level. When we think of grief, we think of death, but grief can be felt because of a number of reasons—the end of a marriage, the loss of a job or career, by being diagnosed with a disease and losing your good health. The end of a friendship. When it comes to the human experience, grief is a thread that weaves through each of our lives. It connects us all in a shared, yet deeply personal journey of loss and longing. It is an emotion that defies easy explanation, one that can render us speechless. We use the word a lot, but I honestly don't believe any of us ever take the time to grieve at all. Grief is something nobody wants to live with, but I pose a question. How come whenever

x   FOREWORD

we discuss "taking a loss," we say things like "Learn from your losses, that's how you win," "You learn more from your losses than your gains," and "If you do not learn from your losses, you will be ruled by them." We believe all those quotes when they apply to losing superficial things but not when it comes to grieving the loss of a life? I know grief can be a very dark place, which is why I thank God my good sister Devi Brown is willing to step into this darkness with grace and wisdom, offering a beacon of light to those navigating the often tumultuous seas of grief.

Devi is no stranger to the complexities of human emotion. She is willing to share stories from her personal journey of dealing with grief to show others that with grief comes the higher consciousness, embodied wisdom. As she once said to me, "Allowing wisdom to bloom is our sacred service to the world. My wisdom because of my experiences is how I serve." And that is exactly what she does on a daily basis. A seasoned wellness expert, a spiritual teacher, and an advocate for inner healing, Devi has spent years helping others explore the depths of their souls. Her voice is both compassionate and unflinchingly honest. Her ability to communicate complex emotions in a digestible way is why I call her "Tupac Chopra." Let me tell you something about Devi Brown. I first met her in 2007 or 2008. She is a natural guide, a natural healer. The first time I touched down in LA, she grabbed me by the hand and showed me the city, introduced me to an emerging crop of new artists from the West Coast who went by the names of Kendrick Lamar and Nipsey Hussle. Everything she did then and does now is with intention, and even as I think about her describing these artists to me, what she was drawn to were the higher levels of consciousness that both these artists were displaying. It wasn't so much who they then presented themselves to be as much as it was about who these individuals were destined to be. They displayed a level of self-mastery that only became greater and more refined with life's experiences. There was a wisdom to be unlocked in both of these young men that would influence generations, and Devi Brown recognized that early because you see what you are in others. Kendrick was always destined to be Kendrick, and Nipsey was

FOREWORD   xi

always destined to be Nipsey, but you have to live life and go through certain experiences (sadly even sometimes death) to attain the wisdom and mastery that will teach you and educate others. That's what makes Devi Brown a master teacher. The Devi who was doing radio, running around in Chuck Taylors, and introducing me to hip-hop artists is the same Devi who is a well-known wellness educator, introducing my family and me to meditation, Reiki, and a whole host of other practices to help with healing and attaining self-mastery. God created Devi to be humanity's North Star. To give us tools to help us navigate this journey called life. *Living in Wisdom* guides us through the process of embracing grief—not as something to be conquered, but as a profound teacher that shapes our lives in ways we never could have imagined.

In a world that often urges us to "move on" or "get over" our pain, Devi invites us to sit with our grief, to listen to it, and to learn from it. As painful as this may be, she reminds us that grief is not a sign of weakness, but a testament to the love we have shared and the connections we have forged. Devi illustrates that embracing grief is not about succumbing to sorrow, but about honoring the fullness of our human experience and getting us to the highest levels of self-mastery.

Living in Wisdom is not just a guide to coping with loss; it is a heartfelt exploration of how grief can transform us into master teachers. It is a call to open our hearts, to be present with our pain, and to discover the resilience that lies within. Devi is challenging us to find a deeper understanding of the journey we are on. When we learn to embrace grief, we realize we are not alone—we are part of a collective experience that connects us all in our shared humanity. Devi reminds us that even in the depths of sorrow, there is always a path to healing, to growth, and to a greater sense of peace. One of the quotes I used earlier, "If you do not learn from your losses, you will be ruled by them"—well, when you embrace grief, you take your power back. In embracing grief, we embrace life in all its beauty and complexity, and in doing so we will find our way back to ourselves and we thank God we have a guide like Devi Brown to lead us home.

—*Charlamagne tha God*

Welcome

Hi, welcome. I am so proud of you for being here. I thank you for coming, and I'd like to invite you to take a moment to thank yourself for arriving here too. For having the courage to take the first small but essential step toward expanding your life and its infinite possibilities for joy, pleasure, wisdom, alignment, and purpose by simply opening this book. For giving yourself permission to explore shedding all the layers that are not serving you and what you are meant to do in this lifetime. For investing this time, even if it's only reading the next couple of pages before you have to move on to the next thing life demands. Whatever your relationship with reading this book looks like, I appreciate it and you.

Take a moment now to get comfortable in your physical space. Maybe that's covering yourself with your favorite blanket or tucking an extra pillow behind your back. Maybe it's lighting your favorite candle or turning on soothing music. Maybe it's simply sitting up a little bit taller, or taking as deep a breath as your body will currently allow. There is no wrong way to do so, and there is no judgment here.

Or if all of that is already making you feel like chucking this book across the room, forget it. I got you. I'm here with you either way. We are, for the next 285 pages, in this together: I as your guide, you as the seeker of your own exponential potential beyond the limitations of suffering or self-doubt, and this book as the soft, gentle space for doing the work that that will require.

xiv   WELCOME

★ ★ ★

One of my favorite things to come out of 2020, if you can imagine having such a thing, is this idea of a "soft space." Not a safe space, a *soft* space. Because despite anyone's best intentions, education, or expertise, there is no credible way that they could have the certainty with which to claim that their space is safe for anybody else. There are simply too many individual experiences we have all lived through, and it is impossible for anyone to intuit what safety means to someone else. I cannot assure you that what lies ahead will not unnerve you. Trigger you. Shake you. Make you want to turn your attention to something—anything—else. In fact, much of what this path requires is that you confront those feelings when the time comes. But nothing before its time. You will not venture forth without first being equipped with the right tools. I am not sending you to slay any dragons without first arming you with the sharpest, nimblest sword. And armor. And a map. Plus a few snacks for the road.

And so, no, this is not a safe space. Nor would you want it to be—because facing the discomfort head-on is core curriculum when it comes to healing. Looking your pain in the eye, refusing to look away, and then finding the beauty and value in that experience is the necessary work. What I can provide you with, however, is the comfort of knowing that I have marked the path for you. The balm of helping you make sense of and eventually feel a sense of ownership of your experiences. And the solace of knowing that every page you turn is bringing you closer to ease. To surrender. To grace. To creation. To a well-lived life unencumbered by pain.

How do I know that? Because I've lived it.

Over the last few years, I have been slammed with loss and upheaval. In a short span of time, I lost people to violence, experienced significant family turmoil, and was severely betrayed by a loved one just as the world went into lockdown and we all collectively unpacked our greatest fears around race, sex, and class.

These experiences not only wove grief into the fabric of my soul but also reopened the deep wounds I'd believed I had healed through more than a decade of profound spiritual and emotional work. Because grief is not new to me. In fact, to say that I had been devoting my life to healing is a vast and unsatisfying understatement. I *embodied* healing. Despite parts of myself and my life that threatened to swallow me whole, I thrived. Not only that, I've helped millions of other people thrive. And yet. When my equilibrium was challenged once again, I had to go back to the well myself.

The thing is, despite all of the work I had done, despite how badly I wanted to power through, despite how many times I'd been told how resilient I was or how successful I'd become despite where I'd been and what I'd experienced—things that may ring true for you as well—I had only begun to scratch the surface of depths I still needed to explore. I hadn't drilled down to the root of the root, the core wound. I was still holding on to limiting beliefs, traversing coping behavioral patterns, and otherwise building a life *around* that wound. And because of that, my usual go-to practices were no longer able to serve me. Sitting in meditation didn't bring me the same solace. Being in my body was too excruciating, too loud. The academic and spiritual texts I'd steeped myself in were just that—written word that could penetrate only my mind and not my cells. If I was going to survive the crushing weight of these fresh traumas that I was spiraling through, in addition to the thirty-plus years of past trauma that it had triggered, then I was going to have to completely excavate my life and forge a new set of tools to better serve the deep restoration I was so desperately in need of:

Tools that would give me a more profound understanding of and relationship with my wound

Tools that would make space for grief instead of denying its existence or even its benefit

Tools that would allow for me not just to intellectually understand the path to healing but to absorb it on a cellular level

Tools that would crack open the sweetness and possibility of life

Tools that would align me with my higher purpose

xvi   WELCOME

Not exactly a week's to-do list.

But I had to start somewhere, and so I started with what I knew. I combined my own intuition and self-knowledge with the centuries of wisdom traditions I had been studying for most of my life, everything from Ayurveda to Catholicism, Buddhism to astrology, Sufi mysticism to plant medicine. I mined my experience working with my teacher Dr. Deepak Chopra and holding space for the teacher community as an educator and executive with Chopra Global.

For two years, I cut anything out of my life that wasn't related to my healing or to meeting my son's needs and my mission to raise him with joy. Then I delved into the deepest level of devotion to myself that I've ever known. Every night after my son went to bed, I'd revisit the supportive practice that I was building in real time, whether that was breathwork, journaling, taking a bath, rubbing myself down with aromatic oils, dancing, screaming, or crying—or all of the above. I forced myself into a steady sleep protocol and tended to my most basic and crucial physiological needs. I learned how to breathe again. I took my body's lead in how it wanted to move and feel.

What I discovered was that what felt best was often described in existing wisdom traditions, such as somatics, yogic pranayama, and Vedic healing. With the help of that timeless expanse of knowledge, I developed my own personalized set of rituals and tools. Practices for releasing old patterns, finding new intention and purpose, creating boundaries that protected me from people and commitments that no longer served that purpose, and understanding that Divine love begins with self-love. And most importantly, practices for grieving and for understanding that to properly do so, continuously and unequivocally, was the key that unlocked the path to healing.

Then, whenever I applied something to myself that felt right, I'd turn around and teach it to my students the very next day. We were healing together in real time, in a way that no one was really talking about before 2020. The "wellness community," as it was accessible to most people at that time, barely had a place for trauma. The BIPOC community often had to wedge itself into spaces that either didn't acknowledge or understand their experiences or just negated them. But more than anything, many of these mainstream practices and modalities undermined or even ignored grief. They often espoused "radical gratitude" or positivity, which in my experience is synonymous with emotional bypass. They didn't recognize that understanding pain is just as necessary and valuable as recognizing love and joy. Which is how I came to know why I was put on this planet in this lifetime: to teach that the point of this experience and of this life is not to erase our pain, but to *embrace* it.

Despite the gritty, shadowy parts of myself I was having to confront throughout this process, I was also living out some of the most purposeful, synchronistic, magical, and impactful experiences I could ever fathom. My life was simultaneously filled with grief and joy, both parts pulling me apart while transforming me into the most authentic, powerful, spiritual, conscious, and fulfilled version of myself. I was gifted with the realization: If I was going to experience hardship—as we are destined to during our lifetimes—why not reap the privilege of it? Why not emerge from it with a higher level of awareness and a more profound wisdom and self-acceptance than what I started with? It was just as the Sufi mystic Rumi so sagely prescribed: "Let darkness be your candle." I've been living in devotion to that wisdom ever since.

Now I invite you to join me.

Living in Wisdom

Just as everything in my life has pointed me to exactly who I am in this moment, including my suffering, this book is your guide to letting your experiences—your suffering—sculpt you into a higher, more evolved version of self. It is about helping you recognize the blocks that keep you from yourself and then dissolving them. And it is about embracing these truths:

You can heal your life while fully living it.
You can learn from life while enjoying it.

xviii   WELCOME

You can cultivate a stable inner peace even amid the collective chaos
we have all been subjected to these past few years—and will
most likely continue to live through.
You can release control and find the flow for your life's unique path.
You do not have to be someone else to find what you're looking for.
You can learn to experience grief and joy as two sides of the same
coin of the human experience.

This book is about pointing you back inside, back to yourself. It is
about it feeling safe, even pleasurable, to look in the mirror. It is a full-
bodied approach—for mind, body, and spirit—using a combination of
spirituality, psychology, and ancient wisdom traditions. Regardless of
whether you're grappling with trauma or Trauma, or whether your pain
stems from generations of tragedy or from simply experiencing the fric-
tion of being a person in this world, I will walk you through the neces-
sary steps for making peace with grief and hurt, recognizing patterns
that no longer serve you, connecting with healing modalities that do,
and reclaiming the kind of love and understanding of yourself that will
permeate every single facet of your life.

While we'll spend plenty of time exploring what exactly these new
concepts mean, this book is less about the learning of wisdom than it
is about the *living* of it. When I was picking up the pieces of my newly
shattered self, I quickly realized the significant difference between
knowing and *being*. I saw how a lack of embodiment—or the actual phys-
ical expression of an idea—had been a barrier to my own healing.

Taking an intellectual approach to healing is something you can
most likely relate to. For example, reading a book like this to learn
about ideas for changing your life. (Although, as you'll see, this is no
ordinary book.) It's the way we *know*, for example, that meditation is a
good thing to do. We *know* that trauma has affected our experience and
that we struggle with feeling worthy. We *know* much of what triggers
us. We *know* that healthy habits will nourish us and make our lives feel
fuller. This list of what we know is endless, and yet, still, life doesn't

change. The goals and dreams go unachieved. Fear and self-sabotage seem to rule, and the little voice telling us that we're not enough seems to always win.

"Knowing" sends many of us into therapy, where we work for years unpacking childhood wounds and increasing our self-awareness, growing the list of what we know to be true about ourselves. We do all the work mentally, but at the exclusion of our bodies. And when we keep wisdom in our minds, breakthroughs tend to stay there. We then get trapped in this knowing, and instead of letting it free us, we stay, stuck, in rumination.

This book is the next piece to put into place for your spiritual awakening. Because when you take your body with you on your healing journey, magic happens. Like a slowly descending elevator, this book will escort the wisdom from the mind into the heart and soul so real transformation can occur. With the practices and rituals detailed in the following chapters—what I like to think of as spells for everyday life—you're going to perform actual alchemy. You're going to create and transform and transcend with the help of these simple but significant tools. Through them you'll learn to:

- Find breakthroughs to old blocks
- Heal childhood wounds
- Move through stagnation, restlessness, numbness, and despair
- Deepen self-acceptance
- Connect to your creativity
- Meet each moment with confidence
- Cultivate joy in your life
- Find power in your authentic self
- Trust in yourself and in your unique life path
- Live in integrity

The fact is, we are constantly dancing between grief and joy. One is just as inevitable as the other. My responsibility, one that I've devoted

xx   **WELCOME**

my life to, is to help you surrender to this truth, honor the discomfort, feel every single bit of it, and expand your ability to do so. We all deserve to know how to connect to and grow a stable inner world that can withstand our outer one. It requires burning the curtain between the persona and the person, expanding your consciousness, and supporting your own humanity through daily practices. Yes, that will require work on your part, but I promise that I'll be there every step of the way. And that you'll walk away feeling more curious and creative, seen and heard, guided and liberated, and inhabiting every inch of who you are.

So I ask you, in this moment: What are you ready to heal for the last time?

The journey begins now, and it is a beautiful one.

Big love,
Devi

Part I

Dancing with Grief and Joy

Chapter 1

Pain as Purpose:
Your Permission to Shatter

The wound is the place where the light enters you.
—Rumi

When I was twenty-two years old, I was hit by a drunk driver. I was heading to a Christmas party when a truck plowed into my Toyota Corolla, crushing it like a roach. The driver took off. First responders had to use the Jaws of Life to pull me out, and my injuries were so significant that I could barely walk for months. I was in excruciating pain because I had no insurance to cover the morphine and rehab I required just to live a semi-normal life. At this time, I was also still in the throes of grieving the loss of my closest friend, Wayne. Four years prior, when I was eighteen years old, just beginning college and learning how to exist in a world that was at many times inhospitable to women of color, he was murdered. Shot through the heart, less than an hour after the last time I hugged him. Ours was one of the most meaningful relationships I'd ever had in my life, perhaps the first to show me what true, unconditional friendship could look like. He taught me to drive; he brought me groceries. Between juggling classes and a job and not having any real community surrounding me at school, I was never fully able to grieve in real time. And while I did begin to open to the possibility that God could carry me through the intense hollowing

4 LIVING IN WISDOM

out that was occurring on repeat every morning when I cried myself awake, I was in agony.

A few weeks after the accident, my mother went to finalize the salvaging of my car, which had been towed, unsalvageable, to the dump. Out of due diligence, she checked inside to see whether there was anything important left to claim. Like most people's cars, mine had become littered with all of life's necessities and detritus, but none of it stood a chance of surviving the crash. When my mom looked in the passenger side, though, there on the dash, completely untouched, was Wayne's picture that I had kept there to watch over me. It had fallen neatly on top of the only other unscathed item: a rosary.

In that moment, in those depths of darkness I was blindly feeling my way through, I could suddenly sense that I was not alone. It made me certain that Wayne was watching over me, and it expanded my sense of God and the Universe. Inexplicably, in the wake of the most terrifyingly awful physical and emotional experiences I've ever had, I felt *safer*. I could see the synchronicity and the way Divine energy could move in your life when you open to the awfulness of it all.

But the real mastery of this idea didn't come until about fifteen years later, when my marriage was ripped apart. Up until that point, every single setback, shock, and upset would barely draw blood. I was somehow able to keep going. This was something else. This struck at a truth that I had never been able to face; it splintered the self-righteousness that I had where I was putting people who had hurt me *above* me. And I just shattered into a million pieces. It was as though someone with a sledgehammer had hit me from the inside. It hurt so much I thought it might actually kill me. I kept having to come up with reasons to move through this intense, unbearable pain because at that point, to be quite honest, I really didn't know if I could. But I knew that I had to let this change me. I couldn't fight anymore. I couldn't resist feeling ashamed and humiliated. I couldn't resist facing this reality of some of my deepest fears coming true.

But in that release, in the thick of one of the darkest moments of my

PAIN AS PURPOSE: YOUR PERMISSION TO SHATTER 5

life, I got just a taste of something sweeter. I couldn't call it joy because I wasn't yet able to access that feeling. It was *freedom*. This awful, painful life that I had been gripping tightly for eight years was finally done. I didn't have to pretend to be perfect anymore. I didn't have to be the bigger, more rational person anymore. That was all lying in pieces on the floor. Not even pieces—the dust of complete and total annihilation. And for the first time, I realized that I didn't have to pick it up.

Normally, I'd always be sweeping up the pieces and gluing them back together as best I could, over and over again, a complete mutation of God's plan for me. But as soon as I looked down at those infinitesimal shards lying around me, I realized there was no point in even trying to get out the broom. It was impossible. The pieces were too microscopic. And as soon as I accepted that, whatever *it* was, I felt relief. Because I never, ever wanted to go back again to where I had been.

Yet, while I knew where I was *not* going, I had no idea where that meant I was actually going, or what I wanted to become. I was in a void, a no-man's-land of becoming. I didn't have any directions for navigating through it. I didn't have any ability to be that or do that. The only prayer I could summon for days was *Please, God, don't let my heart close. Please, please, please; I've worked my whole life to keep it open.* I would not let my heart wither and die. I would slowly bring it back to life. I would let it stretch open, and in the right Divine time, God would show me what I was.

Around that time, I'd started a women's group through my private client practice Karma Bliss. It was at the start of the pandemic, and I was led by God to create something called the "Divine Time-Out." It was birthed from knowing that this moment would be an *opportunity* for all of us to grow. I just kept coming back to that idea in my mind—the opportunity of it all. The chaos, the uncertainty, the fear, the pain; it was like a portal, begging us to all ask ourselves, *What am I being called to become?* I posed that question everywhere—in that group, on social media, on my podcast. Because we were being handed a real gift, as much as it might have hurt.

I realized that when you allow yourself to really be rocked by all of it,

6   LIVING IN WISDOM

when you allow pain to change you, you open up this energetic force field that actually attracts the miraculous nature of the world—especially with the intention and desire to keep your heart open. It can bring in such an onslaught of miraculous energy from people and places. It can unlock an ease that is the Universe's and God's (both concepts I define well beyond Abrahamic tenets, or the language of any particular religion, as we'll talk about in a bit) contribution to us. If we are willing to accept that pain does serve a purpose, and if we're willing to sit with it and witness it, then we're able to come into this expanded experience of self.

People like to say that the healing process after shattering is putting the pieces back together again. What I realized is that the breakthrough *is* the shattering—and then realizing you don't want to be tidied back into a vessel. **Or that you don't want to be contained at all.** I wondered, *What if I'm just here to be broken and bare and raw?* I touched the power of being broken, and it was one of the most gorgeously pivotal, potent experiences I've ever had. It made me see that you'll never be as potent as you are when you're broken so completely that there is nothing left but to master those battered parts and be wide open to what God and the Universe have to teach you.

Before this point, I had a lot of practices in place. I meditated daily. I did yoga. I had a wellness business. I was doing good works. I was being seen and received as someone who had a higher consciousness. But when I finally relented and shattered and realized that I didn't want to plug myself back into old patterns, I also realized that I was going to need new practices to achieve that, ones informed by years and systems of study, but also by intuition, the freedom to create, and devotion to the process. It was from that place of brokenness that I was finally able to grow, to transcend, and to move forward into the unknown with spiritual confidence.

When I was looking for lighting fixtures to add to the sacred healing space I maintain at my home, my dear friend and interior designer

Tiffany Howell brought me to the studio of the artist Jason Koharik. It was an entire aircraft hangar filled with his creations, many of which are sculptures that capture a moment in time. For example, a pillow from his sofa that he'd cast in plaster after a woman, depressed and in tears over a breakup, had collapsed there and cried into it. About an hour later, he'd picked up that pillow, completely unchanged with her indentation and tears, and preserved it. In the corner of his studio, there was a dining room table. On the table was a potted plant in a vase that had broken, accidentally, dirt everywhere. He'd left it there as a centerpiece, a snapshot in time. And the plant, which had touched the point of no return after that irreversible trauma, was now growing again. I saw myself in that process. I saw the power of being both broken and freed from containment. Of the potential and beginning anew as *anything*.

So ask yourself: *What happens if I let myself break completely? What would happen if my soul were to shatter?* Would you hear a voice reminding you of everything you have already survived and reassuring you that, in one way or another, you'll survive this? Where would you go from there?

Allowing the Break Before the Build

Over the course of this book, I will be providing a road map for where to go after you let the pieces hit the floor, as well as all the tools you'll need for receiving the lessons. But first you have *to let those pieces hit the floor.* You have to allow the shattering to happen. Because one thing I've come to know for sure is that this energy, as heavy and leveling as I know it feels, is miraculous energy. It feels so heavy because it is charged, but that also means that you can use that charge for the highest good. For the highest miraculous intention. You just have to be willing to harness that energy and transmute it.

So when you do let the pieces fall, you're not going to plow through until you feel comfortable again. Instead, we're going to build your capacity for grief and suffering so you can learn how to maneuver within them. I'm going to teach you to support these feelings as they pass and

8   LIVING IN WISDOM

reap the wisdom as they do. I'm going to sit with you in the dark and help you make peace with the pain while we wait for the light to gradually seep back in. I'm going to hold your hand while you call out to God, *If you're giving me this to carry, then you have to show up for me too. Where's my joy, God? I want to see it today. Where's my miracle, God? I want to have it today.* And you will. When that light begins to fill your space once again, you're going to see life for what it is, how unfinished it all is, and how unfinished your understanding *of yourself* is in it. And what a clean slate you now have because, whether by choice or not, you had to let it all go.

What you can know is that when you surrender, profound and unquantifiable change can arrive:

- Ease and grace flow into your life—ease in both old and existing relationships, and ease in compassion with the way you experience yourself.
- It activates your intuition on the highest level, allowing you to make better choices more quickly.
- You experience even greater self-respect and personal power.
- You build your self-trust and your capacity to both experience challenges and transcend them.
- You **suffer less**.

When you sit in the shattering, you make yourself more comfortable with what is. So when you heal from this place, you can finally come into acceptance that your life is your life, that your experiences have been your experiences. It doesn't mean that you have to build your identity around your trauma or that it has to be an active pain point, but healing is not waving a magic wand and erasing intrusive thoughts or wiping those experiences from your memory entirely. Because that will never happen, and that is not how life is designed. Our goal here is not to make it so that you'll never be triggered again—you're going to be triggered by these wounds every single day. But the way you'll relate to them and the speed with which you can extricate yourself from

PAIN AS PURPOSE: YOUR PERMISSION TO SHATTER 9

their grip will shift. In the past, you might have spiraled for a day or a week or a month—you may have been pissed for an entire year. When you're operating from this new place of understanding and awareness, that could become twenty minutes, or thirty seconds, or an instantaneous shift. Because you'll be able to observe it and then release it. That's the piece about acceptance that is so valuable and powerful—to accept something doesn't mean that you're okay with it happening. To accept something simply means that it is true, and that it happened. And once you're in acceptance of it, you get to choose how you maneuver within it versus it controlling how you maneuver in your life. **The acceptance *is* the healing.**

Then, when you come into acceptance that this life and these experiences are yours to own, you can begin to connect with your purpose and build your own "spiritual curriculum," or what you were meant to learn (and teach) in this lifetime. It is why, for whatever amount of time I am blessed with being here for, I am committed to doing the work. That work—the breathing, the mantras, the journaling, the meditation, the practices that bring me into alignment with my grief and my joy—is what creates space. The space to feel. The space for potential. The space to *be*. And that is where the freedom is.

Chapter 2

Moving from Awareness to Acceptance

So *how* do we heal? *How* do we get to that place of higher awareness and purpose? If you are like most of the people I have worked with through their suffering, you are wrestling with those questions right now. You, like them, are educated about the tools that exist out there. You, like them, have most likely tried "doing the work." You, like them, could give me all the terminology about your suffering and can tell me where and why it hurts. And yet, as I hear again and again, "I'm still suffering." And so it's time to heal.

The way you're going to do that is by following the process I shaped after my own path to healing. It involves eight crucial steps, each reverse engineered from the wound to the wisdom, from the pain to the medicine. These steps are designed to be layered, to help you build bridges of connection in mind and body, and to follow the flow of what I believe a full, complete healing journey looks like. They are:

1. Grieve
2. Release and Find Intention
3. Retreat
4. Heal and Accept
5. Self-Care and Devotion
6. Set Boundaries, Live in Choice

MOVING FROM AWARENESS TO ACCEPTANCE   11

7. Experience Joy
8. Self-Love as Divine Love

But as you also most likely know by now, these steps are not a checklist. This is not a weekend of vision boarding or a New Year's resolution. There is no medal for completion. Rather, each of these steps is part of a deeper lifelong process that is designed to help you fully embody this knowledge. For that reason, each of these steps could take you years to work through—and that's okay.

The Keys to Healing

While you are moving through these eight steps, you are actually undergoing a bigger, more significant transformation. The slow movement through and repetition of the rituals I will ask you to be doing every single day in part 2 in conjunction with them builds a practice. It is a practice that requires **devotion**, and it is through devotion that you build **mastery**—mastery of **creation**, mastery of **intention**, and mastery of **wisdom**—in order to arrive at **purpose**.

These are the **keys to healing**.

These principles are what are actively reshaping neural pathways in your brain, literally reprogramming you from the inside out. They are how you will be able to climb out from under ruminating thoughts, endless negative feedback loops, old damaging patterns, and feeling stuck. They are the motor behind your ascension from awareness to acceptance. They are the secret ingredients that make the healing process work, and they are ultimately what life is all about.

Devotion

The path to mastery is paved with devotion. I like to describe devotion as a dance with discipline. It is an appreciation for slow, methodical repetition without any expectation of an outcome. It's not going on a diet and anticipating that you'll hit a set goal weight. Rather, it is being in romance with the notion that you have no idea what the destination will be, and then being connected to the process of that unfolding. Because in that process is alchemy; in that process is blooming.

Devotion is discipline but with the added layer of beauty or pleasure. In fact, in some healing traditions, it is believed that the "path of beauty" or the "way of beauty" is its own system of healing. This isn't a far-out idea—hospitals have added healing gardens, or spaces methodically planted with many types of flowers meant not only to invoke beauty but also, more importantly, to nourish the nervous system.

There's a reason we are drawn to aesthetics—beautiful things and beautiful people. Beauty holds power. You can see it in the inverse too: When people, especially women, have experienced trauma or pain, they want to *reject* beauty. Namely because it feels frivolous or silly, especially in contrast to the ugliness or darkness we're feeling inside. And we start to internalize that void of beauty, refusing to look at our reflection in the mirror or the car window and avoiding seeing our physical selves by any means.

Whenever I'm teaching about self-care—that frequently used, maybe even *over*used term that's become so triggering to so many people—I have to break it down for my students. I ask them, "Do you have room to care about yourself a little bit more?" Because rejection of self-care is a rejection of caring for yourself. Which makes a lot of sense if you're coming from a place of trauma—maybe no one has ever cared for you or you've always had to be the one to care for yourself. So the idea of self-care pisses you off. That's your way of getting back at life, by not caring for yourself. *Devotion* is the remedy. Devotion is the slow work and slow build of your own worth, toward experiencing yourself as valuable, experiencing yourself as sacred, and experiencing yourself as holy. It is the difference between the pursuit of knowledge and the pursuit of wisdom. And it is a reclamation of power.

As you traverse the steps of this book, remember that at their core is

MOVING FROM AWARENESS TO ACCEPTANCE   13

devotion. And remember that finding the moments of beauty and pleasure within that discipline and repetition is the key to healing. Think of this process as romancing and building intimacy with your deepest, truest self.

Creation

I believe we exist solely to create. I think about this, nonreligiously though spiritually, through the lens of the Bible and Christianity, which says that God created us in God's image. So if God is the creator of all, and God created us in God's image, that must mean that we, too, are creators. We, too, have been put here on this planet to create, and I don't just mean making babies or content for social media.

I don't mean great masterpieces either. The contrary—I believe that something as small as our *choices* can be a significant creation. I worked with an energy healer years ago, when I was incredibly depressed in my marriage. She said to me, "You have to own your creations." I was like, *What do you mean? I didn't* create *any of this nonsense!* The way I saw it, I was just trying to be a good person, attempting to heal and help my husband. But what this woman made me realize was that staying with him was a choice, one that made me a cocreator in the container that was my own self-destruction.

Every single choice we make is a creation. Every single choice we make curates our experience. This is why it's essential to learn how to make choices from your highest self, the self most in alignment with your truest needs and truest purpose. It's why the healing journey is paved by every single moment that you use your free will to be in practice with and devotion of that highest self.

That's why one of the most grotesque consequences of experiencing trauma is the way it can limit your possibility and potential, because that trauma often limits your choices in some way. God gifted us with free will; it is the governing structure of our existence. It is the essence of why we are here; choice and creation are our purpose. So it is not

14   LIVING IN WISDOM

a coincidence, to look to Christianity once again, that the gravest sins you can commit against another human being are those that rob them of their free will and ability to choose and create. But when you do the work and open the space within yourself, this also opens the potential for creation. Who can you be now? What does that entail? It's limitless. The work creates *limitlessness* potential.

Creation is your cure for karma. Creation is the possibility to change your life, to make entire new worlds, inside and out. Creation, making new choices, is the *only* way to break apart and clear away old patterns, belief systems, barriers, and behaviors that cause you harm. You do that by acknowledging and accepting all of your creations so far, observing where there has been beauty and where there has been pain, and then asking yourself, *What needs to be released now? Moving forward, what and how am I choosing? Is it a nourishing choice? An evolutionary one?*

Creation is also how we serve. Service is why we are here. As you move through these practices, remember: *I am devoted to creation, I am devoted to creation, I am devoted to creation . . .*

Lastly, remember that it is not always the big choices that change your life. Very often it's more so those small daily choices, the tiny shifts in awareness that create the pathways for the big shifts to take root. Every choice you make matters.

A Word on God

I frequently refer to "God" when talking about spiritual practices or connecting to a higher power or purpose. But I am not necessarily referencing a singular deity tied to religion or faith—namely because I don't believe in one religion; I believe in all religions. So when I think of God, I'm also thinking about my higher self, my intuition, and my deeper wisdom. When I think of God, I'm also thinking about the patterns and understanding of all humanity over time. The entirety of creation and

MOVING FROM AWARENESS TO ACCEPTANCE   15

earthly experience. I also think of God in terms of all the unseen assistance we receive in so many different forms, whether that's the saints or ascended masters or angels or energy or chakras. I see God as consciousness itself. It's the container. The only way I can know God is based on what I know of earth and humanity. I look at God as a way of understanding the experiences and the systems of operation here on earth—which is also why God is so different for everyone. I think of God as a benevolent and supportive energy, as facilitating for us experiences that are neither "good" nor "bad"—because God does not have preference or judgment. (I also do not believe there is a "good" or "bad" in the universal understanding, only what we humans assign.)

I once heard that when asked what the point of life is, why we're all here, God responded, "Because I longed to experience myself." Those words sank so deeply into my cells; they completely changed how I thought about the role that God plays in my life. Many of us project this essence onto the idea of God, the belief that God is a parental figure or authority figure or someone we're trying to please. This idea of God simply existing to exist releases all of that pressure. It makes God so *real* because *God is experience itself*. "I longed to experience myself"—is that not the core of every single one of us and all of our creations?

The idea of the mutual longing between us and God and God and us is what I credit for so much of my spiritual growth. Rumi, whose poetry is passionately charged with this same desire, once wrote, "Seek the wisdom that will untie your knot. Seek the path that demands your whole being." Over the course of my healing journey, I have pored over those words, savoring each syllable and sentiment. It ultimately became my mission statement,

16   LIVING IN WISDOM

driving me forth on a higher path in a higher light, moti-
vating me to go to therapy, to meditate, to devote myself
to all the processes. Because, and I still deeply believe
this, it's all God. God is the question and the answer.

Integrity

If devotion to making choices aligned with our highest selves is the
path to mastery and wisdom, then so too is integrity. You simply cannot
achieve mastery, or any progress, if you are not living by moral values
that extend to all facets of your human experience—physical, mental,
emotional, and spiritual. Integrity informs the caliber of every interac-
tion you have, the work you do, and the quality of person people hold
you to be. It is the great up-leveler.

Like any other step in this process, that might be activating for you.
I once posted something about integrity on social media and a young
man replied, "B*tch, shut the f*ck up. We're fucking struggling and
dying; we don't have time for f*cking integrity." I get that.

It's *hard* making righteous choices when you don't have your basic
needs met. When you're struggling financially or in an environment
where none of this is reflected back at you. It's a massive barrier to your
healing, one you didn't even put up. But there is no *change* without
integrity. Every time you make an integral choice or stand as an integral
person, it transmutes the options that are available to you. Which means
that integrity is the place from which your life, and everything in it,
blossoms. It's once again these moment–by–moment opportunities to
have a higher awareness. That is what gives way to living a life that feels
aligned and to having more experiences with grace and ease.

Mastery

Mastery is the boundless, invaluable outcome of applying devotion, cre-
ativity, and integrity to oneself and one's life every single day. It is the

MOVING FROM AWARENESS TO ACCEPTANCE 17

arrival at the most unshakable version of your most authentic self. It is a sense of calm and personal power—what I like to think of as armor from the urge to be a people pleaser or from living in a reactionary state. Because mastery is freedom from the need to control. It is a deep, authentic confidence in yourself, but more than that, it is a deep trust in who and what you are. There's an ease to removing obstacles and getting things done. It's as though the Universe is conspiring to clear the path—which makes sense, because when you are truly your authentic self, you are naturally in service to everyone and everything else. There is a magnetism to mastery, a charisma. A power.

In our society, we like to use the word *expert*, but that is not necessarily mastery. To be an expert is not quantifiable. I've noticed that people are quick to distinguish themselves as "experts." Truly mastering a thing doesn't happen after a weekend course of study. To put this in clearer context, think about the historical implications of the word *mastery*. It used to be that mastery required an apprenticeship, along with precision, dedication, obsession, repetition, and humility. There were countless errors that preceded perfection, and even then, perfection was elusive because mastery is a continuous work in progress. That kind of metabolism doesn't exist as readily for us to see here and now, but that is God's intended path for us. To live in service of and reverence for that mastery of ourselves.

And yet, the barriers to mastery are very real. There's the assumption many of us hold that we don't deserve something better. Or that if we attempt something new, we'll be laughed at. Or we compare ourselves to others. Those limiting beliefs have prevented millions of people from living in purpose and in service and transcending into their wisdom.

Also, the barriers to just *existing* are very real. There have been so many moments in my life when all people can see of my experience is the professional success, being on television, interviewing celebrities, working with Dr. Chopra. What they don't see is the little girl who had to move every few years, often to places where people didn't look or

18 LIVING IN WISDOM

sound like me, and struggle to establish a community. Who attended schools where there was no expectation of going to college, or sometimes even surviving. The latchkey kid who constantly felt vulnerable and alone, worrying myself sick about my mother and whether the two of us would be okay. They don't see the years I spent financially supporting myself through college while working two jobs and an internship, taking the bus for four hours a day, while exhausted, depressed, and starving. People have had no idea what it took just for me to keep going all these years. But when you're in it, *you* know. You know that feeling of *Goddamn, it never stops* or *I can't believe I still have to deal with all this garbage*. But the more you move through the practices we'll explore together, the quieter that voice becomes until you can feel calm inside of yourself.

You have permission to take the things that were once barriers to connection and devotion and creation and to make them part of your mastery; God knows you've earned it. Believe me, I know it takes work. It's taken me my whole life to arrive at this place. But, after consistently working my pain and setbacks into my devotion and creation, I've developed an unshakable reverence for *me*—not in an egoic or self-aggrandizing or arrogant way. It's just that I know what it has taken for me to arrive at myself, and goddamn I am grateful to myself for sitting in it. That's given me a tremendous amount of respect for the core of who I am. And we all deserve to feel that.

I want everyone undergoing this process to have a real respect for what they've been through. A reverence for everything it took to be who you are in this moment. Because the more reverence and respect you have from studying yourself and understanding yourself, the more you transcend that limiting-belief plane. Those experiences no longer shake you from what you're here to do—to be masterful, to be excellent.

There are very few things we can control in life. But you *can* choose to sit with these parts of you, understand them, and love them in a way that leads to a deep respect for yourself. Because when your sense of self becomes less about what happened to you or even the overcoming and

MOVING FROM AWARENESS TO ACCEPTANCE   19

more about the awareness of the profoundness of it all—the awe and respect for the unknown and the understanding that you will never know for certain why anything happens to you or to anyone anywhere else in the world—then you can alleviate your suffering. And you can grasp on a cellular level that you *can* rely on the certainties of spiritual systems, your ability to be present with your experiences, and your ability to move through those experiences and turn them into an advantage and a privilege.

But you cannot come into sovereignty of self, you cannot come into complete alignment with whatever it is that you are without really studying who and what you are. You can only master that which you are in relentless study of, and in this case, it is *self*-study. And that requires an investment of time and practice.

Wisdom

Wisdom is the skeleton key. It is what opens all the doors—to healing, to feeling a sense of purpose. It's why the ultimate goal is to live in wisdom. To live with the **embodied understanding of your experiences and the complete healing of those experiences**. Wisdom is experience itself, the acceptance of that experience, the knowledge distilled from that experience, and the sharing of that knowledge. Wisdom lifts you up in the ranks of consciousness so that you can simultaneously hold a deep understanding of what you've lived through and an understanding of how to be in service to others. So that you can empower others to expand their choices or attune them to the ability they have to make a choice with integrity. To aid them on their own path of devotion to creation in the name of mastery.

It is not often we see true wisdom modeled for us. Namely because it is impossible to achieve wisdom until you've healed from your own pain, because that pain and the process of healing puts us too much in the self to be in service to others. But that's to be expected. You couldn't reasonably anticipate that we'd all rise to the ranks of Christ or Muhammad, speaking in parables because we're so far transcended from our egoic self. But that doesn't mean it can't be the path we're on, or that we can't still benefit from the fruits of merely being on that path. Of devotion to our own mastery. Of relentlessly being present. This is because being on that path, and any wisdom that we gain on that path, connects us to our **purpose**.

What It's All About: Building Bridges and Finding Purpose

Before we get too deep into things, I want to make something clear: *purpose* is one of the most misinterpreted and overused words. Most of the time it's associated with perfection, as in total clarity of what one's purpose is. Or the converse is true—if you *don't* know what your purpose is, you're a failure. That's when the pressure of purpose becomes so profoundly stressful and creates even more of a burden for us. So now, we're either trying to figure out our purpose in a weekend of vision boarding or else we're shamed into believing life is meaningless if we don't have an answer. In reality, purpose is one of those things you spend your entire life trying to understand, and it has absolutely nothing to do with perfection or success.

Another misconception about purpose is that people often think of it in terms of their career or what they happen to spend most of their time doing: "I'm an author." "I'm a mom." "I'm a systems analyst." But purpose is so much deeper. Purpose is your innate essence. In Sanskrit, the idea of purpose, or dharma, translates to "deep knowing." In a sense, it is your soul's mastery and wisdom.

The Formula for Purpose

For every single one of us, the formula for finding purpose is exactly the same:

MOVING FROM AWARENESS TO ACCEPTANCE   21

Purpose is the combination of your innate gifts, your lived experience and the wisdom you have gleaned from it, the skills you have amassed so far, and the ways you are meant to serve.

It has to be all the layers, which is why purpose is our life's work, not something we can figure out in a weekend. You cannot have purpose without wisdom, and you certainly can't have purpose (or wisdom) without acknowledgment of every single experience—the good, the bad, and the ugly—that you've had up until this point. Here, we find ourselves back at the beginning: You cannot have joy without the acknowledgment and befriending of grief. You cannot have light where you have not acknowledged and learned from the inevitable darkness. We are the sum of our experiences, and it is *beautiful*.

It's how we move between the dark and the light that forms the foundation of our healing, which is why I think of building purpose as "building bridges." Because purpose lives in the connections between all of the experiences we've had and the experiences we will have. It's understanding how each piece leads to the next.

But here's the thing: I'm not talking about understanding on an intellectual level. We're not making a laundry list of all the trying things you've been through, or saying, "I'm this way because I didn't have any support as a child" or "I'm this way because I experienced X tragedy." That's being *aware*. You know what happened to you, and you know why you behave the way you behave (or at least you will as you traverse this healing journey). The connective bridge comes in when you can see the deeper context. When you can take the trail a little farther back and reach *acceptance*. The space of acceptance then opens the space of forgiveness. So it's not about what happened to you or who did it, it's about arriving at the mindset that some of these experiences served a purpose for making you who and what you are. Without those things having happened, as unfair as they might have been, you might not have arrived at this moment. You might not be maximizing

LIVING IN WISDOM

the potential of your life, using your experiences as tools, information, and knowledge.

You can form connective bridges when you're no longer just looking at the inventory of your pain but instead are showing yourself the dynamic river of it. It's the difference between reading the book of your life, walking away with a summary, and accepting its stagnant rigidity versus using that book as a guide with forward movement toward new destinations.

BECOMING AN ARCHAEOLOGIST OF THE SOUL

I want you to think of the work that lies ahead for you as a deep excavation. It's not a mistake that a vital part of this process is called "crevice work," something we'll be talking much more about in chapter 3, but for now suffice it to say that in order to move through the necessary stages of healing, you're going to have to do some unearthing and a thorough examination of all the pieces.

This may be deeply uncomfortable if not angering or even repellent work. Some of you may have experienced "big-*T*" trauma—abuse, neglect, violence, generational suffering. Some of you may be navigating **post-traumatic stress disorder (PTSD)**, a mental health condition affecting those who have experienced traumatic events or circumstances that affected them mentally, physically, socially, or spiritually. Some of you may be coping with *complex* **post-traumatic stress disorder (CPTSD)**, which can develop after experiencing long-term or repeated trauma. But even if that is not clinically what you identify with, many if not most of us have had what I call **Complex Lived Experience**, meaning that there may not be one central event you can trace back to as the source of your pain. For many, myself included, it's

MOVING FROM AWARENESS TO ACCEPTANCE   23

a cumulative effect, the layering over time of loss, lack of support, physical pain, emotional betrayal, and on and on and on. And as a result, the events in our lives that may seem like they could be the straightforward and central pain point—a divorce, a car accident, a violation of trust—are instead entangled within the context of every single other layer of pain we've experienced, whether that's within our family, our community, our society, or our epigenetic timeline. All this is to say, trauma, as it is clinically defined, does not need to be present in order for healing to be required—and complicated.

Also, *because* of that pain, you will have what I have come to understand both through my own work and Divine revelation as **"barriers to healing."** When confronted with the necessary exercises required of you to heal, you may want to shut it down—not owing to any personal shortcomings or deficits, but rather as a result of your built-in self-preservation mechanisms. It is easier to put up the wall. It is safer to leave things as they are. It is more comfortable to preserve the status quo.

When I first started working with students to help them navigate their own healing, I thought it was my job to contort myself as their teacher to help them overcome these barriers; I thought I had to be all the things to everyone in order to help them make their way out the other side. I quickly learned that I was not meant to show them—or you—how to dissolve those barriers. I am only meant to show people *how to investigate the againstness they have to something.* That's why, as you move through each of the healing steps in part 3, I've described what these barriers might look like within the context of each step and why they arise. Acknowledging these barriers, understanding where they come from, and honoring them as more information about yourself and what you require is just one more torch illuminating the path that lies ahead to the depths.

24 LIVING IN WISDOM

This Might Hurt a Little—and You're Going to Be Better Than Okay

Oftentimes, someone new to a meditation practice will experience resistance. They have a feeling of just not wanting to do it. And in my experience as a teacher, this is where the most disarmament is required. Resistance doesn't happen because you think too many thoughts. It's because meditation can be incredibly triggering. It's because looking around at the people sitting with their knees touching the floor in Lotus position—a posture many of them took years to master or that may be easier for them simply because they are naturally flexible—can lead to feelings of frustration, irritation, and judgment of the self. If this is you, you may notice the tightness in your hips, and when you do, you may ask yourself, *Why am I so inflexible?* Or say, *I hate my body; it keeps me from what I want.* And for some, it may bring up a traumatic memory or awareness of how you are because you've always had to be hypervigilant.

To that I say: Be with the discomfort. Notice it, time and time again. There's beauty in it, as much as you might need to hear it. But also, it's part of the process. And those knees aren't going to touch the ground by themselves. If it's true healing you're after, you're going to have to stay present with the work, and the work takes time. This process is not a snack. It's not a microwavable dinner. This is slow cooking. It's a long-simmering stew. And it is *delicious*.

When I started, I was sitting with my knees a foot off the ground. For two years. By year three, they were a few inches closer. By year four, a few inches closer. And now, ten years later, I've got my knees on the ground. So don't rush this part or sit in judgment of yourself. Healing is not fast work, and it is not easy work. You will experience cycles when you feel so freaking excited and empowered and easeful, and you will experience cycles where it will feel like nothing is going right, everything pisses you off, and you're mad that you're not seeing radical change. I can feel you. I was you. There is nothing I have described in this book that I have not resented deeply at one point. Gift yourself the

MOVING FROM AWARENESS TO ACCEPTANCE   25

time to continue moving through these cycles and find a pace that works for you. It might feel right to give yourself a year, four full seasons, to investigate a single thought or a wound or an experience before doing anything about it—and that's fine. Because while the work is slow, the healing can happen in the blink of an eye. It is both. It is everything. And it is now yours.

Part II

Practices for Higher Consciousness

Chapter 3

Devotion and the Path to Your Highest Self

The chapters that follow in this part are dedicated to the daily practices that I've curated to accompany this book. But if we're being honest, they pretty much *are* the book. Don't get me wrong, the self-awareness and self-knowledge you will glean from all of the chapters are fundamental for your healing. But without combining that awareness and knowledge with these practices, they will forever remain just that—knowledge. Not wisdom. Unless you are supporting your own process with these practices, the new lessons you'll be learning cannot be integrated into your body and your wiring the way they need to be in order to bring about any kind of shift.

As I've battle tested for years in my own life, these practices are the key to healing. They are essential for unlocking new depths of your understanding of your truest self. All they require in return is that you reach for them every. Single. Day. There is no cheat code. In fact, they *are* the cheat code.

Daily practices—meditation breathwork, gentle movement and touch, journaling, words of affirmation, recapitulation—are what are going to ultimately help you transcend *awareness* into *consciousness*. Awareness is essentially the first crucial step toward healing; in this space, we are aware of *how* we're feeling and *what* makes us feel a certain way. Awareness can be positive, but it's also where a lot of people stall

29

30   LIVING IN WISDOM

out on their healing path. Because suddenly, they feel fluent in their experience and the things that have happened to them. And that feels good. That feels powerful, superior even—a majority of the world is not in awareness.

However, awareness isn't enough to bring about change in your life. It's a catalyst for moving into a higher state, but having awareness alone is a vastly different existence than having the freedom that consciousness gifts you. Coming into consciousness is coming into a state of acceptance, which then guides you toward being able to release the charge of your experiences and access a whole new spectrum of feelings—feelings of true joy, true happiness, true compassion. Consciousness is what allows you to make choices independent from the stories you've always been told or tell about yourself, choices that are aligned with your spiritual curriculum. Moving into a state of higher awareness means you can assume the role of observer in your own life. From there, you can be within free will to connect to possibility and opportunity, who you are, and what your role is in this life.

Until that happens, you will continue to feel at arm's length from your own life. Even when you are in perfect lockstep with your goals and achieving greatness, you won't get to feel any of it. I received that lesson when I was twenty-five years old. I had just moved to Houston, and on my bedroom wall I had pinned a piece of paper that stated my then absolute highest career goals: "Work at Sirius XM" and "work at MTV." I had no idea how any of that was going to happen, but within eleven months of setting that intention for myself, *both* of those entities called me to offer me a job. I went from feeling lonely and isolated in Texas, writing words on a slip of paper and not doing anything specific to make them come true, other than generally working hard while also reaching for some of the spiritual practices that I'd had at that time, to moving to New York and starting both jobs within a week of one another. That's when I first understood the magnetism of intention and that, when you are aligned across several aspects of life and diligently working toward something, there can be ease. I learned that with the

DEVOTION AND THE PATH TO YOUR HIGHEST SELF   31

audacity to want and to put your want out there, those intentions can be brought forward in a multitude of ways.

Then I got to New York. I was now the cohost of a huge morning radio show rooted in the hip-hop community—a community I had been a part of and passionate about for years. I had also been named the lead host of a late-night talk show on one of the biggest TV networks in the country. I was surrounded by an incredible ensemble cast, truly some greats, but I was chosen to be the lead. I was living in an incredible apartment in the center of Manhattan. I could afford things that I'd never in my life been able to afford. I was surrounded by people celebrating me and telling me what an incredible life I had.

And I was so. Damn. Unhappy.

It was the first time I glimpsed performative happiness and joy. I felt so unconnected to all of it, like I could blow it all up and not care.

My mom came to visit me shortly after I moved to New York—a visit I was really looking forward to because it had been a couple of years since I'd been in one place long enough to spend real time with her. Almost immediately, I was pulled out of my body. I suddenly felt activated, volatile, and destabilized by just her presence. I was upset that I felt so upset in that moment; in hindsight, this was largely because I hadn't yet connected with the memories or experiences from my childhood that were causing friction in my adult life. This feeling of unhappiness when I had everything I thought I wanted was what kick-started my investigation of my own trauma, of the reserve of pain that was sitting just below the surface, and of my barriers to joy. In that moment, it dawned on me—if I didn't get into this deeper, gnarlier stuff as part of my healing, if I didn't let myself feel the bad, then I'd never be able to feel the good too. Nothing would ever feel like enough—even my biggest dreams coming true.

So it's time for you to recognize that awareness is not enough. It's a beautiful beginning, and it does take courage to give language to things that need to be said out loud. It takes real bravery to actually change

32   LIVING IN WISDOM

your circumstances. I'm asking you to take a huge leap of faith to jump into the unknown of this process with absolutely no way to control it or what you might find there. (Not as though you have control over anything else, but a perceived notion of control is a pretty powerful thing standing in most people's way.) For a lot of people, awareness has become a new kind of self-avoidance. It's just more sophisticated language for you to perform with, and to ultimately keep yourself from yourself. It might make you sound or feel like you've really *gone there*, but I'm going to give you the brutal truth here: it's faux depth.

The only way to actually develop different feelings—not different thoughts, *feelings*—is to build a system of practice that supports the intention of change, one that rewires your ability to make new choices based on the new knowledge you receive, and also supports you while you undergo this slow and difficult yet rewarding and beautiful evolution toward the desires you have for your life, both internally and externally.

This Is the Cheat Code

I have a friend, Kai, who is an incredibly special person. She's truly gifted—brilliant and magnetic. The second she thinks of something, it manifests into the world. She's achieved just massive things with such little effort because that is the truth of her innate power in her life. Over the past fifteen years, she's read what seems like every book about reaching higher consciousness. She's gone on psychedelic journeys, partaken in ayahuasca ceremonies, psilocybin, and therapy-supported ketamine, many times over. She's sought the expertise of therapists, gurus, and guides—all at the top of their game. Everyone talks about how aware she is, but she feels that she is alone. Because even though she has completely outpaced her peers in terms of how she understands her experience, never once has she been able to step outside of her therapized box. Never once has she developed a practice to support any of these experiences she's having outside of the confines of her teachers' offices.

DEVOTION AND THE PATH TO YOUR HIGHEST SELF   33

She's never been able to create an actual change in her day-to-day life, in the kinds of people she brings into her life, and the way she's able to feel in her life.

Then she finally came to me. We'd both been on this healing journey, and we both have similar childhoods and trauma. We've each been a safe haven for the other to understand one another profoundly. So she asked me if she could come over for some energy work and get my thoughts on how she could fix the way she was feeling. As we were sitting and talking, I described my philosophy and my process as it relates to cultivating a practice, giving her a lot of recommendations for what I thought she should be doing every day—the exact same tools I use.

She sighed and gave me the most exasperated, exhausted roll of the eyes.

I said to her, "You seem disappointed."

And she said, "Well, yeah; I know all of that."

"Well, do you do any of it?" I asked. No, she did not. And instead of greeting this actual, objective solution to her problem, the problem that led her to my doorstep after years and years and years of searching, she wanted something else. She wanted another intellectual cure, another book that was going to explain it in a way that *finally* unlocked her mind and freed her for good. But *these tools* are what creates change. *They* are what creates that shift.

I explained to her what I leave you with as well: Your past is never going to change. Your experiences will never disappear, no matter how mindful you become. But the way you relate to them *can* change. The way you hold that charge in your body can change. And that's what creates the freedom for new experiences and choices. Part of this higher consciousness is accepting that all of this is what it is. The freedom is how you feel about it. How present and current it feels in the decisions you make now. And how you hold your self-worth. That's where happiness begins to slowly grow and bloom from.

The reason why welcoming in these practices is so hard for so many of us—it really is the thing people struggle with the most—is that it is the only way to wrench us out of our disassociation with our realities

34   LIVING IN WISDOM

and with our bodies. What pisses off people, including my friend, is that you can't get away with simply reading another book. And you definitely can't outsource it.

WHEN NAVIGATING TRAUMA AND ABUSE

For some of you, this process of self-courtship can get kind of gnarly. Your path may include making peace with truths that no one should ever have to come to peace with. And what we're beginning to understand about abuse is that if you experienced any form of it in childhood, that makes it feel difficult to make your way back to your purest origin story. You can adapt and create other expressions of yourself, but that sacredness of childhood you were not given access to may feel elusive.

I say this to acknowledge that if this is your experience, you are not alone. And that acceptance of this truth helps. Feeling the unfairness of it all helps. It will bring in awareness that in and of itself creates the necessary space for your process to unfold. Because once you have that awareness, you know where the pain is. And through these practices, you get invited to take that awareness a step further and actually create change. You may also consider exploring these deeper themes with a therapist, doctor, or other trusted individual. This work is heavy, and you should not have to bear that weight alone.

Crevice Work and Power Washing the Spirit

The fundamental reason why these practices are so deeply effective is that they are what I like to call **crevice work**. It's the practice of getting into the tiny nooks and crannies of who we are and undergoing a

DEVOTION AND THE PATH TO YOUR HIGHEST SELF   35

self-excavation. It is the essential deep cleaning of the emotional sludge that resides within us, persistently lingering in every little crack and fissure.

This work is a lot like getting your car detailed. The person cleaning doesn't start by getting into your car and vacuuming the interior. They first attend to the big surfaces with a scrub, then—if you've paid for the deluxe package—they start pulling things out of the car, layer by layer—the floor mats, the car seat, the tissue boxes, the trash—and *then* they start cleaning the spaces in between. This is that same process, but for your soul.

The first stage comes after you've moved beyond that initial call to live life on a different kind of frequency or in a more mindful manner, when you're just developing that awareness. You then start to realize how the way you're showing up in your material life—in your career, your relationships, your family—is disjointed from the awareness you've gained, because you haven't yet moved beyond all of your friction points. You begin to understand you are the sum of every experience you've ever had. You can see how that accumulation has become this big mountain inside of you, and you're going to need to slowly and methodically clear it away, layer by layer. You're going to need to dig deeper and deeper through each of those layers down to your truest self and highest consciousness—like you're excavating through the layers of the earth, seeing each millennium of history told through forcefully compacted strata of rock and silt. As each of those layers accumulated in your soul, they slowly carved you out, distorting your original form. Now is the time to clear them out.

As you begin the unearthing process, you'll naturally start by clearing away some of the larger, easier-to-grab rubble. You'll be able to zero in on experiences that altered you and shaped every subsequent decision you made—a divorce, a breakup, getting fired from a job. What often happens once you get the bigger pieces out of the way is that you immediately begin to feel a little space free up—and it's tempting to say, "That's it, I'm done." But oftentimes those first few rocks are just the

36   LIVING IN WISDOM

by-product of what is buried deep in the core. You'll know this because you'll continue to see the same patterns of your behavior—patterns that we'll work together to identify and heal—show up. For example, you might think you're just healing from an unhappy marriage or a divorce, you work it out in therapy, and you finally come to understand, *Ah, this is what happened in our relationship and who I became as a result.* But then things don't necessarily change in your next relationship...because you only healed the wound from an even larger experience that you haven't even touched yet. So you have to dig to a deeper layer until you've reached what is considered to be the root wound or what I like to call your **original wound**, which inhabits that deeply buried core. It's also what you can draw a straight line to from pretty much any situation in your life that constantly creates friction—every relationship that is unnourishing and not evolving, detrimental behavioral patterns that can't seem to be altered.

Sometimes, the origin of this wound is straightforward. For me, my work began with examining my relationship with someone who emotionally neglected me, which I then traced all the way down to emotional neglect in childhood, due to my mother's treading water as a Black woman navigating financial struggles and single motherhood in America. Not only that, she was doing so alone because of challenges in her own family system, in addition to being abandoned by the father of her child.

For others, it might be more subtle. It could be a parent who is strictly budget conscious—potentially as a result of their own core wound—and that made a significant imprint on your brain and affected how you think about prosperity and worthiness. That's not going to change simply by gathering the courage to ask for a raise at work. It changes only if you continue spending time unearthing your connection to that way of being. And *that's* when you get into the crevices. That's when you can start to get into the tiny spaces and the sludge and residue of your experiences that have settled in there.

Meditation, breathwork, lovingly moving and touching your own

DEVOTION AND THE PATH TO YOUR HIGHEST SELF   37

body, journaling, practicing words of affirmation—these are your highly specialized tools that are designed for getting into those hard-to-reach spaces, clearing them out, and keeping them clear.

Ayurveda, the ancient healing tradition, often prescribes Sanskrit mantras, or repeated phrases or "seed words," for meditation. It's not unusual for my clients to want to know the meaning of these words and mantras I give them to practice. But it's not so much the literal meaning of these words that's extraordinarily deep as the *vibration* that that mantra releases in your body. It creates an intentional energy.

If you practice yoga, think about the feeling you get when everyone chants "om" in unison at the beginning and end of class—the delicious vibrational energy that comes forth when all of your tones meet in orchestra and you experience it from head to toe. The word *om* itself doesn't hold as much meaning as its vibration, which is thought to be the sound of the Universe.

All of these practices, all of these systems, are creating a vibration inside of you that shakes loose the dirt and sediment in places where the sun don't shine. The beauty of that function is that if you reach for them every single day, even as you come into higher consciousness and feel like you've cleared out a majority of that rubble—these tools are going to continue to find those little particles of dust, which, if you just let them linger, would eventually accumulate and accumulate until that mountain starts looming again.

This is why, when you clear the big stuff out and stay in the highest alignment of yourself, it is imperative to continue to devote yourself to the work. Eventually, this daily maintenance will allow you to simply wipe away those little smudges. And then, when new obstacles and challenges present themselves—which they inevitably will, because life— you won't have to dig through all the rubble first before dealing with that challenge. You won't have a septic tank beneath the surface that needs to be emptied before you deal with that new issue. You'll only have to sweep the corners and pick up a little trash.

38   LIVING IN WISDOM

Do you know what that dedication to keeping things clear and aligned with your life's purpose on a daily basis is called? Devotion. Devotion to self is one of the most powerful shifts you can experience. Not because there's something wrong you're trying to fix, but because you are surrendering to the idea of *this is what's best for me, and I'm doing it with joy and acceptance*. It is holding your practice and yourself with reverence. And you deserve that.

What These Practices Look like in the Body

What all of these practices have in common is that on a physiological level they help regulate your nervous system. The nervous system, which has nothing to do with feeling nervous and everything to do with the nerves that the human body requires to function, is in the driver's seat of how we feel at any given moment. It is in constant surveillance of and communication with your external and internal environment, receiving, processing, and autonomically (i.e., automatically) responding to meet your needs. When your body is exposed to trauma, stress, or just what it perceives as stress, it goes into either hyper- or hypoactivity: "fight" (physically or verbally challenge the threat), "flight" (run away from the threat), "freeze" (play possum), or "fawn" (try to please the threat). The amygdala, the part of your brain responsible for perceiving threats, sends out a distress signal, causing the hypothalamus (also in the brain) to activate the sympathetic nervous system by sending signals through the autonomic nerves to the adrenal glands. In a hyper state, these glands respond by pumping the hormone epinephrine (adrenaline) into the bloodstream, which causes a cascade of physiological changes: The heart starts beating more quickly; pulse rate and blood pressure increase; breathing becomes rapid. Extra oxygen surges to the brain, and glucose is released into the bloodstream to give the body a big dose of fuel for this amped-up all-or-nothing state the body is now in. Conversely, in a hypoactive state, you experience the opposite: a restriction of blood, breath, and alertness as the body tries to tune out the experience it has to deal with.

DEVOTION AND THE PATH TO YOUR HIGHEST SELF   39

The problem is that the amygdala is really good at its job, and this ancient appendage has not yet caught up with modern times. So every time we get an overwhelming email, sit in traffic, or think a friend is upset with us, these same systems are triggered as though we're faced with a life-or-death problem. When your system spends too much time in this state, it suffers on a physical level. In a hyperactive state, that can mean high blood sugar, high blood pressure, digestive issues, anxiety, and risk of stroke and heart attack. In a hypoactive state, that looks like dissociation, depression, anxiety, and numbness.

If the nervous system is our first point of contact, the basis of our human interface, then imagine what is happening to your emotional and mental well-being if your nervous system is in a constant state of hypervigilance. That distorts your perception and keeps you stuck in the same cycle of unproductive decisions, whether that's the dissociated, emotionally depressed, ready-to-surrender framework of hypoactivity or the impulsive, ready-to-destroy wavelength of hyperactivity. In either case, you are not able to access a clear channel and stable connection with self.

However, when you reach for these practices on a daily basis, you're not only nourishing your nervous system and allowing it to reset to a more resilient, less reactive baseline, you're also recalibrating your inner GPS. You'll have a much more finely tuned sense of what is right for you, what is not, and how to meet your needs. This part of you that is designed to plug into the ether and sense what is coming—the closest thing we have to a sixth sense—can start to tap into a much larger, deeper consciousness. It is your inner highway to wisdom. To your innate gifts. To the Divine.

Another way we become stuck is a result of our neural pathways. Our brains are made up of thousands of neurons, or nerve cells, which are connected to one another by these beautiful branch-like extensions called dendrites. When you develop a new habit, your brain multiplies the number of dendrites to reinforce this new connection—the equivalent of a neurological shortcut. Over the course of our lives, purely from

40   LIVING IN WISDOM

making the same choices over and over, our brains forge these neural pathways. It's like a well-worn path traveled many times—smooth, the path of least resistance. I like to think of it as a Slip 'N Slide, or a chute from Chutes and Ladders. We don't even need to complete the full thought before our brain plugs right into these connections.

When we develop habits rooted in creativity or skill, these pathways are phenomenal. They allow you to perform mastery with ease instead of starting from scratch every time. But when you're stuck in the negatively reinforced grooves of ruminating thought or a traumatized body, those same connections can become one of the biggest hindrances to transcendence. Over time, these pathways become calcified and increasingly difficult to change—which is why it is imperative to create change as soon as you come into awareness that it is necessary for you so you can take advantage of the brain's innate pliability.

The practices that follow are essential for changing the road map in your brain. They are the powerful catalysts for forging new habits, connections, and associations. Every day that you come to the meditation cushion, that you leave a breadcrumb trail for self-study in your journal, that you reset your nervous system through breathwork, that you experience the gentle pleasure of self-touch, and that you lift your mind out of negative loops to rest on affirming thought, you will be charting a new course, toward growth, toward empowerment, toward resilience, and toward joy.

Chapter 4

Connecting with Your Practice

There is nothing like returning to a place that remains unchanged to find the ways in which you yourself have altered.

—Nelson Mandela

The practices that follow in this part of the book are for the wooing of your soul. It is the soft, slow romancing of your own little inner flame that's there—even if just flickering embers—and building it into a roaring bonfire. It is your love story that is unfolding with you through these practices. At first, it can feel scary, the same way real love with another person can be scary.

I was talking to one of my friends who is one of the most beautiful people but is also single and deeply desiring partnership. She wanted to daydream with me about her ideal partner or relationship, and so I held space for her to list all the things she thinks she's looking for: an alpha male breadwinner who can provide and protect the financial security of the partnership, yet also an evolved, self-aware househusband who can swoop in to carry the everyday load of responsibilities when her plate gets too full, as well as someone who can anticipate her needs without her having to ask for a single thing. I gently pointed out to her that it sounds like she wants someone to father her more than be a romantic partner, and that it might be impossible for someone to meet all of her needs *plus* his own needs.

42 LIVING IN WISDOM

I suggested that maybe, just maybe—and she really didn't like this—she needed to examine why she needs to outsource that type of unconditional love. It's completely understandable; our core need as humans is to be deeply seen and understood by other people. And not only that, we're looking for a sense of unconditional love. But unconditional love only exists between a parent and child and us and God. It's the only place it *can* exist—and that's not even a guarantee, or an appropriate expectation of how your child feels about you! It's a once-in-a-lifetime experience people may or may not get, and it in no way, shape, or form is natural for a relationship between two adults.

If you weren't afforded the opportunity to experience unconditional love as a child, it can feel unfair to have to go through life never having had that. I know you want and deserve for that need to be met. That you crave that sense of security and acceptance. If that is your experience, I understand how challenging and confusing a feeling like that is to hold, and I am sorry. It is so unfortunate what happens for so many of us, to have to go through life feeling at our core that our deepest needs were not met. But you have to come into acceptance that if it didn't happen in childhood, then that kind of love is not going to come from another person. You cannot reasonably expect that from someone else. You cannot control it or force it into being. You have to concede that the unconditional love story is between you and you.

I know how triggering this truth is. But as soon as you make peace with it, as soon as you see that you can do that for yourself, that's when everything shifts. It not only welcomes more mutually supportive relationships into your life, but also offers the kind of security and sense of well-being that you have been missing through most if not all of your life.

It's also very freeing. When I realized that I'm not meant to unconditionally love anyone but my son, I felt a huge weight of responsibility lifted. I don't want to be expected to be someone else's caretaker, nor do I have any expectation of someone doing that for me.

CONNECTING WITH YOUR PRACTICE   43

★　★　★

And so, just as you would build a relationship with a partner, you have to build a relationship with yourself. Practices and processes are the way to do that. It requires diligence and time and expectation and disappointment and cringey-ness—just as building a relationship with a partner does, but even more so. Much more.

The process of creating a relationship of unconditional love with yourself allows you to find space within your own body. That overcrowded feeling of all the unmet needs, unexpressed feelings, and repression will begin to slowly open and release, like a slow draining—not unlike draining the infected pus from a wound. Suddenly, you'll find space, specifically space to bring in whatever it is that you need in this moment and every moment that will follow.

My biggest desire for you in forming a relationship with your new practices is that you can find the sweetness and slowness. I want you to take the pressure off yourself—remember, self-work is not meant to be quick; it is not meant to deliver instantaneous, large-scale results. For one, that's not real. And two, it's not sustainable. You are building a relationship with *yourself*, one constructed from the most unshakable foundation of intimacy and care. That requires developing trust over time with patience and tenderness.

Soon after I started adopting more of these practices into my life, I was talking to one of my teachers and telling him about the urgency I felt surrounding what I knew was my higher calling and how badly I wanted these changes to take root. He said to me, "Devi, this is your life's work. It's supposed to take your whole life to do." Suddenly, I didn't feel like I had to rush through, trying to get to these bigger epiphanies. I didn't have to slay the dragon all at once. If I wanted to, I could give myself an entire year to explore just one facet of my spiritual curriculum. This slowing down made the process so much more human for me, and so much more beautiful. I could be in flow with it without judgment of where I'd been and where I was going and when.

44   LIVING IN WISDOM

It's important to take the slow and steady path to adopting these new practices. Big changes can feel really unsafe; they pull us into a "new self" before we've fully laid the stabilizing foundation within our inner experiences. Consider one of my executive clients: He had been the CEO of a Fortune 500 company but had left that job to start his own company. We worked together for three days, through several experiences that were radically upending him, and he had significant breathethrough moments. By the end of our time together, he felt a noticeable improvement in his mental clarity, as well as relief of his chronic pain. I sent him home with a literal toolbox full of implements that he could reach for in his own practices—crystals, incense, meditations, and a journal, plus biohacking tools such as a sleep protocol and recommendations for improving his overall health—and when we parted ways, he was fired up and ready to continue the work we'd done together.

Normally, I check in with my clients about a week after our session, but we weren't able to until a month later. I asked him how his practice was going, and he admitted he hadn't even opened the bag I'd given him since arriving back home. He hadn't meditated. He hadn't journaled. I asked him, "Okay. When are you going to start?" I pivoted to (very gentle) tough love mode. "What is this for you?" I asked. "Let's talk about this 'againstness' that's coming up." He started gushing about how amazing our time together was, but I gently interrupted him. "Let's stop that," I said. "I believe you. *And*, you know what you need to do to prepare yourself for this new moment in your life. So what are you avoiding, and why can't you do it for yourself?"

Ultimately, it was the shift that was so terrifying for him. This ascension to an even more elevated version of himself. He could see it and taste it—and it tasted good—but to embody it was a different story. Because even if it's something you've been waiting for your whole life, if you're yanked into it and you haven't had time to slowly make it your own and push against the discomfort, it feels like you're living another life. It can feel kind of fraudulent, like you don't know how to wear this new kind of outfit you've put yourself in. And that leads to instant

CONNECTING WITH YOUR PRACTICE   45

rejection—your body wants to reject it; your brain wants to *eject* it. Then, eventually, you interpret it as something not working.

Also, oftentimes, we're simply not ready for some of the truths that will be revealed along the way. There's a reason why people say that in order for counseling or therapy to actually be effective you need twelve consecutive sessions. Twelve hours to move past the venting and purging and into the slow unraveling of deeper core issues. To begin to loosen the cemented ways of being. Quickly pulling yourself out of that not only would be extremely difficult in less time, but also could be incredibly unsafe. One of my teachers once gave me the sage warning that I as a healer needed to be extremely careful when I reveal things to people, because I might be telling them something before they're ready to receive it. I could be sharing something that they still need a month or a year or four years' worth of work to do before they're equipped for it. No matter how valuable the insight, it can't be a solution for them if it's not their most aligned timeline to receive it. The same goes for this process and the information you'll uncover, which can only be a solution if you're prepared to receive it. Which is why I so firmly believe that everyone deserves the dignity of their own version of that process, and why everyone should respect the time that it takes to unravel the complexities and nuance that exist in their inner world (and why we should have the utmost respect for and patience with others navigating their own).

Staying Flexible

You already know by now that rigidity is not the thing when it comes to this work. The trick is balancing the necessity of the work with the reality that life will occasionally have to intercede. Unanticipated changes will occur; emergencies will arise. When they do, these practices will be here for you as you need them, with no expectation of you other than what you are able to give them. There is no guilt in needing to momentarily step away.

46 LIVING IN WISDOM

About a year ago, I was heading to Mexico to lead a retreat—a signature event for me that I genuinely look forward to every year. As the plane was taking off, I learned that a woman in my community—a kind, creative soul and devoted mother who was a new friend I'd made through our sons' friendship and whose family I'd also gotten to know—had been murdered, allegedly, by her husband, who as of this writing is standing trial. The horrific news sent me emotionally reeling as I tried to simultaneously hold the grief for the three boys she left behind, the abyss of sadness that her body had been so devastatingly desecrated, and then the familiar jolt of PTSD as a result of the far-too-many people I've lost—often in tragic ways—over the course of my life.

Upon landing, my primary responsibility was tending to the demands of the retreat and the women who were expecting me, rightfully, to show up and support them in a deep and meaningful way. It was putting on makeup and a beautiful dress to attend a dinner with a group of people who wanted to talk about the purpose of life and joy and healing. It was leading a goddess meditation on the beach.

And I was dying inside.

My right eye started twitching. I developed a rash. I was in physical pain, but there was nothing I could do to meet my needs at that time. And while I knew that I had built up some emotional endurance because of my practices, I also knew that if I was going to get through this moment, even if I needed to dial my practice way down, I was still going to have to meet my most immediate needs. At the very least, I needed to ground, and I needed to cry.

I first created boundaries that felt right to me at the time, which is its own practice we'll talk more about in chapter 17. I would still need to be present and honor the commitments that I had made, but I knew I could also step away during sessions I wasn't a part of. I felt no guilt about that, because ultimately, I was going to be enabling myself to show up and support everyone else, and to my mind, it is more important to not disappoint yourself than to not disappoint someone else, if you have to choose between the two.

CONNECTING WITH YOUR PRACTICE   47

Every day I made time for what I could. I would wake up at 5:00 a.m., ahead of a 7:00 a.m. group meditation session, to take a hot shower and rub myself down with oils and lotion. I could do some slow stretches, listen to an intentional playlist, and give myself the opportunity to just weep. I would do some mirror work, gazing deeply at every physical element of myself in the mirror, because when you are isolated in your grief, it's essential to bear witness to yourself. To witness your humanity. I would sink my feet into the grass to get grounded. I did everything I could to just be present with myself until I could find my supportive community and really unpack all of this.

Yes, I know that sounds like quite a bit of intentional practice that I could tend to, but for what I was holding, it barely scratched the surface. In no way would it have been enough to carry me through that grief. I needed at least another thirty minutes to an hour a day to meditate, to soak in an Epsom salt bath to detoxify and surrender and float to the top. To cry. To let my nervous system reregulate.

The bottom line is that I am giving you a new set of tools, and these tools are going to serve you wherever you are. Sometimes you cannot carry each of these tools with you, and that's okay. The important thing is that you know they are there, and that you do ultimately return to them.

A Lifetime of Work, the Work of a Lifetime

I want you to approach your practice through the lens of curious exploration. And not only that—exploration over the course of your *entire lifetime*. While it's true that I will be giving you some structure so that you can grain proficiency in each of these modalities, I ultimately want you to take a more intuitive path. There's no reason to look at this with the rigidity of a drill sergeant. There is no "right" and "wrong" way to do any of it. How liberating is that? *You cannot get this wrong.* Even if some days it's just choosing not to scroll through our phone when we sit down for a moment. Even if it's just sitting and eating a meal in silence. That is a self-care practice, that is a spiritual practice, and that is in deep

48 LIVING IN WISDOM

support of your mental and emotional well-being. Will that continue to serve you if that is all you're making time for? Not optimally. But just as life ebbs and flows, so will your practice.

You can also play with when you reach for each of the elements of your practice. I personally have a very extensive practice, so I choose to split it up over the course of about four hours each day. What works for me is waking up with the sun around 5:00 a.m., meditating, and then doing a few things that feel supportive of the day—maybe yoga, maybe affirmations. Sometimes I'll give myself a bit of time after I finish working to just sit at my desk and process the day through journaling. Then, in the evening, I set aside another block of time for winding down, such as lighting some incense, taking an Epsom salt bath, and doing cycles of breathwork. But I let it be fluid, and I let my intuition lead. Sometimes I just go to my sacred space with the intention of being in there for one hour and seeing where it leads me. Some days that could be meditation and journaling. Some days that could be an entire hour of stretching. Or sun salutations. Or just reading some pages out of a spiritual book and seeing how it feels, maybe journaling afterward to see what comes forward. Or simply holding silence for myself. All of these elements are valuable parts of the practice, and none of it has to be super structured.

You simply have to let your practice develop, be in observation of how you uniquely respond, and make adjustments over time. It is not meant to be a measure of success but rather a companion, something in your constant presence that offers familiarity and comfort as you revisit it over and over again.

Mastery will come when your practice evolves into your own unique recipe or prescription. As you build your self-trust and are able to identify your needs separate from ego, when you are able to communicate with your authentic self and feel the things that spark that flame, you can fully let intuition take over your practice. Then you can begin to treat it as the living, breathing organism that it is.

Your practice is meant to flow and change and to expand and contract based on the seasons of life you happen to be in. Sometimes it's

CONNECTING WITH YOUR PRACTICE   49

going to be smaller and more refined and to the point, and there are times or days when you can really luxuriate in it and give yourself over to half a day of practice and notice the nuances in the ways it fuels you. The beauty of exploring your practice and this lifestyle of devotion is that you get into the fibers of your own nuances. You really get to know what makes you come alive, what makes you feel supported.

Just as your practice will shift and change with each season of your life, it will also naturally shift and change with each season of nature. Committing to this lifelong pursuit in alignment with and support of your spiritual curriculum while also allowing it to follow the rhythms of nature is such a powerful way to integrate new wisdom. It's why I strongly encourage you to give yourself a full cycle of seasons, a year, to try on these practices, noticing how they change as the seasons change. Every season has its own vibration; every season commands a new wavelength; every season brings up its own things. While you're witnessing all these aspects of creation, you'll also be witnessing how it affects your own practices.

Many traditional wisdom practices and ancient systems do this intentionally, whether it's tethering rituals to the full or new moon, equinox or solstice, mercury retrograde or eclipse season, or the in-between space of seasonal transitions. Bringing your awareness to the unique energetic subtleties of these moments lends even more nuance and depth to your connection with them. There's fall, with its shedding and turning over and settling down. Shifting into winter, there's a burst of hustle and bustle of community, gifting, and joy as we move through the holidays. Then we're called to nest, to be swaddled, fed, and nourished in hibernation, awaiting an awakening. To seek warmth and comfort in body and spirit. When you move into spring, which is considered to be the energetic equinox and is when the world wakes up again, you see the things you planted drive up aboveground and bloom. And then you come into the spice of summer, the heat. The intense dryness or humidity, depending on where you are. There's also a sense of freedom and

50   LIVING IN WISDOM

connecting to the dog days of summer during your childhood, with the sun setting well into the evening. It's playful and fun, while also bearing an intensity.

As you practice throughout the year, ask yourself, *How do I relate to my patterns through the energy of this season? How does my spiritual curriculum relate to that? What triggers am I noticing?* You can ask yourself how you relate to your pain while you also are experiencing the abundance and beauty of spring or the almost sluggish intentionality of winter or the playfulness of summer. How does your body feel when it's moving more? Less? What somatic effect does your movement practice have in spring versus winter? These observations are what will bring you into mastery and self-trust, while offering you a whole new way of relating to your life.

At the end of this first year, you may feel that some significant shifts have already taken place, but be aware that going through this cycle twice—two years—is what it takes for these lessons to really stick. This has been my experience, and that of nearly all my clients. It can take two years to peel away the layers, going deeper and deeper to the core, gaining even more understanding or attaining more release. This two-year cycle offers you the room for this work, to test you in every way as it relates to your awareness of this healing and apply it to all the facets of your life. You'll be invited to master it in every category that it shows up for you—something we'll talk more about in chapter 13.

With this knowledge in hand, I want you to begin to let go of the idea of completion. This is not twenty-one days to a new you. This is not habit hacking. Yes, repetition and holding yourself accountable will create some necessary structure. But trying to give this work and the resulting mastery the restraint of time or an end point does it a disservice. It's the slow unfolding that makes this kind of work real and sustainable and authentic and lasting. So sink into that slowness. Release all the ideas of control or perfection that you see in everything else in your life. Understand that that does not apply here. That's not the best fuel for this kind of work.

CONNECTING WITH YOUR PRACTICE 51

Instead, look at this practice the way an artist paints. It's the observation of something. Then it's the sketch of that thing, the beginning formation and the taking shape. Then it's deciding what media will do it justice and capture it just right. Figuring out which tools will bring this creation forward. Sitting with the pains of it not coming out right. All the drafts. And then, the masterpiece. The great work.

Chapter 5

The Pillars of Practice

Sever the ignorant doubt in your heart with the sword of
self-knowledge. Observe your discipline. Arise.

—The Bhagavad Gita

The practices outlined in the following chapters are nonnegotiable for
transformation. They were the essentials that changed everything for
me, and since sharing them with my students and my community, I've
witnessed over and over again how fundamental they are. These prac-
tices are your tools for alchemizing choice, creation, self-devotion, and
self-mastery—without which there is no wisdom. Without wisdom,
there is no ability to dance between the realities of life and the joy of the
human experience. Allowing these practices into your life will unlock
the greatest, deepest, most significant peace, satisfaction, and resilience
that one can know.

The pillars of practice are:

Meditation
Breathwork/Pranayama
Journaling/Self-Inquiry
Affirming Statements and Qualitative Words
Movement and Touch
Recapitulation

THE PILLARS OF PRACTICE   53

In the following chapters, I'll be walking you through the fundamentals for each and how to apply them in a simple, foundational way. This will be your practice as you wade into part 3 and begin peeling back the layers of the healing process. Within each of those chapters, you'll find variations of these practices that will best support you as you spend time with these specific themes and challenges. There will also be suggestions for additional practices that help you go even deeper into your study and increase your receptivity to these vital shifts.

As you incorporate these practices into your life, I'd like you to think about how to do this in a way that works best for you, that puts you at the center of what this experience is. I can give you the tools and teach you how to build the boundaries, but *you* make the remix. *You* learn how to meet your needs, even if that has never been role modeled for you. Ask yourself what you can do to bring yourself relief/comfort/catharsis. Then tinker and adjust. Think of yourself as a gardener or farmer, amending the soil of your land and tending to it to produce the most abundant yield and the biggest blooms. Following that intuition versus following my word because I said so (although, yes, there are a few *I said so*s just to make sure these practices are effective) is what will help you cultivate a powerful self-trust that will be your constant companion on this journey.

Creating the Container

The first step in creating a practice is to set the stage, or create the container. I like to call this a sacred space. You could also call it your Zen area, your well-being area, the place you go for your daily practice or your daily routine—however you'd like to think of it without *over-thinking* it. No matter how small the corner or nook, carve out a place where you can, again and again, sprinkle your energetic seasoning. It should be practical to you, somewhere you can easily ground and restore each day within your regular rhythm of life. I have a sacred space in my bedroom where I do my daily meditation, but then I also have a sacred

54 LIVING IN WISDOM

space in my office—which I call my office altar—where I have crystals such as fluorite, moldavite, selenite, and mookaite; a sacral chakra bell; and other totems for invoking creativity. This space could be on a windowsill, in a drawer, or on a counter. It can be in a corner or in a closet; it could be an entire room. It just needs to be a space that you are going to intentionally put items into that, as Marie Kondo would say, spark joy. Maybe that's some candles or a throw or some pillows. Maybe a photograph of a younger version of yourself that you want to spend time with or a family photo or heirlooms for an ancestral altar. Perhaps you have a Bible or other spiritual books that bring you joy. It could be giving a small offering to a particular deity such as Ganesha or Shiva, or a teacher such as Christ or Krishna, depending on what your belief system is. You'll also want to think about ways to enliven your five senses—have some copal, palo santo, or sage to burn; include chimes, singing bowls, or bells whose frequency is pleasing to you.

Each of these elements helps create an opportunity for you to remove yourself from whatever you are currently connected to in the world and be brought into your present awareness. This is a space where you are in full command of yourself and fully in the moment, which is essential for your emotional, spiritual, and mental well-being. What you're really creating here is an opportunity for touching what's called "the gap." It's a term that's sometimes used when describing the pause between thoughts that you occasionally get to experience during meditation. It's when you can find stillness on both a biological and mental level and touch what Deepak Chopra has coined "the space of pure potentiality." It's where you're able to unlock your deepest levels of creativity, self-sovereignty, and also healing for whatever you happen to be working with in this lifetime as your curriculum. That can arise from simply being quiet and still, just sitting comfortably and taking in the sensual pleasures that you've surrounded yourself with.

However you choose to create your space, the important thing is that you honor the ritual of returning there. Not just physically coming back again and again, but also showing up with intention. As difficult as it

THE PILLARS OF PRACTICE   55

might be at first, do your best to not go rushing in and out of your practice. Extend the container for your practice to the five minutes before and five minutes after any sequences as a buffer so that you can really ground into that experience. At the very least begin and end with a couple nice, deep belly breaths.

This intentional return will become just as important a part of your practice as the meditations or breathwork or movement itself. Now, after many years of my own practice, I know that I need to hear that sound bowl every day; I have to smell sage every day; I have to have access to fire every day; I need to meditate with a crystal such as golden healer's quartz, arfvedsonite, or copper—because these elements are what help me hold the center and be my best self. Even when I travel, I always have a little pouch with the tools that give me the same exact energy.

That act of honoring what you require upholds your practice. It is the act of *being in relationship with* your practice. That's a large part of why these individual practices are so effective—because there is no way to become a higher version or more healed version of yourself without being in practice with relationship itself. As you keep returning to your space and yourself over and over, you're building that relationship. Because your practice is unchanging, you'll be able to witness yourself in contrast to it. It could be the evolution of how willingly you come to the space, how you're feeling emotionally each time you come and go, or how you physically feel. When you're just beginning to meditate, you haven't yet released the tension from your hips, so it can be challenging to sit with crossed legs. I remember seeing a picture of myself around that time, and I was so surprised to see my physical body in that moment—my knees were hiked up in a V shape; my shoulders looked like they could touch my ears, and there was so much effort in my face. Now when I see photos, my thighs and knees are flush with the ground, my hips are settled, and I've let go of the tension in my shoulders. There's laxity to my jaw, and a whole new look on my face. That was me building and witnessing a relationship with my meditation practice.

56   LIVING IN WISDOM

That is what it means to be in process with something—anything—and respecting it with your devotion.

The other beautiful aspect of this sacred container is that by returning to it time after time, you'll be accumulating a stored energy there. On the days when you're not able to connect with your practice or reject it outright (normal, natural, no judgment), you can simply sit in your space doing nothing. Or hug yourself. Or cry. However you are called to be in that moment, know that you are completely free and safe to do so.

Chapter 6

Meditation

A meditation practice is essential for you to crack open. Of all the practices we're unfolding here, meditation is the one people choose to do the least. It's always the one that gets left off the list. But it's the one that ties *all* of this work together and fast-tracks your ability to access your superpowers.

Meditation is an interesting challenge. On its surface, meditation seems so simple: Sit. Be still. Close your eyes. And perhaps at the beginning, you *think* you want to do it because you know intellectually how amazing it is for you—and then you start to resent it and hate it. Because the practice requires you to truly cultivate an immense amount of inner discipline to remain still in your body and in your mind, even though you don't want to and it feels triggering and uncomfortable. Meditation can make you go, *Damn it, I don't want to be doing this right now. I'd rather be doing literally anything else.* But when you stay with it, you crack through a layer where you'll actually begin craving meditation, like your body needs it. As you build your capacity for that stillness and quietness, a meditation practice will eventually ignite a pleasure response, a bliss response. It feels the way athletes describe a flow state or hitting a rhythm, when you surmount what you thought was the peak and then finally lock in. Eventually, you start feeling a deep satisfaction. Pride that you can do this, that you can do hard things.

58   LIVING IN WISDOM

The miracle of meditation is that it is the most fundamental exercise of consciousness that results in the expansion of the consciousness. Meditation stretches your ability to hold two competing thoughts or ways of being or even truths at one time, until you are able to simultaneously experience the intense edges of human emotion at the same time: grief and joy. On a micro level, meditating takes you beyond your day-to-day stress so that you can zoom out and hold the duality of your experience. So that you can acknowledge a day that has held maybe disappointment, sadness, frustration, or anger but maybe also enthusiasm and contentedness. When I was in Mexico, having just found out the news about the tragic death of my friend yet also dropping into an experience of holding space at the retreat, meditation gave me the ability to allow myself to feel joy while also feeling an extreme amount of pain and grief.

Meditation is the bridge that connects your internal and external selves. It facilitates the ability to reconcile how you're feeling inside with what is happening in front of you and then choosing how you show up and be present for that thing. It's what allows us to move in alignment with both of those realities and notice where in our relationships we're manipulating, where we're pleasing, where we're projecting. It's an observational mechanism so that you can make new decisions based on who you are and who you want to be.

How the Body Responds to Meditation

The benefits of meditation are not just emotional or psychological. A meditation practice has been proven to reduce stress and improve memory. Meditation stabilizes heart rate, regulates blood pressure, and increases creativity. It also makes your mental function more efficient; in any given situation, you can quickly and more easily choose the tools you need to respond. Whereas before, life may have felt like it was happening too quickly and you didn't know how to respond to a stressor, meditation acts as a sort of internal sharpening and has the effect of alchemizing time. It's like the Matrix, allowing you to slow an experience so you can ask, *What do I want? How will I respond? How will I experience this?*

Meditation also allows you to expand your awareness so that you can focus on what is true *right now.* When we're in a state of stress, we're also summoning forward our entire history of stress. It triggers every previous stress or unmet need that came before it. That is, coincidentally, why it can be difficult for people to empathize with one another when they observe someone experiencing stress that seems, to them, incommensurate with the experience. That's why they say things like, "It's not that big of a deal." But that is how stress functions for all of us.

Through meditation, you can learn how to zero in on what is in front of you right now without bringing all of the baggage of your entire life experience into the mix. Focusing your attention on a very specific thing, whether it's an object, mantra—a repeated sound or phrase— breath, or visualization, foundationally allows your body to reset to a state of calm without even thinking about it. It lets your body do what it does best in its most vital, natural state, and then creates a rhythm or cadence that your body will begin to automatically adopt without needing to be asked to. It will start to greet stress in that way. It will start to give breath where the need is.

I saw this at work in real time recently, while reviewing a recording of one of my podcast sessions. I'd been in conversation with a trauma-informed yoga facilitator who specifically works with women who have been sexually assaulted and sexually abused. As we were talking about some of the barriers sexual abuse survivors might have to meditation and yoga, we were traversing some pretty difficult and triggering conversations. I noticed, though, that I was unconsciously bringing my breath *all the way down.* And not only that, I was using a breath style meant to push out charged energy. I could witness myself doing those things—while I was mentally engrossed in the conversation, my body

60   LIVING IN WISDOM

knew what I needed to do in a moment that could have otherwise pulled me out of the present. If not for that, the conversation could not have gotten as deep. In a triggered state, I might have started speaking more quickly, rushing through that topic, or else I may have had a more blasé response to try to avoid the conversation—like, *yeah, yeah, yeah, got it.* Instead, I was able to be available and fully present, which then created space for my listeners to be present. In meditation, your body practices that habit and ability, like stunt doubles who practice how to fall properly so that they don't inadvertently hurt themselves.

Focusing on something other than your thoughts also frees you from the rumination loop. For overthinkers—which is most of us—we find ourselves thinking, *If I just revisit that thought one more time, I'm going to get the solution or get to the bottom of it or break through it.* But when you consider this through a more aligned place, maybe through the lens of your spiritual curriculum, you'll realize you've been thinking about this stuff since you were a kid and all through adulthood, so there's really no way you're getting to the bottom of it by thinking about it *more.* To break out of this, you work on choosing to consciously let go of those thoughts and distance yourself from the addiction cycle—because this rumination and overthinking can be like an addiction. Whenever I experience these thought loops during my meditation practice, I offer myself the following: *You've so courageously thought of this so many times and in so many ways; there is no stone left unturned about this issue and how you relate to it. You're now free to let it go.* Focusing on a breathing technique or mantra or doing a body scan offers you that same kind of escape hatch, pausing the loop of thought, even if for just a brief moment in the beginning of your practice.

There is evidence to back this up. Meditation prompts the brain to shift from high-frequency, high-alert waves to the slower, more relaxed alpha and theta waves that are linked to deep, calm focus and sleep. So when these thoughts do surface, you don't have an intense, hypervigilant attachment to them. It's more like watching a cloud drift by or gently swiping to the next.

When you first begin to meditate, you'll spend a lot of your time just battling your thoughts. It will feel distinctly challenging, and there's a reason for that. Oftentimes, when you sit still to meditate, it is the first moment of stillness you've had all day. When you don't have the distraction of constant movement, conversations, work, parenting, screen time, etc., all the thoughts you've been holding at bay come careening in. All of that worry and anxiety and preoccupation hovering over you waiting to be looked at and processed comes flooding in. That's in large part why people are so intent to distract themselves in the first place—quiet and stillness leave too much opportunity for the thoughts to overtake you. Almost everything in our modern lives is a tool of avoidance, so the nature of just stopping can be incredibly triggering. But that doesn't mean anything is wrong. It is completely normal to not enjoy that feeling. It's also normal when you're in meditation mode for those thoughts to feel really dense, like they're an actual part of you. It's common to feel as though your thoughts are your actual identity and your actual personality. So there's a heaviness because it feels like there's a deeper connectedness to your thoughts that says something about you.

Meditation also brings forward anything you've been avoiding or don't want to see. It's why some beginner meditators just cry and cry for months. If you don't typically cry as an emotional response but all of a sudden are weeping every time you meditate, and want to stop because you think there's something wrong, know that that's part of the beauty of it! You need to give yourself the space to be yourself and with what is true and present. Slowly those tears will stop, and you'll shift how you relate to the root of those hard emotions.

As you practice meditation, your frontal cortex, the part of the brain that processes all of our sensory information about the surrounding world and gives it a value, goes off-line, in a manner of speaking. This is to say, your thoughts will become less and less invasive, and you'll become capable of separating yourself from the thoughts you're having about yourself.

> ## MINDFULNESS VERSUS MINDFUL AWARENESS
>
> The concept and practice of mindfulness became mainstream about thirty years ago, and somehow became synonymous with meditation. Mindfulness, the practice of being aware of your thoughts and feelings in the present moment, is a wonderful concept, but it's the actual opposite of what's happening to us when we're in a meditative state. "Mind-fullness" conceptually is not what we're going for. This is not the experience of a full mind. Rather, meditation is about *mindful awareness*. You want to be aware of the full mind, and then be able to shift your consciousness and your behavior and your presence as a result of your awareness of what is full inside of you.

When Meditation Doesn't Feel Safe

It is undeniable that silence and stillness can be triggering. For almost every single one of us, it is a vastly foreign and jarring experience after constantly being in motion. Quiet seems to be the opposite of what we value in society, and so every day we receive nonstop validation to go, go, go, distract, distract, distract, stimulate, stimulate, stimulate. It is the flow in which we have the most experience and practice, but just because silence and stillness feel mildly uncomfortable in contrast does not mean that they are not right for you.

However, from a trauma-informed lens, sitting with your eyes closed can be very, very scary and unearth unprocessed pain. For some, revisiting this practice little by little will allow you to slowly disarm yourself. For others, especially those for whom there has been predatory trauma, I recommend alternative ways of being in meditation that you can explore in tandem with a mental health professional while you get grounded in your safe space and rebuild trust in the body. This may be a low eye gaze meditation where you keep your eyes open but keep a soft, low gaze that allows for peripheral sight. Or it could feel nice to practice a guided meditation with a companion holding space for you so that you're not alone. You could also try practices that, while not technically meditation, facilitate a meditative state or a state that creates freedom in your mind to explore and go where it pleases. That could be walking in silence, connecting your eyes to beauty such as finding the flowers or splashes of green. It could be coloring in silence and getting lost in the creativity, or another activity you do with your hands such as creating a collage or a mandala with found objects. There are many ways to access this work; I invite you to explore and play until you find what feels right to you.

Your Meditation Foundation

Each chapter throughout the rest of the book will have its own unique meditation practice to support the chapter's core lesson. Consider this practice as your foundation, your home base. It is the most basic expression of the practice but is no less potent in its simplicity.

As you begin your practice, I would like you to commit to **daily twenty-minute** meditation. This is the minimum amount of time proven to have a measurable effect on the brain. So, while I do believe intuition plays a role in how you build your practice, I don't believe in giving you a pass to meditate for only five minutes a day. I think we do ourselves a disservice when we try to make things snackable—we're not getting the real benefits, and it keeps us in an intellectualization mode that acts as a barrier to an embodied experience and the wisdom that comes with it. Twenty minutes a day should be your starting point. And then, as you build the discipline to sit still for longer stretches, you can work toward thirty minutes twice a day—this is the ultimate goal. If you can unlock a morning and evening practice, you will see monumental and accelerated results.

Choose either morning or evening for your meditation. For a morning meditation, try to accomplish it first thing, before you get your day

64   LIVING IN WISDOM

going (and before you look at your phone). Meditating in the morning sets the tone of greeting the day with a relaxed feeling and clear thoughts, and the ability to make higher choices with your consciousness.

By contrast, an evening meditation is about releasing the choices of the day. Ideally, you find time to practice before dinner, at the end of your workday. When I was commuting home from an office, I would sit in my car before I left work and meditate right there in the parking lot, or I'd sit in the driveway when I got home. That allowed me to come into a place of regulation and take the day off before I settled back into the experience of my life and spent time with my family.

As you prepare for your meditation, remember the only rule is to stay present, even if you want to stop. That's it. Stay in it, even when you're deeply uncomfortable. Other than that, there's no wrong way to do it. Just notice yourself. Every time you give yourself the chance to be in the discomfort and be present in the noticing, you're giving yourself the chance to be fully in practice. Remember, thoughts coming up is normal and to be expected. Your goal is to arrive at the gap. Find the space between one thought and the next, wherein you take on the role of a silent observer. This will bring you into the space of inner choice and awareness where you can, over time, see things from an expanded vertical view; you'll be able to see all your thoughts at once and then pick and choose where your attention will go.

If you've maintained a meditation practice, what follows may be a helpful refresher. If you're new to it, let's take it step-by-step. Find your way to your sacred space where you've set the container. Come into a seated position that feels comfortable to you—with your legs crossed or straight in front of you, or kneeling with your back against the wall. Props, such as meditation cushions, folded blankets, or a BackJack meditation chair, are a great way to get more support and not get distracted by unnecessary discomfort. If at all possible, do not lie down to meditate. You want to arrive at a place of *active* yet relaxed awareness.

Sit with a straight spine and a soft belly. You're going to notice that your body will want to shift and change throughout the practice, and that's completely fine. Notice if you're getting hunched over, and allow yourself to slowly reset your body without thinking too much about it.

Set your hands on the tops of your thighs or on the floor next to you, depending on how you're seated, with your palms facing up. This puts you energetically in the state of receiving. One of the biggest obstacles to creating a life that feels more nourishing and abundant and full is that we're so used to caring for the self and doing for the self that we cut off the ability to receive—acknowledgment, kindness, help. So, in this moment, you are making yourself available to receive the synchronistic capabilities of the Universe. As you sit in this meditation, you can bring your mind to that receptivity, as well as to surrender: *I am not trying to control everything around me right now.*

Now start to connect with your breath. Start with a very simple, quickly calming "take five" or 5-5-5 breathing technique: five seconds breathing deeply from the belly, up into the chest and to the top of the head, then hold for five seconds. Slowly release out of the nose for five seconds. Repeat this for at least three cycles, but aim for three to five minutes of this. Then return to nice, easy breathing.

For this foundational meditation, the only real direction I have for you is to continue to focus on your breath. Focus on the rise and fall of your chest. Begin to make peace with your body in a still experience. Notice what's uncomfortable. Build your capacity for discipline by finding an adjustment but staying in it anyway. Notice how much you're thinking and your discomfort about how much you're thinking. How cringey you might feel. Then let it all go and bring it back to the breath.

If you'd like, you can work with a mudra, or a ritual gesture made with your hands, to heighten the energetic intention of your meditation. In Vedic wisdom, energy moves through the channels of our fingers, connecting our own energy with cosmic energy. There are hundreds of mudras, each of which with its own "prescription," such as building inner strength and courage, transforming ignorance into wisdom, or shielding oneself from negative energies. I've included some of my favorite mudras in part 3, which are intended to be used as companion practices with each chapter's lesson. Or, if you prefer, you can simply rest your palms face up on your thighs in quiet receptivity.

You may also choose to work with a mantra, or words or sounds that are repeated to assist with concentration in mediation, according to the Vedic tradition. A common mantra for new meditators is *So Hum*, which translates to "I am" or "I exist." Say it aloud a few times, allowing the tones and vibrations to resonate in your body. Then continue repeating it in your mind as you also maintain awareness of your breath.

Use this meditation as an opportunity to release the roles you play in your everyday life. Release work, release desires, and just sit in the present and notice who you are when you're not responding to the world and people around you. If at any time you get caught up in thought, don't overthink it. Don't open your eyes, just notice and bring it back to the breath. Just breathe. So Hummmm.

Come out of the meditation by bringing your hands into prayer position in the center of your chest, letting the thumbs touch your breastbone where your heart is. Take in a few more deep breaths, then let your eyes slowly gaze open. Take a bow of self-respect for giving yourself the opportunity to be in that moment.

Building a Foundation for Practice: Setting an Intention

As you come out of your first meditation, I'd like to invite you to set an intention for your life for the duration of your experience with this book and exploring these practices. By creating an intention, you're giving yourself the opportunity and the right to have a desire, to have a foundation for who and what you want to be and to experience. It's an incredibly important piece of this entire puzzle because it's what opens you up to moreness. But what's truly incredible is the way you're opened up to the ability to have more *without having to come up with the solution or the structure for how that will happen.* When you create an intention and are not also trying to immediately come behind it with a plan, you open to the limitless potential of the Universe around you and outcomes you can't fathom and facets of growth that aren't anywhere in your awareness because you don't yet know they exist. Think about it from a practical perspective: To say to the Universe or God that your intention is to know your highest self and to have access to a version of yourself that is grander and has more depth than what you are now—it would be utterly ridiculous to imagine that you could know how to get there. Because let's be honest, if we did, we all would.

I like to say that intention is the horse drawing our cart, the cart being ourselves. This is the most essential way to relate to your spiritual journey because the belief that you are the one drawing the cart is performance and won't create change—namely, it won't build self-trust. An intention, on the other hand, disarms you from the notion that you need to be responsible for everything. It allows you to build intuition and sink into that trust. Energetically, you are building community with the systems, people, and practices that allow you to call forward everything in this life and in this world that can assist you on that path. You are shifting your faith toward those channels and away from the hypervigilance or constant state of control that keeps us stuck. There is no possible way that you can ask for a change you don't know how to accomplish and be required to come up with all of the solutions. This is where you surrender to the unknown with only the desire to receive that change. It is the first step to unlocking the greater ability to be with yourself and transform yourself. Intention is just such a holy, sacred prayer. It creates space for creativity to arise from the deepest truth of who and what we are—that's all that synchronicity is: the creation of things coming up to be made manifest.

The key to setting an intention is to make it purposeful but vague. It should be something you want to explore but without getting too specific—this is not a vision board. It is not *My intention is to get my dream job/get married/buy my dream house.*

Instead, as you come out of your meditation—a way to ensure that

68   LIVING IN WISDOM

you are in a truly relaxed state in which intuition can arise—complete this sentence: "It is my intention to ___." Greet the end of that statement with what is true and not contrived. It should be disconnected from performance. It should not be something you think you should say or be. Even if it does not make sense to the conscious mind when it comes forward, don't edit it. Don't try to revise. *My intention is.* It could be to heal. It could be to feel loved. To *be* love.

For one of my earliest intentions, which I have saved in a sacred box along with many others, all that I could bring forward was my intention to surrender to the truth of my life. I didn't quite understand what that meant or why I was saying that. I could have greeted it with a criticism: *What do you mean? You* are *living your life. Living your truth.* But by honoring what had come up for me and following that mandate to surrender to the truth of my life, I could come into a state of enoughness and not constantly seeking or admiring or needing more. I could recognize what was true and unique for my life and for me. It took me out of comparing, measuring, looking across the street, and constantly evaluating what I was when compared to others. *Miracles* unfolded from that one statement. It gave me a true understanding of who I am, what I'm meant to do, and the people who are meant to be cocreators of my life and me of theirs.

Reach for your intention now. Write it on the inside cover of this book or in your journal as part of your covenant with this process and filling these pages with your sweat, your tears. It is all waiting for you.

Chapter 7

Breathwork/Pranayama

We don't normally give a lot of thought to breath. By design, humans' breathing is governed by the autonomic nervous system and doesn't require you to be any more aware of it than your heart beating. And because we are not required to think about our breathing, we frequently do not. We take for granted this enormous life-giving process as just being *there*. Consider for a moment that whales, which are also mammals, do not have autonomic breathing. They have to think about their breath just to survive. It also means they can't sleep for long periods of time because their bodies cannot automatically meet their needs for breath.

Not only do we not think about our breathing, we assume that we're all breathing correctly and supporting our bodies and organs and brains at an optimal level. But owing to our fast-paced lives, pollution, and the way most of us walk around in an altered dysregulated state of fight-or-flight, we are often not getting the oxygen that we need because of the quick, shallow breath pattern we fall into whenever we experience physical manifestations of stress. When we breathe that way, it's not possible to provide our brains with adequate oxygen, which then means that our brains can't function at their highest capability. If our brains aren't functioning at their highest capability, then neither can we as our innate selves. And neither can our spirits. Or any of the ways that we want to be in the world and meet any of the physical, mental, or emotional goals that we have.

70 LIVING IN WISDOM

So let's just say that breathing unconsciously is essentially the bare minimum. You're alive. You're moving through the world. But to breathe consciously is to improve our lived experience exponentially. Breath is our life force. It is what allows you to activate your parasympathetic nervous system, leave a state of stress, and enter a state of calm. The breath can improve your body's functioning by delivering more vital oxygen into your blood and organs, decreasing the stress hormones cortisol and adrenaline, increasing oxytocin (aka "the love hormone"), lowering blood pressure, increasing blood flow, easing gastrointestinal symptoms, and boosting overall immune function. Breath expands your awareness and your ability to problem solve within your body. It's what gives you the opportunity to release charged thoughts and feelings. Breath is, by spiritual design, a sacred instrument that moves in and out of the body. I like to think of breath as being a material, biological manifestation of what we know as the Holy Spirit. To breathe with intention is to deepen your connection within and without.

Breathwork has been recognized for thousands of years in wisdom practices. Specifically, in yoga, breath is associated with *prana shakti*, or life force or life energy, hence the name *pranayama*—the practice of focusing on the breath to elevate the prana shakti. Pranayama also appears in the Bhagavad Gita, one of the most sacred Hindu scriptures, and the thousands-of-years-old foundational yogic text the Yoga Sutras of Patanjali, which indicates to me not only the power of living in flow with the breath and recognizing it as essential for vibrancy and vitality, but also the power of breath specifically in service of goals of transcendence. For that exact reason, especially looking at this practice through the lens of trauma, breathwork is essential to healing. It has the ability to transcend traumatic experiences, discomforts, and stressors housed in the body. It has the ability to *move* things in the body, not dissimilar to how we think of wind. Breath, like wind, is a vehicle of creation. Think about religious texts—God *breathes* life into things. Breath is one of the more transformative tools that we have access to.

How Breathwork Functions in the Body

Breathwork brings you back into your interior experience. That's why it's so important, especially for self-development, because so many of us are operating outside of the body in an almost dissociated state. When your nervous system is activated, when you're stuck in a loop of ruminating thoughts, or when you're exposed to higher stressors—perceived or real—you exit your body. And when that happens, you may experience a numbness or a lack of feeling, which is not the ideal space to be operating and making decisions from.

When you center your focus on the breath, which is one of the core tenets of easing into meditation, you're bringing yourself down and grounding into your physical reality. All humans, separate from any social construct, experience their humanity in three specific ways: the mind, the body, and the spirit. Breathwork unifies these functions. It's one of both the quickest *and* most profound ways we can come into what's known as an integrated or embodied state of being—or when mind, body, and spirit, or soul, can be experienced simultaneously.

Breathwork balances the brain's energy, creates a feeling of more internal space, and allows for more elevated choices from that space. It's as though after receiving information or stimulation you have more room to process the information and respond in a way that feels ideal for you. Because of that, breathwork is instrumental for metabolizing emotions and healing emotional pain and trauma. It has been successfully used to address addictions, stress and anxiety, negative thought patterns, anger issues, chronic pain, the emotional effects of illness, grief, and post-traumatic stress disorder. It helps us develop life skills, particularly our executive functioning, which typically develops in early childhood around the age of six and can be stunted for a number of reasons. Executive functioning is crucial for working memory, cognitive flexibility, abstract thinking, and emotional regulation and self-regulation. Breathwork stretches our capacity for discomfort and the ability to make choices in the midst of it. It helps us develop or increase our self-awareness. It

72 LIVING IN WISDOM

potently activates the body's intelligence so we know what our needs are from moment to moment and can ideally meet them. It enriches our creativity. It can improve personal and professional relationships. It increases confidence, self-image, self-esteem, joy, and happiness.

Breathwork is the magic that makes it all work.

Your Foundation Breathwork

There are many types of breath patterns and practices, all of which can be used in different ways to deliver different benefits. Some are calming and centering, while others are energizing and revitalizing. The practices I've chosen for you to begin to explore here are those I use most often for myself and my students, which I find bring great rewards in everyday life, and that are easy and accessible to do on your own. When practiced daily, they support the lived human experience and all the stressors and stimuli that come with it.

To begin, I'm going to introduce you to four types of breath. The first two are traditional pranayama patterns typically explored in yogic philosophy, so they might sound familiar if you've taken yoga classes. The second two are more modern techniques that have become popular in mainstream Western applications. My intention is for you to read through each description and begin to familiarize yourself with these resources. Unlike other Pillar Practices, such as meditation and journaling, breathwork isn't something you necessarily need to limit to a sacred space or time of day, nor should it be limited to once or twice a day. There are so many moments and transitions that breathwork can ease and elevate—waking up, going to work, preparing for a meeting, preparing to reenter your home space after being at work all day, going to sleep, needing an afternoon boost, recalibrating after a stressful moment—and you should feel empowered to reach for breathwork for every single one of them.

To start regularly incorporating breathwork into your routine, begin with the moment you open your eyes in the morning in order to

BREATHWORK/PRANAYAMA 73

get into your body. Then do the same in the evening. That's two opportunities for breathwork that don't even require your leaving your bed. I also suggest using breathwork to drop into your meditation practice. Beyond that, try engaging with it in all different scenarios and notice its effect in real time, in real life. Try it on the subway. Try it in the car. In the elevator on the way up to the office. Try it standing. Try it with a hand on the heart when you're feeling anxiety. With each of these breathwork sequences, feel free to work with it until you feel a shift, or if that's too open-ended, aim for three to five minutes. If you hit that five-minute mark, by all means, keep it going. In its own way, this is an excellent exercise for tuning in to what your body needs and wants.

The beautiful and surprising truth about breathwork is that its benefits compound the more you are in practice. Eventually, it will become muscle memory; you'll start to notice how your body will reach for these rhythms on its own when it needs regulation. I experienced this in my own practice, how it started coming to my rescue without my having to think about it. My body would simply activate whatever breath sequence I needed because I knew them by heart. Some of the most miraculous moments we can have on the healing path are a result of our being in cocreation with our bodies and our practice without requiring an active, hypervigilant mind. It's our body's way of reminding us that we can loosen the reins and trust.

Remember, as you try on these new breathing patterns, you're stretching your capacity to be aware of your body and to be with any discomfort that comes up. Just observe whatever arises, and resist the temptation to judge it. It may surprise you how challenging something as seemingly easy as breathing can be. You might notice a tightness, or that it makes you feel emotional, or that you feel a sense of disruption or an internal shift. It doesn't mean something is wrong. Dare I say that it means that everything is actually right? Because your body is allowing itself to reset.

Challenge yourself to take just one more *sip* of air. And then another tiny sip. And then expand, expand, expand from those sips. Before you know it, you will have excavated your chest and lungs into a spacious

74   LIVING IN WISDOM

cavern you can fill and empty. You'll also notice how well-oiled your body feels from the inside; things will move more easily—digestion, emotions, ideas—once you begin flooding your body with life force and oxygen.

Dirga Pranayama (Three-Part Breath)

This breath is phenomenal for beginners, particularly before meditation or yoga, because it quickly settles you into your body and connects you to the present moment. I love this breath pattern for starting your day before you get out of bed, as well as ending your day just before falling asleep. In fact, it's one of the few breathwork practices you can do lying down.

Start by lying on your back in a comfortable position. Start breathing through your nose into your belly, and notice as your belly slowly expands. Just when you've got enough breath to fill your belly, right when it starts to feel full, let in just a little more breath through your nose until it fills your rib cage area. Next, slowly move that breath up your body toward your chest, letting in a little bit more air to completely expand across the heart.

Now exhale very slowly through your nose, first releasing the air from your chest, then your rib cage, and finally from your belly. Allow your chest cavity and your belly to deflate.

Repeat for three to five minutes. Or more, if it feels nice.

Nadi Shodhana Pranayama (Alternate-Nostril Breathing)

This is one of the most famous pranayama techniques and also one of the most powerful. It enhances concentration and focus, reduces anxiety, and gets you really centered in your body, making it a great practice to reach for throughout the day. In particular, this practice is meant to bring balance among mind, body, and soul—as well as between masculine and feminine energies.

At first, this pattern can seem a little bit more complicated than others because there are hand movements involved, but it will eventually come naturally to you. To prepare, start in a comfortable seated cross-legged position. Place your left hand on your left knee, palm facing up. Now, rest your right hand gently over your face. Situate your pointer finger so that its tip is on your third eye, which will naturally align your thumb with your right nostril and your ring finger with the left. Take a moment to exhale completely, getting all of the breath out of your body. Use your thumb to gently close your right nostril, and take a deep inhale into the left nostril. At the top of the inhale, release your right nostril and close the left nostril with your ring finger. Exhale completely through the right nostril. Inhale again through the right, switch, exhale through the left. Inhale left, exhale right. Repeat the full cycle (in, out) for three to five minutes or more, if it feels nice.

Box Breath

This is a more modern breathwork practice, and one I use with most of my clients when they're first getting started. It also happens to be one of my personal favorites; I engage with it frequently throughout the day. It's specifically great for calming stress in real time and taking the edge off quickly. It's true that all breathwork can do this, but I find the active engagement of box breathing in particular is very effective at pulling you out of the cycle of stress and ruminating thoughts. Plus, it reduces the feeling of stress in the body—pounding heart, clenched jaw, tight chest—so you will notice not just an unburdening of emotional stress patterns, but total physical relaxation as well. It is, quite simply, a powerful reset for returning to a relaxed state. Also, box breathing resets your innate autonomic breathing pattern. Oftentimes, when you're stuck in a stress loop or doing too much too quickly, your breathing will get very shallow. This practice helps not only pull you out of that, but also ingrain more deeply how your body wants to be breathing when you take your hand off the wheel. More significantly, this breath can be your lifeline back to regulation if you're experiencing true distress, whether emotionally, psychologically, or physically.

But you don't have to be in the throes of stress or distress to reach for this breath. It can be hugely beneficial for performance, endurance, and concentration. Box breathing is used by athletes preparing for competition; a former Navy SEAL turned motivational speaker credits this style of breath for getting him through the excruciating physical and mental demands of his training.

Box breathing has four equal "sides": breathing in, holding that breath, breathing out, and holding that exhale—and doing each for the same number of beats, in this case four. Start by getting into a comfortable seated position, or if you prefer, you could do this sequence standing. Take a deep inhale through your nose for four (slow!) seconds. Hold the breath at the top for a count of four, then slowly release through your nose for four seconds, and hold once again at the bottom for another four seconds. Repeat that sequence until you feel a calm regulation take over your body. I suggest a minimum of four cycles, but it's also a beautiful practice to stretch for as long as five minutes.

Pursed-Lip Breathing

This final breath is particularly useful because it helps control shortness of breath. We don't often realize when we're short of breath, even though we so frequently are. When we're not breathing, we're not bathing our brains and organs in the oxygen they need, therefore making it hard for them to function optimally, which is why shortness of breath makes it more challenging to create enough space to uproot and push out any emotional stressors.

Pursed-lip breathing is what to reach for whenever you're in a moment of anger or emotional overwhelm, or even just exerting a lot of physical energy. This practice will not only slow your breath rate, it will also keep your airways open for longer after you're done, which decreases the amount of effort it takes to breathe. And by encouraging nice, deep, full breaths as your default breathing, you'll be physically bringing in more ventilation to move out old air and make space for fresh oxygen. Emotionally, you're releasing negativity, misinformed beliefs, and traumatic experiences, creating space for what you are becoming.

Begin by finding a comfortable seated position, either in a chair or on the ground with crossed legs. Alternatively, you can lie down, if you like. Relax your shoulders as much as possible. Now, purse your lips together like you're blowing on hot food. Slowly breathe out through your pursed lips. (You'll notice that this is the only breath sequence that includes breathing through both the nose and the mouth, just a taste of a different experience.) Then take a nice, long inhale through your nose, and this time when you exhale, push it out through your pursed lips for twice as long as it took to inhale. Aim to inhale for a count of anywhere from three to five seconds, and then double it for the exhale—whatever your chest has the capacity for. Over time, as you work with this breath, that capacity will expand and this will get easier.

Repeat until you feel a sense of dropping into your body, getting regulated, and being present with your internal experience. I suggest spending three to five minutes in this sequence. Or more, if it feels nice.

Chapter 8

Self-Inquiry/Journaling

I'll begin by saying I know how deceivingly complex and unapproachable journaling can be. I've had a lot of journal trauma—my mom read mine when I was fourteen. It was the innocent transgression of a mother simply wanting to know more about her highly emotionally guarded daughter, but it set us on a ten-year cycle of distrust. Believe me when I tell you I understand that you might have some barriers around the idea of expressing on paper what has only lived inside you. But journaling is sacred and necessary work.

At its core, journaling is nothing more than writing down your thoughts and feelings in order to understand them more clearly. Simple. And yet, decidedly not. What naturally happens during this process is that the innermost truths of your life—your secrets, fears, and anxieties—all come to the forefront. This is the crevice work. Everything needs to be shaken loose so that it can come out. By writing everything down, you're giving yourself permission to face those truths. That does not always look good. Sometimes the truth of our lives is the trauma of our lives. It's the things we want to forget, the truth about our behavior or our reactions, which can feel shameful and guilt inducing. It brings forward all the things we feel inclined to dislike about ourselves. But by laying them out on the table, by saying the things out loud to yourself and being able to see clearly the patterns, bridges, and deeper truths, you'll implicitly understand that so much of that doesn't have to define you, and that you can forgive yourself for the things that didn't have your consent in the first place, such as behaviors and thoughts influenced by your trauma. You have to be present with all of it for that to happen, though. You have to witness the reality that is both inside and outside of yourself.

Doing so will give you deep access to processing yourself and your experiences. It's like opening a valve inside of yourself, creating the necessary space to consider your stories with the kind of objectivity that sparks transformation. In many ways, journaling is a mechanism of release. It creates a pathway of ease between you and yourself, yourself and others, and yourself and the world. That ease has been reflected in research; studies have shown that journaling alone, even without meditation, can reduce stress and improve not only your mood and sense of well-being but also the way you relate to your life.[1] And inherent in making all of that possible for yourself is a deep self-respect and self-trust.

The alternative is continuing to live with these truths and allowing them to keep a viselike grip on every choice and experience you have. I attended a retreat where a woman in her seventies shared a story about abuse she experienced during her childhood, and it was as charged as if it had happened yesterday. She was still holding on to it so tightly. It was a profound moment in my own journey; I decided then and there *I will face my truths*. The idea that something could live so presently inside of you for so long was so sad to me. Every experience this woman had had over the course of her seventy-plus-year life had been filtered through that one reality.

The woman facilitating the session said to her, "Just because you're choosing to let it go doesn't mean it didn't happen. It doesn't mean you didn't pull through that experience." Which is such a beautiful reminder—we don't need to hold on to pain as part of our identity. If this is something you can relate to, I know how it can feel like so much was required of you, how much of yourself and of your life you had to devote to that pain. Releasing that pain does not mean that people won't

80   LIVING IN WISDOM

see that strength. Or that hard work. Or that your experience is diminished. Or that you won't be anyone without it. The power of regular, if not daily, release is that it gets you into the cadence and muscle memory of being able to let things go. And letting your witnessing be enough.

Despite its challenges, journaling is courageous and sacred work. You're documenting your existence, as though carving your name into an old tree. You're saying, "I was here. I existed."

Documenting oneself is the creation of our legend, of our myth. It is, I believe, the work that pushes humanity forward. Think about the great minds of the past and how they created monumental paradigm shifts—Vincent van Gogh, Frida Kahlo, James Baldwin—they did that by documenting themselves. Journaling is what allows us to view our own human experience, which is a profound opportunity to give your soul in this lifetime and is a large part of why I think we're here.

What I love most about journaling, though, is that it allows you to become your own case study. You can clearly and in real time see your thoughts and experiences, your perception of them and reactions to them. You can then turn on your self-scientist brain and assess all of that data: What are the equations? What are the patterns? Identifying those patterns allows you not only to begin to release them, but also to reverse engineer how you relate to things moving forward, putting you back in choice.

Journaling Without Judgment

There are many ways to access journaling—some people journal with the intention of capturing moments of their personal history, or just detailing their daily experiences. For our purposes, we will use journaling as an active mindfulness tool for self-growth and processing, which gives us access to a wider range of techniques. You can get really specific and journal about how you're relating to that singular thing in your life or story, and continue to revisit it. You can do daily gratitude journaling and see what comes to the surface. Some find it helpful to journal their

SELF-INQUIRY/JOURNALING   81

wants or desires, giving themselves permission to have wants. For some of us, having the audacity to desire is a barrier. Journaling our desires gives us the opportunity to explore what the act of wanting looks like in both a micro and a macro sense, the big things you desire and the little things. Journaling can take on another dimension when you add images—drawings, paintings, doodles.

When I journal, I use a bullet-point style and simply make observations about what feels relevant to me, anything and everything. I also make use of voice memos, which I find helpful when I'm in transit, or not feeling well, or just can't find a pen and paper. If you do record journal entries, I highly recommend you transcribe them so you can review them later. Regardless of the style, be sure to date each entry so you have a clear record of when you recorded those thoughts, which will eventually become a resource for you.

Romanticizing or novelizing our thoughts can be a hindrance to growth. Journaling in this way externalizes the practice, as we imagine someone else will be reading our words. The exercise then becomes about perception and performance. Instead, trust your writing. Don't try to manipulate or contort it. Don't self-censor. Just let your thoughts come through in their purest form, whatever that looks like. Commit to being yourself in this process in the most transparent way possible, and don't take your journaling to mean something about you. Don't evaluate what's coming out on the page. Just let it be the truth of whatever it is, and then release it. Then start a new day and do it again.

If you do find yourself worrying that someone might read your thoughts, it can be helpful to protect your entries in whatever way you need in order to feel safe. If you're writing in a journal, lock it away. If you're writing on your phone, make the app accessible only by password. While burning pages to release them is often used in ceremonies, I don't recommend burning papers or deleting things. This might have its benefits, but only once you've arrived at a place of true understanding, when what has arisen for you through your journaling has been released from your body and decision-making. Ridding yourself of all

82   LIVING IN WISDOM

of it too early just becomes a bypass, but it's not that simple. You can't just burn something and make it go away. You have to be with it until you're able to fully process it.

Your Foundation Journaling Practice

I recommend coming to your journaling practice in the late afternoon or evening, when you can begin processing the day. Ideally you would meditate first, but it is very effective to practice the 5-5-5 breathing from page 65, or perhaps just a short meditation. A small practice to help you get centered and out of the loops of thought about the day.

I prefer to journal in my sacred space, but anywhere quiet will work—or with sounds you enjoy—where you can feel grounded and anchored in the present moment, able to get lost in your thoughts. It could be at a park, at the beach, or snuggled in bed (which is great as part of the recapitulation process, page 106). Occasionally I will journal at my desk at the end of my workday so I can get some things out.

Aim to spend anywhere between five and thirty minutes, depending on whether you catch a flow. Once you get the hang of journaling, oftentimes five minutes will be enough to get everything out. Do not feel pressured to do this practice every day—especially if you tend to experience anxiety about "falling behind" or feel like you have to catch up for missed days. Commit to three days a week, and then settle into a cadence of doing it every time the urge arises.

For this first practice, before you make your way to part 3, I'd like you to spend time answering this self-inquiry prompt: *Who am I being called to become right now?* Not *Who do I want to become?*—that's too connected to your controlled thoughts and evaluating mind. Really sink into *Who am I being pushed to become even if I'm doing it kicking and screaming?* Let yourself sink into being here with this book, with this process, and write to that prompt for five to ten minutes. Take stock of who you are now, how you feel about your life, how you would like to feel about your life. What do you need to release in order for that to be true?

As you move through this book, you may be tempted to look back at previous journal entries. It is, after all, an excellent resource for self-study. However, I would like for you to be discerning about how you explore these past entries. I want to make sure that when you revisit them, you are doing so in an objective research capacity. It is because you are ready to process that information and use it to identify patterns and build connections. It is *not* because you want to be a tourist of the pain. If you sense that that is your motivation, keep moving forward. Then, when you come into a space where you feel like there's enough room for you to integrate that wisdom, you can begin to look back and objectively review these thoughts, experiences, and patterns through the informed lens of your healing experience.

Chapter 9

Affirming Statements and Qualitative Words

The next pillar I'd like to introduce you to is affirmations, or rather its full name, *affirming statements and qualitative words*. At their root, affirmations are a simple but powerful way to affirm, encourage, and support something that is important to us, in this case, our healing journey. This tool is particularly imperative for our work on ourselves, because ultimately we do that work alone—even when we're working with a facilitator such as a therapist or healer. Add to that the fact that healing is difficult, uncomfortable, and often slow going, and it becomes clear how effective a salve it is to be affirmed. Affirmations are also another way we can show up for ourselves and be able to meet our own needs, which is part of the healing process itself.

For many, being affirmed is not something we have a lot of experience with. Most of us are on this path *because* we had that trauma or challenge of not having that need met. That doesn't necessarily look like neglect or abuse, it's just that affirming is often associated with words that people say to us and that feel particularly good when they come from an authority figure, such as a parent or someone whom we hold in high regard or esteem. But even if you have received external validation, that is not the level that affirmations are operating on. Rather, truly affirming statements and qualitative words have the power to penetrate to the deepest parts of ourselves. They speak to the very quality of us, the worth of us. It's the kind of feedback that tells us more about who we are, our choices, what we do well, and what we could use some help with or could work on. Affirming requires the person administering it to have a certain amount of personal awareness, integrity, generosity of spirit, and complete selflessness. There is no ulterior motive to affirmation. All of which is why the most potent affirmation comes from ourselves, and it's important for us to find ways to meet that need.

Modern Alchemy

That said, there are obstacles we will need to clear first. For many people, affirming words can be very triggering. We all have different ways that we define the same words—whether we're looking at them from a cultural perspective or a personal and experiential one. But particularly how you've engaged with a certain word or idea in your life will inform how you relate to that word. Even something as simple as the word *love* could have very, very different meanings from person to person because of how that concept was modeled and explained in real time—or not at all.

But consistent use of affirming language coupled with your healing process makes coming into self-love and mastery some of the strongest alchemy you can access. Some cultures believed that there is such a thing as word magic/spell casting/manifesting that's generated through the coupling of language and intention. That's the power of calling something into your life. Christian Scripture puts forth that the power of life and death is in the tongue. I deeply believe when it comes to our own personal journeys with ourselves that we can break ourselves down or masterfully build ourselves up. That starts with language and how we relate to it.

How Affirmations Function in the Body

Positive affirmations are simply short written statements that use words that are meaningful to you. These words should bring you joy, bring you truth, and bring you motivation and inspiration. They can help you

86 LIVING IN WISDOM

lighten your load and brighten your outlook on the world. When you say them to yourself regularly—and their power lies in reaching for them regularly—they create a kind of potential around you. They grow not just your self-esteem but also your self-belief and your self-trust. They connect you to the solar plexus chakra and your sense of deserving and self-worth. They connect you to the heart chakra and your ability to receive love. They expand you, help you stand a little taller. They combat negative self-talk and powerfully break ruminating systems of thoughts. In fact, they're a great tool in real time to counter negative thoughts you're having about yourself or the world.

The power in affirmations lies in their regularity and consistency of practice, which allows you to dive deep and get to know yourself through your word selections—the words we use in affirmations, the words we're choosing to identify with or work toward, represent different qualities or experiences that we want to have. At their most basic level, affirmations can be something like those simple, short, sweet statements we saw coming out of the last iteration of the New Age movement. Things like "I am abundant," "I am healed," and "I am love." And those are beautiful. But it's necessary to get a little more surgical with the process and make it a lot more supercharged and active, and therefore useful.

We'll talk about how to craft your specific affirmations when we get to your foundational affirmation practice later in this chapter, but in general, they should feel like cloaks that we are wrapping over our bodies and then walking through the world with. They really serve to give us energetic protection and energetic guidance. In the bestselling book *The Seven Spiritual Laws of Success*, Deepak Chopra writes about the Law of Pure Potentiality and the Law of Synchronicity, and those are the experiences you have with a thoughtfully crafted affirmation. You have an ability to tap into limitless nature, to move forward and create with more assistance from the Universe. It's the feeling of "I can't believe that just happened; that's such a coincidence!" Or "Oh my God, I wanted this and it just fell in my lap." Because affirmations connect us more firmly with our authentic self and our mastery. When you're

AFFIRMING STATEMENTS AND QUALITATIVE WORDS 87

in purpose, the Universe conspires for you. Your desires spontaneously appear in your path with ease. That's how life should feel all the time! Those kinds of experiences let us know that we're on the right track and working toward alignment.

Working with mantras during meditation is often confused with affirmations, as we learned in chapter 6. As I've shared earlier, mantras possess a vibrational quality whose resonance provides healing in and of itself. They also serve to bring you back to the focus of the moment, which is staying in your meditation and not getting lost in thought. During a retreat, I'll commonly instruct, "If you find yourself drifting off into thought, gently bring yourself back to your mantra and repeat it." Affirmations work in much the same way, but they're not called mantras because (1) they're not in Sanskrit, and (2) they're often much longer, with very specific meanings. But affirmations have the same effect of bringing you back to the goal, to the intention, and to what you want to heal. They also serve as positive and supportive reminders of what you really want for yourself—what you desire, the experience you're craving.

Another way to think of affirmation is as a companion for intention. The same way you can use intention to get yourself on a chariot moving forward toward your healing goals and desires, and the same way intention is one of the first steps you can take toward putting something out into the Universe—affirmation is the practice of intention. It's intention in real time. That's the work itself taking shape and taking form. There's a quote that I love: "Where intention goes, energy flows." You can say the same about affirmations.

How Affirmations Evolve

Before we craft your affirmation, let's first identify the most effective way to work with them. I recommend that anytime you make an affirmation, you use it for a significant length of time, saying it every day for an entire quarter, or year—however long you need until it clicks into place for you. There comes a moment when you are invoking the power

88 LIVING IN WISDOM

of your statement, when you can actually observe yourself living that statement and it's no longer something you're working toward or longing for, but rather it is present and being lived. At this point you can lay that affirmation aside and construct a new one.

As with much of this work, an affirmation has the highest chance of clicking into place if you give yourself four seasons to work with it. The New Year is a time when people are naturally attuned to this kind of shift and goal setting, so I often lead my clients in this exercise around that time. But to me, the New Year is not a time of powerful transformation. According to older calendar systems, and certainly ancient wisdom traditions, the time of new beginnings is not in the dead of winter when creatures are preserving their energy and hibernating and there's no natural growth. There's no *life*. No, the time for transformation is in the spring, specifically the spring equinox, when life bursts forth.

I also believe that our birthdays are our New Year. That is the marker from which I track my life and my growth through my cycle of life. Astrologically, it's a potent portal day, a day on which you're just a little bit more electric and connected to yourself because it's the beautiful, miraculous day you entered the planet—something your body remembers. Your birthday can be a significant opportunity to be in transformative energy and to supercharge the intentions that you have.

That said, you can feel empowered to shift your affirmation practice anytime you are called to, especially as you navigate your healing journey. As you start to click different parts of yourself into place through each layer of healing and release, you'll be ready to choose a new area of growth and may want an affirmation to support that. For example, you may have been working with an affirmation that was aligned with healing the pattern of the way you approach your family. As you develop mastery over that dynamic, you may start to notice similar patterns coming up at work and how you're giving your power away there. At this time, I would sunset the affirmation you were using to change your family dynamics and create a brand-new one that supports building inner strength and purpose in the work environment.

AFFIRMING STATEMENTS AND QUALITATIVE WORDS   89

Affirmations are particularly useful for some of the deeper crevice or shadow work, the trauma work. But affirmations can also be used for the more earthly, material things, such as working toward creation, working toward your purpose, working toward the desires and intentions you have for your body or for your community.

Repetition is what makes affirmations work. You're giving yourself a constant reminder and reinforcing a particular message. You're integrating this belief into your neural pathways and changing grooves of thought, creating a new belief system that can take up residence in both brain and body. That requires time to be in practice, and it requires time to take root.

Your Foundation Affirmation

The way I learned to connect with affirmations might be different from others you've encountered, but this is the style that was imparted by two of my teachers, Drs. Ron Hulnick and Mary Hulnick. I've given the style I learned my own remix, which has supercharged the practice for me and those I work with.

First, read the list of words I've provided on pages 90–91. Choose words that stir something inside of you and speak to qualities you'd like to have. Really drop down into asking, *Who am I becoming? Who do I want to become? Who am I being called to become?* It should be as though you are trying on a new aspirational version of yourself. As though you're letting the Universe and your own soul know what qualities you're trying to cultivate in yourself.

And then pick one to two of these words. Go with words that you'd like to embody. For example, *beautiful* and *generous*, or *forgiving/forgiven* and *original innocence*. The more honest you can be about the words you're longing for and craving, the more powerful it will be for you.

Some of these words might seem silly. They might even seem antiquated or funny to use in your regular life. But it's so important to leave yourself open to those big, beautiful, expansive, poetic words because it

90 LIVING IN WISDOM

makes the overall process feel so much more sacred. Allow your vocabulary to open. Affirming yourself may feel ever-so-slightly out of reach at first, but use this feeling to compel yourself to evolve and aspire to have more, to become more. If some of these words are new to you, explore their definitions. The more you can equip yourself with knowledge of how these words work and what they represent, the better—and not just for you, but for the entire world, so that everyone can receive the powerful gift of your newly accessible language. Because if you've used that word for yourself, there's a good chance you'd use it for someone or something else as well. That's not only deepening your knowledge, that's deepening your emotional language as well.

If you find a word that means something you connect with but the sound of it isn't pleasing to you for some reason, be empowered to find a new word with a similar meaning to take its place. We're getting creative here.

Qualities and Affirmations

Abundance	Confidence	Enoughness
Acceptance	Conscious Cocreation	Enthusiasm
Aliveness	Cooperation	Equanimity
Attunement	Courageous	Expansive
Authenticity	Creation	Fearless
Awareness	Creativity	Forgiving
Awe	Delight	Freedom
Beauty	Devotion	Fulfillment
Boundaries	Dignity	Generosity
Bravery	Discernment	Gentleness
Brilliance	Divine	God
Cheerful	Effervescent	Goodness
Cherishing	Elegance	Grace
Community	Empathy	Gratitude
Compassion	Enlightened	Grieve

AFFIRMING STATEMENTS AND QUALITATIVE WORDS 91

Harmony
Healed
Healing
Heart
Highest
Holy
Honest
Humility
Humor
Inspiration
Integrity
Intuition
Joy
Joyful Discipline
Kind
Liberation
Light, Lightness of Being
Love
Loving-Kindness
Loyalty
Luminous
Majesty
Mastery
Noble

Nurturance
Observer
Original Innocence
Passion
Patience
Peaceful
Playful
Poise
Potent
Power
Preciousness
Presence
Prosperity
Purpose
Radiance
Refined
Release
Resilient
Respect
Reverence
Sacred
Self-Acceptance
Self-Respect
Self-Worth

Soul-Centered
 Leadership
Sparkle
Strength of Heart
Surrender
Sweetness
Tenderness
Transparent
Trust
Truthful
Unconditional Loving
Understanding
Unique
Unknown
Valued
Vitality
Wholeness
Willingness
Wisdom
Witness
Wonder
Worthiness

Now, think about how you individually relate to the words you chose. Take a moment to observe and journal about what each word represents to you. How have you experienced that word? What has it meant to you? Then move to your sacred space, if you aren't already there, and sit in meditation for just a couple of minutes. It's important to have the space and silence to be with yourself in calm, regulated energy. Enjoy a few deep breaths, and then after that final exhale, open your eyes and look at the words.

92   LIVING IN WISDOM

★   ★   ★

What you're going to do now is craft your affirmation, but not like the simple single-sentence statements I first learned how to create. Instead, I like taking those words and using them to create a detailed mission statement. The only "rule" in this exercise is that your statement is in the present tense, as if these things are happening or have already happened to make it your reality. Then you're going to start with *I am*. Now you can begin to slowly craft your affirmation. And I do mean craft, as though it's a piece of clay or a painting or a sculpture that you're slowly forging and bringing forth. It's almost like you're activating those words, making them present, and then giving them forward momentum.

This process will take tinkering and honing, stepping back for a moment to consider it, and then fine-tuning. At first it might feel uncomfortable, particularly if you haven't had to write very much since high school or college. But this distance can make this affirmation practice so satisfying because it kind of activates that younger you. Having to design a paragraph the way you did in English class, with a beginning, middle, and an end. Continue asking yourself, *How can I make this come to life? How can I make it even more descriptive and communicative of my goals? How can I give each and every word intention and meaning so that it can expand the intention and meaning of the affirmation?* Say it out loud a few times. Roll it around on your tongue. Revise. Say it aloud again; revise a little more. You'll know when it is right and ready. You'll know when it hits. As though you are saying *exactly* what you mean.

To turn your affirmation into a practice, say your statement aloud at least three times a day. Once when you wake up, once in the middle of the day, and then again before bed. That's the minimum; you can reach for it as often as you like. I also recommend writing your affirmation down in a beautiful or artistic way, maybe on a creamy, high-quality piece of card stock or another piece of paper you find pleasing. Place it somewhere visible where you'll see it frequently. Tuck it somewhere playful so it catches your eye every so often and makes you smile. Put it by the front door so you remember to read it before you leave, or put

AFFIRMING STATEMENTS AND QUALITATIVE WORDS 93

it on your phone. Keep it on a piece of paper in your wallet. Write it on the bathroom mirror. Eventually you'll have it memorized and be able to recite it at will, but visually taking it in enhances its power.

Repeat your affirmation over and over and over and over again. If you can build it into your practice as mirror work—looking at your face, looking into your own eyes, and witnessing yourself—even better. Try saying your affirmation while you're doing your skin-care routine or getting ready in the morning or for bed.

When you say your affirmation, do it authentically. The first couple of times, you may feel like you have to deliver it in a bold, theatrical way. But get used to saying it in a deeper, more loving way. Sometimes it can feel almost casual, but other times you might be called to give it more intensity. Your relationship with this practice will change from day to day, mood to mood. But it is there for every version of you to recite as though weaving a prayer.

Your affirmation is just for you. I recommend saying it to yourself in private and creating a safe container to nourish the desire and intention without having anyone else's energy on it. This can be incredibly vulnerable work, especially because it is usually structured around your bigger pain points. Once it clicks into place for you, you can share it as you're called to. Perhaps from a place of understanding of what it did in your life and how powerful of a tool it was for you.

Let's go through two affirmations together as a practice. First, I'll share one of the original affirmations I wrote in my own style that was very powerful for me. The words I chose to work with were *precious, mastery, authentic,* and *joyful discipline.* To help you better understand this process, I'll explain why I chose these particular words. I resonated with *precious* because it was at a point in my life when I was doing a lot of re-parenting or inner child healing, and I was working with a lot of the wounding and pain from my childhood. So the idea of feeling precious was something I desperately wanted to feel about myself and my body. And I hadn't, up until that point, had many experiences where I felt

94 LIVING IN WISDOM

valuable, protected, or cherished, and *precious* seemed like such a beautiful idea to me. The way you hold on to something that's precious to you. I wanted to hold myself and my childhood versions of myself, my little girl, as precious. And not just to me but to God.

I chose *mastery* because I've always been drawn on the path of mastery. I believe in doing things well. I am designed and built to have a refined ability to see detail, and I love the process of that refinement, of improvement. When I crafted this affirmation many years ago, I wanted to continue to forge that path. I wanted to sort of expand past patching things up for myself over the course of my healing journey. I wanted to be in mastery of the different facets of the work I was doing on myself.

I chose *authentic* because I believe authenticity is the highest calling for us. When we are our authentic self, we are also our highest self, and it's when we're released from the collective consciousness and the relentless caring of what so many people around us are thinking. You're not consumed with how you're being perceived or observed. I wanted that word present because I was ready to have more experience with authenticity, for others and for myself. I was looking to be in more environments—especially in work and friendship—where it was safe to be my most authentic self.

The final word, or phrase, that I chose was *joyful discipline*. I really just fell in love with this idea because discipline had always been challenging for me. It always felt like a lack. It felt like another way to withhold from yourself or irrationally pressurize yourself. I also knew that I wanted more discipline in my life, but I wanted to relate to the word differently. So *joyful* discipline stood out. What's important to note here is that your affirmations should contain words that are activating for you, just as the idea of discipline was activating for me. Take an opportunity to examine those words, close your eyes, take a breath, and ask yourself, *What does this feel like inside of me? Where do I feel it?* In my case, I shifted from "I *have* to do this" to "I *get* to do this." It was a reminder to feel joyful about these tasks and these rhythms that I was looking to undertake and connect with because I knew that it was evolutionary. I

AFFIRMING STATEMENTS AND QUALITATIVE WORDS 95

knew that it was in pursuit of the version of me that I was dreaming of, craving, desiring, and working toward. That shift in perception was a game changer for me.

So I took those four words and got down a couple of drafts before I arrived at:

I am a precious child of God, living in the mastery of my most loving and authentic self, creating with joyful discipline and leading from my soul's center.

I would read that to myself over and over and over. I invoked it. I called it to me. I watched myself, over time, start to embody it. I felt it clicking into place. I felt the Universe conspiring to bring it into existence almost immediately, both through my practice and through my good works. The way I've related to it over the years has really changed. I've seen it evolve and grow and change forms. It has touched and continues to touch every single area of my life and of my work. It has radically changed me from the inside out.

I approached this second affirmation in a slightly different way. It's shorter and highly specific, because I wanted something to use almost like a talisman, like a sacred trinket I could keep in my pocket and use for protection. This affirmation came to me at a time in my journey when I was noticing that I was bumping up against people in my life who were kind of irritated by my light, by the energy surrounding my seeking of healing and wholeness. The worst versions of themselves would be on display, aggressive or apathetic. At the time, I was traveling a lot, and this was exposing me to others who were not embodying the best versions of themselves; when people are in those in-between, transient spaces, they don't care about being good to one another because they feel like they'll never see each other again. That layer of anonymity can bring out the worst in people.

So I was desiring to feel other people's highest self. I wanted to attract people to that understanding of themselves and then to magnetize them to me in a way that I could *experience*, not just feel. I also wanted to affirm that my heart was open enough at that time in my life to receive that highest version from others—and then reflect it back to

96   LIVING IN WISDOM

them. For this affirmation, then, the word or phrase I was drawn to was *highest version*. The affirmation became:

I attract, experience, and receive the highest version of every being whom I encounter.

When I tell you that it works like magic . . . it works like magic. Taking a couple of deep breaths and offering these words to yourself when you're in a charged situation—it can be miraculous.

That's why affirmations are effective. They attract experience. In this case, it's receiving the highest version of every being whom I encounter.

The magic in creating an affirmation does not come from its perfection. The magic comes from nonjudgment of yourself and others. The magic comes from it being you.

Chapter 10

Movement and Touch

This is *the* pillar of integration. It is the name of the game of the book, moving the healing down from the intellect and mind and into the body. Especially as you're in the early awareness phase, this set of practices—stretching, self-massage, dance, movement—will help you move into the most holistic view. They're going to help feed and nourish your whole self so that you're able to feel your feelings and stop disassociating—disassociating with feelings on either end of the spectrum, "good" or "bad."

In the wake of trauma, particularly complex trauma, we leave our bodies. You can be physically standing in front of someone, but your spirit, soul, and feelings are not really inside. They're just kind of hovering above, waiting to feel safe. So, so many people are walking around in their bodies but *operating* from outside of them, and as a result, they feel numb. Or stuck in the freeze response, or the fight-or-flight response. Sometimes even stuck in martyrdom, creating an identity out of their suffering. When you're not staying present in your life, you're not able to connect with your body's intuition or your "gut reaction" to your experiences. Touch and feeling help ignite that reintegration.

The practice of movement and touch integrating experiences into the body has been codified as a therapeutic modality called "somatics," a term coined by professor and theorist Thomas Hanna in 1976, and it has come to encompass an entire field of study that was popularized

98 LIVING IN WISDOM

by Dr. Peter Levine. *Soma* is Greek for "body," so somatics is just that: the practice of being in the body. More clinically, it is the practice of interoception, the awareness of what's happening inside of us. Somatics operates from the understanding that the body keeps a score on a cellular level and that we have the ability to release emotions, information, and energy that have not been sufficiently processed and are now trapped in our physical tissues. So what's required is sitting with sensations happening within the body while consciously moving or touching the body, which then creates healthy dialogue among mind, body, and spirit.

Somatic work must be a companion to any work that you do, because it is the most powerful way to stay connected to the truth of your experience, especially for people with complex trauma. We get so good at persevering and being resilient that we start believing with our entire brain we're over something, or past an experience, but the body can't lie. It can't be trained the way you train your mind.

How Movement and Touch Work in the Body

Touch and movement are regarded as two of the most powerful modalities in both Western medicine and ancient modalities such as Traditional Chinese Medicine and Ayurveda. They have been proven to improve spiritual, mental, emotional, and physical well-being. They regulate your nervous system. They reduce cortisol (a stress hormone), lower your blood pressure, and improve immunity and bowel function. With touch and movement, you are better able to move into a relaxed state, inviting in more and better quality breath. Touch and movement help you sleep better and relieve pain. They help you feel more sensually connected to yourself and your nature. They help you cultivate awareness, a sense of safety, and a release of damaging, pent-up emotions and thoughts, particularly if you've experienced physical abuse, sexual abuse, or neglect. They help reduce symptoms of PTSD, CPTSD, anxiety, and depression. Touch and movement also stimulate circulation, which is particularly beneficial for the lymphatic system, the part of the immune system that helps remove toxins, bacteria, abnormal cells, and metabolic waste. By enhancing its circulation and drainage—something that lymph fluid requires an external assist to do, as it does not have a central pump like the heart pumps blood—you're boosting the health of every single other system in your body. This daily support is incredibly important not just for healing but for sustaining healing long term. That's what makes these practices even more powerful—even after you're "done" healing, they facilitate your being able to live in your purpose and exist as your highest self.

These physical practices also lead you to self-discovery. You get to learn how you feel. What kind of pressure you like, how your body feels to move in certain ways. Where you hold tension and how to relieve that tension. How to bring pleasure to your own body in a nonsexual way (although discovering what appeals to you sexually is important too). You're communicating with your body in its own language and then inviting it into the experience that the rest of you is having, which then builds your ability to embody those experiences and master them. You cannot underestimate the power of supporting yourself with your own hands and making yourself feel loved in your own body.

When Movement and Touch Don't Feel Safe

Like a lot of self-care practices, which we'll talk about in more detail in chapter 16, this pillar can cause friction if you've spent a lifetime having to meet your own needs, especially your needs of intimacy such as touch. If you've always had to provide that kind of care and support for yourself, you may find that you, on some level, resent that you had no one else to provide that for you. Or you flat-out reject the need to do it yourself. The more you practice being in relationship with yourself, the more you invest in developing a relationship with yourself, the more you begin to see yourself as worthy of receiving this type of care—which you most certainly are—the more seamless this self-love

100 LIVING IN WISDOM

becomes. For more guidance on how to navigate this resistance and any negative associations that come up for you, see pages 195–196.

Movement and Touch: The Basics

Movement and touch support my day. They support my sleep. They are what make me feel good. They bring my body, spirit, mind, and heart pleasure and relief.

I naturally discovered the power of this practice in the first two years of the COVID-19 pandemic. I was in the house alone with my young son, so after he went to bed, I decided I needed to dedicate that time to whatever I was called to do in that moment. Something that has always been so powerful for me is music, so I found mixes from a DJ collective called Soulection on Apple Music. It was called *Soulection Radio*, the mixes lasted exactly two hours, and I was so drawn to the artistry of it. Each mix was made of songs I didn't know well or hadn't heard in a while, and it was a perfect mash-up of Afrobeats, house, dance, R & B, and jazz you could tell was crafted with so much intention and care. For the span of those two hours, just listening to the music created a kind of effortless healing container for myself.

And so for nearly two years, I'd put on one of those playlists and give myself over to it. My only commitment was to be with my body for that entire time until the mix ended. I would massage myself, stretch, do mirror work and say affirmations to myself, speak prayers over my life. I'd journal, take Epsom salt baths. But so often what I found myself doing was dance. In that safe space of my own, I just let my body *move*— shaking, jumping, giving freedom to every limb. I was in total autonomy of my physical expression. I started noticing that my body was evolving. The chronic back pain I'd lived with since I was sixteen years old was lessening, and recovery time between flare-ups was shorter. The restriction and tightness I used to have in my hips when I would walk or sit was easing. Prior to this, whenever I would dance, I always felt like my hips were locked up and almost unavailable to me. That dissipated.

MOVEMENT AND TOUCH   101

Regular movement gave me access to my own femininity and my ability to experience myself as a woman with grace and ease. I felt so much more lightness. All of this came from dancing it out around my house. Yes, with daily devotion and dedication, but it really can be that simple.

You may already be engaged with some somatic practices that are naturally systematically healing, such as yoga, Pilates, tai chi, dance, various styles of martial arts, even sports. These qualify as somatic practices because you're being given verbal prompts that lead your mind to search for where these cues are housed in the body, which results in your brain integrating with your body. This is why I'm particularly fond of yoga, where you have different postures or asanas to get into, each one a varying degree of difficulty. It takes quite a bit of mental disarming of oneself to submit to the practice, so as you're working toward mastery of the postures, you're essentially building physicality from the inside out.

Pilates is similar, but I'd say even more so. To me, Pilates is one of the most incredible things to ever have been created by humankind. Joseph Pilates developed a system of being incrementally aware and in mastery of the entire body through a series of subtle, targeted movements. He honed this practice to improve his own physical strength in the wake of struggling with poor health as a child. Pilates gives you a masterful control over your body, which many of us have never had before. It gives you a greater sense of all your parts, what they're doing and how they work. And to do that, it, too, requires a mindfulness that stems from the inside out. You're coming into that awareness from the innermost part of your being. Once you find that truth and clarity on that level, the physical body follows.

Self-touch also rewires the mind-body connection and is incredibly important on the healing journey. For example, hugging oneself to self-soothe or self-massage, which in Vedic healing is called abhyanga. Slowly stretching your body, maybe using a foam roller. Using hand placements or mudras in meditation, such as gently pressing one palm

102 LIVING IN WISDOM

to your heart and the other to your sacral chakra or womb space just beneath your navel. Or placing a hand on your throat or solar plexus chakra.

Don't underestimate the power of your own touch and your ability to hold yourself and witness yourself. Looking in the mirror and massaging your knees and shoulders and feet. Threading your fingers between your toes, massaging the back of your skull where your neck meets your head, where your vagus nerve resides. The more you can find comfort in doing that, the more you'll feel like you've met a new person entirely. The more you'll be engaging with your body in new ways. And the more you'll be touching others, emotionally and physically, in new ways.

I'd also put therapeutic touch in this category—"educated" touch by someone else, which was a big part of my journey when I was moving through a lot of the deeper traumas in my life under duress. I was grateful for having the time and ability to fund semi-regular deep-tissue massage, acupuncture, hand massage, foot massage, scalp massage. I even took the time to receive deep, long hugs from people I trust. For some of you, the idea of someone else touching you might be a ways down the road of your journey, but remember that human touch is its own language, and when we don't engage in that language, we also suffer. Studies have shown that experiencing "touch starvation" or the deprivation of physical touch can cause feelings of emptiness and loneliness, depression, anxiety, stress, difficulty sleeping, low satisfaction in life and relationships, and the inability to form secure attachments. We don't always have someone available to us to meet this need, but giving yourself the goal of cultivating trust with just one person who can provide that, whether it's someone you're in relationship with or a professional practitioner, can have tremendously positive outcomes.

The thing is, all of these seemingly small acts of movement and touch create a powerful ripple effect throughout the body. On one level, spending time to give your body the care and support it deserves has the potent ability to facilitate release. Because your body deserves to feel your presence and attention. But on a deeper level, some studies have shown that this kind of touch also signals a feeling of safety and trust within us. Warm, gentle touch can calm the cardiovascular stress that accumulates in the body. It regulates the nervous system, and it also triggers the release of oxytocin and dopamine, aka the "feel-good" hormones. Oxytocin is often called the "love hormone" or "bonding hormone," because it is released in both mothers and babies when they touch skin to skin. So, in a sense, self-touch creates a moment of bonding between self and self. Over time, the more you access this practice, the less awkward it feels. The easier it becomes. The more necessary it feels to have every day.

Your Foundation Movement and Touch Practice

Similar to breathwork, this is an intuitive practice that may look completely different from day to day depending on what your mood or body requests, so there is no set sequence or recommended "prescription" to follow.

That said, as with any Pillar Practice, begin by getting grounded with breath, which creates an energetic pathway for disarming your body, allowing it to open and release as needed. I also strongly encourage you to spend time to be present with your hips in any movement or touch practices that you choose. We hold an incredible amount in our hips—trauma, emotions, a center of gravity for our immune system— plus what we require of them as the fulcrum of our physical body. Keeping them loose, open, and supple is essential support for our spiritual, emotional, and physical wellness.

Similarly, giving attention and care to your hands and feet can feel rewarding on these same planes. Think about the way we use our hands now—our fingers and thumbs regularly scrolling, typing, holding our phones for dear life—our hands often develop tightness and pain points. Tending to these vital appendages when administering self-massage—or even in a spare moment while sitting in traffic or on hold

104   LIVING IN WISDOM

on the phone—not only is beneficial for their functional use, but also puts us in closer connection with the spiritual portal that is believed to flow through the hands and feet, particularly in Vedic and Kabbalistic traditions. You'll notice that when you spend time doing this how easy it is for the rest of the body to come into alignment and how much more achievable release is.

If anything, the takeaway here is that small moments of intentional touch throughout the day can create a significant shift in your overall feeling of wellness.

Chapter 11

Recapitulation

Recapitulation may sound like the simplest of the Pillar Practices, but it is one of the most powerfully expanding tools you'll have in your kit. This largely has to do with the surprising amount of intention and presence that it requires.

Recapitulation is a therapeutic technique that potently combines multiple healing modalities, such as visualization and cognitive behavioral therapy. It is much like it sounds—a recap. It is a slow, methodical, unattached, uneditorialized, nonjudgmental review of your entire day, including every tiny detail that unfolded in the preceding hours. This is what will really help you understand how you are moving in your own life. It builds your capacity to be in life as the observer, to objectively look on as you navigate interactions and experiences and observe your patterns and your choices. And as you gain more practice, recapitulation even helps you hit the pause button as needed in order to quickly reach for the most aligned reaction or choice in a particular moment. In some ways, recapitulation is what creates your ability to become a time traveler in your own life, allowing you to be an active, real-time participant in who you are becoming.

You're also training yourself to become more present in these details every day, which is a crucial shift out of the fight-or-flight mode or dissociative state that so many of us perpetually inhabit for a multitude of reasons. Recapitulation helps us drop down into the experiences to

106 LIVING IN WISDOM

experience them while at the same time seeing the bigger truths of our lives, unadulterated by ego or emotion.

Your Foundation for Recapitulation

Recapitulation is best suited for the very end of the day. Maybe while you're lying in bed, or it could be during your evening meditation. While being mindful of maintaining deep breathing, slowly walk yourself through the moments of your day, intentionally conjuring the details of the minutiae but not giving in to the very real temptation to reverse engineer, repair, fix, control, or otherwise manipulate this objective recollection, or even come to a specific understanding. You're just here to observe.

Begin with thinking back to opening your eyes in the morning. Try to remember what happened when you woke up, how you felt, what you noticed. Then continue from there. For example: *I got up, brushed my teeth, washed my face, did my morning practice, went downstairs.* Did you have any interactions with your family? What was your flow of the day from there? *I picked up the dry cleaning, called a friend, we talked about such and such, I went to work, talked to so-and-so, had lunch, worked out.* Think about what you ate—how it tasted, how it felt. Think of all the events and interactions and experiences that brought you to where you are at the present moment. Then maybe give gratitude for another day on this planet, if that feeling is available to you, and rest.

Part III

The Path to Living in Wisdom

A Note About This Process and the Four Pillars of Healing

We've spent the first couple of sections of this book talking about what can only be described as some high-level stuff. Awareness. Acceptance. God. Mastery. Purpose. It's a lot. It's effective, it is sacred, it is unconditional, but it is quite a bit to take in. So I want to talk more about this process, why it works, as well as why the eight steps in this section are structured the way they are—and how this is not an à la carte menu. There is a method to the madness.

The progression of each one of these steps has been thoughtfully and methodically arranged, moving you all the way from the pieces hitting the floor to putting them back together in the most aligned way possible. It's not unlike navigating the developmental milestones from infancy to childhood, with each begetting the next and each one crucial to the next one's success. Healing is no different. To get to your purpose, you have to first understand your pain.

That said, this journey is not a linear one. While I will be introducing you to new ideas and concepts in each chapter, the effect is more like a spiral than a line. Thematically, many of these chapters echo one another, wrap around one another, and that repetition is not an oversight. Rather, as you move through this process, these same ideas and concepts will consistently come up for review. And each time they do, you will be considering them through a new lens of understanding, perspective, and integration, which gets your synapses firing in new ways and ultimately forges new neural pathways.

109

110   LIVING IN WISDOM

However, your understanding of these ideas and concepts doesn't just happen on the intellectual level. This is where the second layer of this process comes in: the practices you learned about in part 2, before we even get to that first stepping stone. That's because these daily rituals—the meditation, the breathwork, the journaling, the movement—are what will be delivering these ideas directly into your cellular network to literally rewire your brain. So you need both. This is all part of what I call the **Four Pillars of Healing**.

What I've learned through my own experience and through a decade of working with others is that healing cannot be successful unless it is done on four levels: **mental**, **physical**, **emotional**, and **spiritual**. In order to achieve true well-being, your health in each of these categories must be attended to. *We* are each of these things, therefore our healing has to be each of these things.

The beauty of the pillars of practice is that they echo the pillars of healing; they each support your physical, mental, emotional, and spiritual well-being. To reach for these practices is to ensure, innately, that every day you are filling every one of these "buckets" in a balanced way. There are affirmations to nourish your mental health. Journaling creates a very specific creative flow that's in service to your emotional *and* mental health. Meditation is supporting and enhancing your spiritual well-being. And gentle movement and self-touch bring the body into the conversation. That's not to say that each of these practices doesn't provide benefits for any other categories—because they most certainly do—but they make up one beautiful, balanced, harmonious whole.

When you embrace daily practices and lessons with devotion; when you build mastery over your choices because they are coming from an informed, aligned place; when you live with intention; when you vow to do all of this excavation and expansion in search of wisdom in the name of you higher purpose—you will have met this book where I have asked you to meet it. And lifelong change will be yours for the taking.

Chapter 12

Grieve

Grief can be the garden of compassion. If you keep your heart open through everything, your pain can become the greatest ally in your life's search for love and wisdom.

—*Rumi*

I've shared how my healing process couldn't begin until I succumbed to the pain, burnout, betrayal, and unrealized dreams and finally let the fuck go, shattering into a million unrecognizable, uncontainable pieces. It was *messy*. It was also unlike anything I'd ever experienced before. Because, like most women, I had a viselike grip on *should*s and *have to*s. I prided myself on how hard I worked and how little I slept. I had no time for myself because I had to hustle twice as hard just to prove myself as equal to my male counterparts. Meanwhile, I was nurturing everyone but myself, playing the role of the good wife and the good daughter and the good mother, rarely saying no, rarely taking up more space than I needed to.

But I also *thought* I was healing. I meditated, I did yoga, I taught other people how to meditate and emotionally regulate, and I lived my life in a deeply devoted, educated, aligned-with-my-higher-consciousness way. Although I had done a lot of the work—therapy, retreats, training— because I was still insisting on remaining in control and "keeping it together," the work I did was essentially surface level, or else reactionary only to the fissures as they appeared, never rooting all the way down to the source of the fracture.

111

112   LIVING IN WISDOM

I could sense that compromised foundation; I could feel its instability. But I thought if I built a sound enough structure on top, I'd never really have to shine a light at those parts of me I thought I'd made peace with. Besides, there was no time to cry.

Then, when the load got too heavy, when the effort of keeping everything upright became unbearable, I finally submitted. When I wasn't being a parent to my son, I was in my room, crying, pleading to God, on my knees saying, *I can't take it anymore.*

The thing was, after giving myself the permission to break fully and come face-to-face with my suffering, I didn't feel worse. Instead of feeling empowered by having moved beyond my trauma, I was empowered because I was *in* my trauma. Just as we talked about in the early chapters of this book, permitting the shattering meant that I could sift even deeper into the rubble in order to clear it away and vacuum out the spaces in between.

That is what happens when you allow yourself to grieve. You have to allow yourself to touch grief, feel it, and let it move through you. I'll be the first to tell you it is not easy, nor is it comfortable or convenient. But it is necessary.

About five years ago, I lost yet another friend, Nipsey Hussle, suddenly and violently. It was a friend I loved deeply; we had come up in the world together during a special time in the Los Angeles music scene—me as a young radio personality and him as an emerging artist. I watched him find his voice as a musician, a leader, and a modern-day prophet, lifting up those around him and pouring his soul into humanitarian work and community activism. In that moment, for the first time in my life, I completely lost my faith. Up until that point, I was committed to walking a path with God; in many ways, I had never *not* loved God, had never not surrendered and worshipped God. But after suffering this particular blow, I stopped, as though I was choosing to starve God from my life. I woke up every morning angry with God. Every single morning. I was the numbest I'd ever been.

At first, I tried to muscle my way through. I refused to grieve this loss—probably because it made me face what seemed like an impossible fact—that I had lost so many of my peers who mattered to me, that I'd had *seven* friends in my adult life who had been killed. So I pushed the grief away. I somehow found ways to compartmentalize, tapping scarcer and scarcer reserves of enthusiasm and focus. Until I couldn't. I was getting sick in a way that I couldn't shake, with painful autoimmune flare-ups, extreme muscle weakness, and spasms. My body was struggling to absorb essential nutrients, which was damaging to my physical and mental health. I was living in a perpetual state of holding, holding, holding to the point where my back—already subject to significant bouts of chronic pain from my accident—was gripping onto something I could not be rid of.

I finally went to see a healer and said to her, "Get it the f*ck off me." I just wanted to be rid of the pain. But at the end of the session, when I woke up on her table, I still felt so dense and heavy. She said to me, "Your heart has some words for you, and it wants you to know it will get better. But it's really sad, and you have to let it be sad for however long it wants to be sad."

That was the shift. For the first time, I saw my body as having to process just as much as my emotions do. It was the first time I realized that my body had a voice and that it had its own timeline. And so, as I felt myself shatter in the wake of being profoundly betrayed by someone I loved, I had this tool to reach for. It was simply the knowledge that I needed to give my body the dignity in the grief that it deserved. There was no pushing through this pain. It was not about intellectualizing it or trying to make sense of it in any way. It was, simply, about feeling it. About surrendering to time. Which was a powerful awakening for me because I realized until I did just that, I wouldn't be able to flow in any other areas of my life. I would only continue to suffer.

It's time for you to let go, to let your pieces hit the floor and to grieve. Maybe you're grieving the thing that didn't happen, or the experiences you didn't have. Maybe you're grieving trauma, abuse, or poverty.

114   LIVING IN WISDOM

Maybe you're grieving all the ways your needs weren't met and how this has played a role in your inability to make choices or the way you feel about yourself. Maybe, like many women I work with, you're grieving the barriers you've encountered simply because of the year you were born—being unable to have the career you desire, sexual freedom, or autonomy of any kind. Maybe you're grieving something that no longer exists for you, or past versions of yourself. And then there's our collective grief that we're experiencing on a societal level—holy war, climate crisis, degrading institutions, unraveling childhood heroes. Just being alive right now—constantly bearing witness because of the immediate and pervasive access we have to everything, everywhere, all at once and feeling the pains of the human experience—is enough to warrant your attention at this juncture of your journey.

I co-taught a class on grief with my friend Sah D'Simone a few years ago, called Dying the Daily Death. It was about recognizing grief in the everyday—contending with the realization that nothing is permanent; nothing, down to each moment, lasts forever. I think the most tangible way we experience this is through our children and recognizing every morning when they wake up, they are somehow changed from the day before. During the first few years of my son's life, which was such a blend of tragedy and magic, I would take pictures of him every single day. Every night I would pore over all the pictures I'd taken up until that point and see so clearly how he was growing up, and I'd sob. One evening, he had gotten into bed with me. He was about three years old, and I was reading to him. He was just so *excited* about being there with me, sitting on my lap, listening to his favorite stories. He looked up at me with the biggest smile, the kind that takes the effort of your entire face. In that moment, I was so profoundly tickled and grateful to see myself through his eyes. Then, after we were done reading, we snuggled in my bed, nose to nose. Even though it had gotten dark, there was the faintest glow from behind the curtains, which illuminated my son's face just enough for me to see that he was still beaming that big, breathtaking smile. And as I lay there, tears silently streaming down my face, I desperately tried to remember every molecule of that moment because I knew I'd never have it again—never that same exact light or that same exact smile. It was dying a daily death. A moment where I could hold both the joy and gratitude and love with the sadness and the grief. What I've come to learn is that everything has a layer of grief to it, even the best moments. To understand that is to respect grief, while also beginning to accept how it is a bridge to opening ourselves to more of the really, really good stuff.

No matter how you are connecting with grief, it is the unavoidable first step toward your healing. It is only from this place that you can begin to palpate those wounds and triggers and traumas. This is where you begin to form an understanding of what pain is and why it's just as holy and as valuable as love and as joy. It is where you make peace with grief.

Grief as a Rite of Passage

You have only to look at ancient wisdom traditions to understand how necessary and present grief is, and how impossible it is to remove it from the fabric of our lives. It is just as much a central part of life as any other milestone or celebration. In Vedic and Hindu traditions, both the community and the family participate in a series of rituals over the span of days and sometimes weeks. Prayers are offered; mantras are chanted. There is an order to things. Indigenous American culture is much the same. In fact, of the 574 federally recognized tribal nations in the United States, there is a wide range of unique bereavement practices. The Lakota mark a distinct period of mourning with crying, singing, wailing, and cutting their hair.[1] The Iroquois, who divided themselves into a number of small clans, would surround a mourning clan with support to help console and tend to ceremony preparations.[2] In Abrahamic culture, there are protocols in place for navigating a distinct period for grieving, not only for sending off the deceased in a sacred and meaningful way, but also for tending to the mourners and helping them mark a

116 LIVING IN WISDOM

very specific time when they are meant to dedicate themselves solely to feeling their grief.

The immense value of grieving can be seen even more clearly when you look at what happens when culture no longer supports grieving. In Japan, secularization or decreasing religious observance has meant that fewer families are participating in the Shinto or Buddhist rituals around death that had been in place for thousands of years. Also, the country has been experiencing an epidemic of *karoshi*, or "death from overwork," the result of a chronic imbalance between demanding grind culture and restorative practices.[3] So despite its people being known for their longevity, Japan has one of the highest suicide rates in the world.[4]

The body, the spirit, the mind, the heart—they know when emotion has not been properly processed.

When Grief Stagnates

The resistance to the unpleasant situation is the root of suffering.

—*Ram Dass*

For most of us, grief—whether or not it's surrounding death—is not part of our culture. In fact, many of us are conditioned to "keep it together," not wanting to burden other people with our emotional experience. Some of us were raised in families where crying was considered a weakness, or our adults didn't have the tools for emotional healing themselves. Or in more extreme cases, no compassion or tenderness was modeled. Some of us get caught up in the loop of toxic positivity—"Focus on the positives!" "Lead with gratitude!" Some of us are just in shock and calcified by the emotional overwhelm of our pain. It can create a numbness that gives a false sense of security and allows you to convince yourself that you're fine or that something doesn't affect you—something I experienced for years.

Some of us naturally gravitate toward emotional bypass, because it's neater. We're terrified that, when we open the door to grief, we won't be able to find our way out of it again. We don't know what else will come up, which feels out of our control and terrifying. That's why a lot of people avoid meditation, because they think, *If I create space to feel uncomfortable, what else will I feel and will I be able to get it to stop?* What all of these scenarios have in common is that it's just easier to avoid seeking grief.

We reject grieving because it hurts. Grief is disruptive to the flow of your life, how you show up as yourself, how much you're able to accomplish, how you're perceived. It doesn't fit into the perfectly curated life that we're trying to project on social media. In a world of surface-level connection, we're not incentivized to dig deeper, to risk things getting messy, and potentially alienating the people we think we're in relationship with (more on that a few steps down the road).

But the most significant barrier to grieving is literally not having the space or container for it. In our current world, where productivity is queen, there is no room for grief. If you lose a spouse or a parent, you maybe get three days off work before you're expected to be back to business as usual, performing at the same mental and emotional level as before you experienced a loss. Meanwhile, those three days are barely enough for you to even regain consciousness, let alone move through your pain in any significant way. And so we continue the cycle, for one reason or another, of not resolving our grief.

But, as we well know by now, the body keeps the score. Grief—much like anger, resentment, and other strong emotions—that has not been allowed to run its course and is instead pent up inside of you will come out one way or another, often through chronic or acute mental and physical health issues. Unresolved grief can compromise the immune system, causing it to make fewer immune cells to fight infections or to have higher levels of inflammatory markers—meaning the body can't defend itself from illness as well, or it can make existing illnesses worse, especially autoimmune disease.[5]

We now know that individuals exposed to childhood trauma have an increased risk of developing autoimmune disorders and that people living with psychological stress—especially from PTSD—are more likely to have an overactive immune system.[6] You can actually chart the physical impact that unresolved emotion is having on more vulnerable communities, particularly women, most specifically women of color. In the late 1980s, Harvard psychologist Dana Jack identified that the common pattern among those patients with depression was a tendency to self-silence, or being more likely to compulsively take care of or please others while inhibiting self-expression.[7] Well, in the United States, between twenty-four and fifty million people suffer from some form of autoimmune disease and *four out of five of these people are women*. And in 2022, a team of researchers from the University of Pittsburgh found that women of color who strongly agreed with statements like "I rarely express my anger to those close to me" were 70 percent more likely to experience increased carotid atherosclerosis, a cardiovascular plaque associated with higher risk of heart attack.

Other studies have connected self-silencing to irritable bowel syndrome (IBS), chronic fatigue syndrome, and cancer—again, particularly among women.[8] Carrying grief in the body can also resemble chronic mental health conditions such as anxiety or depression, leading to feelings of worry, helplessness, hopelessness, anger, irritability, obsessing, addiction, hyperalertness, apathy, and suicidal ideation, such that grief informs the way you emotionally respond to everything else.[9] Researchers have found that our psychological pain can actually morph into and increase the experience of physical pain.[10] In fact, severe emotional and physical stress can trigger a heart condition called Takotsubo cardiomyopathy—also eloquently known as "broken heart syndrome"—which mimics the symptoms of a heart attack.[11] It is also possible to experience an actual heart attack as a result of a grief response because of how grief increases blood pressure and heart rate, tightens blood vessels, and increases the risk that plaque in your arteries will dislodge and cause a blockage.[12] Grief also messes with the very cores of your health—your sleep and your gut. Overwhelmingly, people experiencing prolonged grief also experience sleep disturbances.[13] And when your sleep is off, almost every single aspect of your wellness goes out the window—mental health, digestive health, immune health, cardiovascular health, endocrine health, hormonal health. The same exact thing goes for your gut, or the keystone of your digestive system, which researchers now know can be negatively affected by psychological factors such as—that's right—grief.[14]

Grieving to Create Flow

I'm not going to overcomplicate this simple truth: You cannot move forward with your healing until you grieve. As we discussed in chapter 2, this process is identical to the way we think about babies and their developmental milestones, with each step being foundational for the next. At some point, you'll experience impeded growth if you don't hit those milestones when it's biologically or energetically appropriate. You can't satisfactorily get to the next healing milestone without resolving this one first. You can't bypass a step and expect to get the big breakthrough. Each of these steps is meant to create small yet incremental shifts that expand your capacity to hold consciousness, to grow, and to have awareness. To skip any one of them is to sabotage the entire journey.

What I've also observed is that if you have not come into a certain amount of awareness—not necessarily being fully healed, but aware—by middle age, the opportunity to shift and change your life can be more limited. By that time, your neural pathways have begun to set, which means your brain is much more likely to take the well-worn route when it comes to assessing thoughts and experiences.[15] Also, because of the inevitable ebb and flow of life, you tend to not have as many new experiences—new people you meet, new places you're going, new activities you're trying, and as a result, there aren't as many opportunities to stretch yourself or to be in practice with these new understandings

120 LIVING IN WISDOM

outside of your well-worn grooves of comfort in order for them to take hold and create a new mindset.

I say this with compassion and love: go grieve.

How, When, and Where to Grieve

At first, grieving might not feel intuitive because we're rarely allowed to fully experience it. But many elements of it will feel familiar—like a good cry that can no longer be contained or a primal scream. But mostly, grief—the forms it takes and how it will look on its way out—is completely unique to you. As you explore your relationship with grief, prepare for what will come up. You may feel humiliated or ashamed by certain thoughts and feelings. You may feel disgusted with yourself, weak, angry, or resentful. Conversely, you may feel empowered. It is all natural, it is all okay, and it is all inherent in the human experience.

What you can do is allow those thoughts and feelings to move through you and embrace whatever the energy looks like on the way out. Don't judge it, and embrace the fact that you cannot control it. Only the Divine knows what it's supposed to be. The sooner you can surrender, the easier it will be for you. Remember, not only is all of this expected of you, it is *required*. The surrender to grief is required for it to clear.

To accomplish this, you have to meet me halfway. Just like anything else worth your time—meetings, the gym, health appointments—you have to pencil in grieving. I'm not sure I could have told you how necessary that is until, during the pandemic, I had to juggle being a mom and running a business and creating content and helping other people trying to heal and just being present. So I set appointments for grieving on my calendar app, whatever time I had—sometimes thirty minutes, sometimes two hours—to plumb the depths of all the layers of my grief. I'd be intentional about the space and would light a candle and some incense, put on my grief playlist, focus on my breath, and allow all the intrusive thoughts to come forward without any narration,

GRIEVE 121

interruption, or judgment. Everything I'd been trying so hard to keep at bay would pour out, because I'd given myself the time and space. To weep. To scream into a pillow. To be disgusted with myself. To be tender with myself. To ask for my own forgiveness.

During this time, I was also hosting *Self-Care, Simplified*, a weekly one-hour Instagram Live series with the Chopra community. I'd devote that time to diving into practice, specifically as it was in service to people during a time when everyone needed tools. I would be able to show up to these expansive sessions armed with what I was navigating and honing at home, and using that as a place from which to receive and understand what other people needed from me.

The cumulative result of this experience is what led to the fine-tuning of the "recipes" for grief later in this chapter. With them, you'll be able to move in and out of these rituals seamlessly on a daily basis because you will have already created a container for grief, or prepared a sacred space. From there, you can choose how you want to connect with yourself, whether you construct an altar to your grief, take a grief bath, or simply reach for a prayer or affirmation tailored to grief plus some self-soothing tactics and letting it all flow.

And then, when you're ready, you'll release.

Practices for Grieving

Before easing into any of these, ask yourself, *What is my intention for this practice?*

Meditation for Grieving

Start by sitting in a comfortable position, taking five deep belly breaths to ground yourself in your body and in the present moment.

Now begin a body-scan meditation with your hands in your mudra of choice. (See Anjali Mudra below.) Incrementally move your focus from the top of your head to the base of your spine (your crown to

122 LIVING IN WISDOM

your root), gently releasing any physical or emotional tension points (such as in your jaw, neck, shoulders, or heart) that you may notice as your attention travels down your body. Throughout the meditation, notice your breath. If at any time you find yourself connecting to your thoughts, bring your awareness back to your breath and the rise and fall of your chest.

Let your practice stretch anywhere between five and twenty-five minutes. Allow the length of your meditation to gradually increase over time as you feel more settled into your practice.

ANJALI MUDRA

Anjali mudra is the hand gesture of pressing together your palms in front of your chest. Some call it the "namaste" position or prayer "hands," and it is a gesture used for both greetings and farewells (which is particularly interesting in the context of grieving). The joining together of the palms is said to provide a connection and unification between the right and left hemispheres of the brain, calm the mind, ease anxiety and stress, and improve focus, all of which can help you enter a meditative state that is receptive to the Divine in all things. In fact, this mudra is often translated in Sanskrit as "I bow to the divinity within you, from the divinity within me." It is meant to promote a feeling of self-respect, a respect for others, and gently encourages the heart to open.

Begin by sitting in a comfortable position. Lengthen your spine and extend the back of your neck by lowering your chin slightly. With open palms, slowly draw your hands together at the center of your chest as if to gather all of your energy into your heart. Repeat this movement several times, contemplating your own metaphors for bringing the right and left sides of yourself—masculinity and femininity, logic and intuition, strength and tenderness—into wholeness. Continue with your meditation practice, holding this mudra, but also rely on your own intuition whether you prefer to allow your hands to open with palms up in a state of receiving.

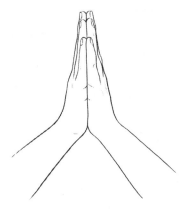

Movement for Grieving

This practice can be done standing or seated. Start by placing the palm of one hand on your heart. Close your eyes. If seated, ground your body into what lies beneath you (a chair, the floor). Take a few centering breaths slowly in and out. Then let your lips part after the next inhale, and exhale with a sigh through your mouth. Repeat three to five times.

If standing, slowly sway your body from the waist up from side to side while continuing to hold your heart. If seated, slowly sway your body from the hips up from side to side.

Affirmation for Grieving

I am anchored to the present moment and grounded in my human experiences. My heart is open to feel, my spirit is free to release.

Journal Prompts for Grieving

What have I been feeling lately?
Where in my body do I feel it?
If the feeling were made of a substance or material, what is it made of? How does it feel in my hands? How does it smell?

124   LIVING IN WISDOM

Creativity for Grieving

Go outside, visit an open area such as a park, backyard, or field. Connect your eyes with the openness of the space. For a few moments, let your eyes stretch open a bit, exposing more of the eyeballs themselves. Walk around at leisure without a clear directive. Connect to the feeling of space around you. Slowly observe your surroundings, taking in the nuance that surrounds you without applying too much thought or judgment to anything in particular. Settle yourself on something that brings a small smile to your face.

Repeat as often as needed.

I am a precious child of God living in the mastery of my most loving and authentic self, exercising joyful discipline and leading from my soul's center.

Chapter 13

Release and Find Intention

Seek the wisdom that will untie your knot. Seek the path that demands your whole being.

—Rumi

As you'll recall from the previous chapter, when you allow yourself to go to pieces, you make it easier to begin exploring the rubble. This step is the beginning of that exploration, and it's a two-parter: you're identifying the patterns of your behavior that are no longer serving you and letting them go (release), and then identifying what you need more of in your life and inviting that in (intention). Another way to think of this is as understanding your **spiritual curriculum**. It's understanding your specific course of study for achieving mastery. That's going to look different for everyone because our behavioral patterns or coping mechanisms are all different, as are our wounds, and our needs. This is where you will start to craft your unique curriculum—beginning with identification, like an archaeologist doing an initial pass over their worksite. Eventually we'll start to more closely examine the findings in a more active way, but for now, we're easing into observation.

When I first started coming up for air from my grief and began noticing my own patterns, I realized that they often showed up as people pleasing. That was my dynamic with my family systems. I was the child of a mother who did it all and was never meant to do it all, much less

RELEASE AND FIND INTENTION 127

under the thumb of the cycle of poverty and oppression. I had no dad as a counterbalance. No aunts or uncles. Not one living grandparent. The care and attention I received was sometimes whatever was left over because that was what reality demanded. I was required to change shape in order to fit, which turned into my being self-sacrificing to nearly a masochistic level. I would bypass my own feelings because it felt more important to try to fix or save or endear myself to others. From there, I could trace a straight line to my original wound, which was emotional neglect in childhood and then emotional abuse in adulthood. When I understood that, coupled with all the loss and difficult circumstances I'd experienced up until that point in my life, I could see that my spiritual curriculum was to better understand that pain, that grief, and that void. I was meant to come into acceptance of the darker side of life—the truth that the human experience innately includes pain and grief. With that knowledge, my path was to show up as a mentor and a guide to help other people do the same. Through years of devotion and study, I've become even more attuned to what that looks like—because I was searching in the right place. I learned that my life was *meant* to be challenging because my purpose was to transmute that trauma and alchemize it in order to serve humanity.

The beauty of this step in the healing process is that it provides you with a road map. When you identify your spiritual curriculum, you're identifying where you've been and where you need to heal, and you're identifying where you're going or all the ways that you're meant to be living in service of your higher purpose. That's meant to give you hope! It's the carrot dangling on the stick. Don't want to do all this work because what the hell is the payoff? It's *purpose*. That's the beacon. That's what will make life happy and good. That is the point of being here. So crack this code, and you'll know how you're naturally meant to be in flow with your life and with others. And when you get there, life becomes a lot easier to bear.

Everyone Has a Life Path

That is the simplest, most beautiful truth—everyone has something they're meant to be and a way in which they're meant to contribute. And how you figure out what yours looks like is by identifying your patterns, your wound, and your intention—and, by extension, your purpose.

Like grieving, you're still working on touching the parts that hurt and allowing for a release. Where these two steps differ is that grieving is focused on your feeling something and moving it out as a fundamental, primitive biological response. Here, you're releasing the patterns of behaviors and thinking you developed as a *by-product* of or coping mechanism from your not having had that unhindered, unedited experience with emotions for what has probably been a long time, if ever. So it's a little less innate and requires a little more discovery.

In traditional therapy terms, you're looking for your "breakthrough" moment. It's the isolating of the coping mechanism. It's connecting the dots between your original wound and how it's showing up in your life right now—maybe it's people pleasing, maybe it's your desire to control situations or other people's emotions, maybe it's always holding yourself back with limiting beliefs. Whatever that pattern looks like for you, that's powerful information for you to use; that pattern is hindering your connection with yourself, and you cannot master any dynamic in your life until you are in complete alignment. You're going to have to die the good death.

Stop Arguing with God

You only lose what you cling to.
—*The Buddha*

This step of the process is where ego enters the chat. Your experiences in the grieving stage were between you and the pain in the space

RELEASE AND FIND INTENTION   129

where you chose to safely navigate and express that pain. It was a conversation between your pain and your inward-facing self. Now we're opening the aperture and seeing how pain affects your outward-facing self. We're examining how you in some way try to control the perception that other people have of you, or how you're regarded or spoken about. It's the external world versus an internal experience. When you start poking these tender spots, when you start disrupting the flow of these deeply held "truths" you've constructed for yourself, the ego... does not like that.

Of the people I work with one-on-one, 100 percent of them struggle with the ability to release control. That is the barrier. It might look different for each of them, but beneath their individual struggles are the ways they're trying to manipulate other people or situations for no real reason or benefit except their own comfort of control. And believe me, when we start to shine a light on that, the way people try to justify that behavior and the self-righteousness involved is truly something to *see*. I get it—I'm not going to pretend that I wasn't people pleasing my way through relationships, swooping in with that savior complex and being completely unable to receive any criticism or negative feedback because I felt like I was above reproach. And that's *okay*. These patterns have existed to protect yourself in some capacity. So in a way, they are doing their job to shield you from some element of pain. But ultimately, they are keeping you directly in the throes of your pain.

Interestingly, this is by far more of an issue with women than with men. There's a lot of layers to explore there, but primarily, it's because so many women are conditioned *out* of knowing how they truly feel. That ability or right was taken away from them. Not necessarily as a big-*T* trauma; sometimes as a function of having a parent who didn't have the capacity for discomfort, so they shut down any big emotional experience (crying, being upset). That creates a level of disconnection inside the body that makes it difficult to experience *anything*. And if you have deep-seated discomfort around not knowing how to feel or how to submit to the feelings you do have, then the next best thing is to either bypass those feelings, attune yourself to other people's feelings instead, or make everyone around you behave in a way that allows you to feel comfortable or is pleasing to you. Because you're being triggered by a history that no one knows about but you—sometimes *including* you! It's all inherently manipulative.

When you don't take responsibility for these patterns, you're ultimately misleading others. Consciously or not, you're taking away someone else's ability to have their own experience when they interact with you because you're not being entirely truthful in how you're showing up. You're challenging the integrity of your connections with other people. And you're most definitely risking the self-loathing these patterns create when they take root and wreak havoc on your physical, mental, and emotional health. Because to resist is to suffer.

Typically, if we don't release, we are beholden to unhealthy karma or the fate of our future existences in new lives, unhealthy relationship dynamics, unhealthy personal patterns, the continuation of generational curses or trauma, and self-sabotaging behavior. There are also physiological patterns of unreleased stress that eventually cause inflammation in the body.[1] It accumulates across all of your bodily systems, creating stagnation and imbalance that will manifest as disease. That could be irritable bowel syndrome, dorsal vagal collapse, autoimmune disease, mental health issues such as depression and anxiety, general aches and pains, or low energy levels and fatigue. Bottom line: it takes a lot more energy to hold on to the past rather than releasing oneself to the present or future.

If you can stop resisting release, if you can surrender, you will finally unshackle yourself from the script that's been previously written. Whether that's ongoing cycles of generational trauma or individual experiences, you are allowing yourself to rewrite the story. But to do that, you have to stop arguing with God. You have to give up control. You have to *shed* and give yourself the gift of the constant state of surrender, or what I like to think of as the daily death. Because, really, who

RELEASE AND FIND INTENTION 131

are we to argue with the Divine? Are you going to get into it with God about who is in control? Because you will lose every time. You'll suffer every time.

So often we interpret the word *surrender* as giving up or being defeated. In reality, to surrender is to stand in your sovereignty and the depths of your power. To surrender is also to stand in your dharma. Loosely translated, *dharma* is "purpose," but more accurately it's the deepest inner knowing that's available to us in this life. So to surrender is not to fail, it is to allow yourself to be held by forces far more vast than you can fathom—and then to see yourself and God the most clearly. It is your being in empowered choice, saying, "Now is the time I'm going to recognize the energetic potential of this moment and allow myself to rest."

I know how difficult it is to feel the feelings. The way I relate to that is with my own depression. It's not always pleasant. But when you give yourself the permission and access to feel your feelings in real time as they're making themselves available to you, there is so much freedom— real, real freedom—and self-love and self-awareness in doing that. Those feelings become your deepest spiritual teachers.

We are trained to run from what is dark. But what has been the most transcendent experience in my life is understanding that darkness can be the invitation to find the light. Darkness has been one of my most beautiful teachers. In those moments when I wanted to give up, where I felt sure that this pain or grief or sadness or anger would engulf me— that's when I have learned some of the greatest lessons of this lifetime and potentially all of my lifetimes. Because I have kept my heart open. And I stopped arguing with God.

Step 1: Release

If you want to fly, give up everything that weighs you down.
—*The Buddha*

132 LIVING IN WISDOM

Once you're willing to shed and release, the opportunities to do that will present themselves without your even having to try. You'll become deeply present with whatever it is you want to know. You'll start to really see your patterns or coping mechanisms and how often you reach for them. And you'll be able to follow those patterns all the way back to your original wound—the key to unlocking conscious, targeted healing. And eventually, as your understanding of that wound grows, you'll be able to let go of these patterns that are no longer serving you.

In order to tune in, start looking for behaviors that are simultaneously controlling (of yourself or someone else) and protecting you from having a real-time, attuned emotional response. For example:

- Emotional control or suppression of people around you versus regulating your emotions for yourself
- Emotional control or suppression of yourself in order to please others versus having your authentic reaction without concern for how you will be perceived or whether someone will withdraw
- Attachments to outcome and attempting to control scenarios versus allowing things to unfold as they're meant to
- Limiting beliefs (an outgrowth of trying to control outcomes because they keep you stuck) versus inhabiting your authentic self

Once you're holding that pattern in your awareness, take the time to walk yourself through the other areas of your life where it shows up. Then be in practice by noticing it every day. I assure you, once you get into this rhythm, you're going to see your patterns in real time—and it can get cringey. *Oh my gosh, did I just try to suppress that person at Starbucks? Did I just manipulate that person at work?*

But having a breakthrough in that first, more obvious area of your life is only the beginning. I love explaining this dynamic because it brings people a lot of peace and allows them to let go of a lot of guilt or negative self-talk. The truth is, very often after you start to heal in one

RELEASE AND FIND INTENTION   133

area of your life, you're invited over the next year or two to redevelop your relationship with the other facets where that same pattern shows up. For me, that looked like initially noticing how I was people pleasing in my romantic relationships. I was ignited by that realization because of how much awareness it granted me and how I was able to trace that straight back to my original childhood wound. I remember feeling so damn good and able to date so much more freely because I could let go of that pattern in that particular context.

But then one day I got a work email that got me feeling anxious and so completely caught up with what that person wanted that I wasn't advocating for myself—and then it hit me: *Ooh, this is what I've been doing in love.* It was starkly apparent in that moment how my tendency to play it safe, make myself smaller, and not advocate for myself wasn't confined to my relationships. So I had an opportunity to settle into the discomfort of that disconnect—and it really is a disconnect; I had still managed to feel successful and empowered in my career. Then I looked at how this pattern showed up in my interactions with my family and with my friends. Every time I took a step back to observe, I was presented with a new facet of this pattern. I consciously chose not to interpret that as a failing but rather as an opportunity to get deeply familiar with *why* it was showing up the way it did.

Begin observing where you see your patterns surface. And then, using your pillars of practice, and other healing modalities we'll be talking about in more detail in chapter 15, you'll have to address and heal that pattern in each of those spaces, as though you're slaying all the dragons, one at a time (and potentially more than once). Don't worry; this doesn't necessarily mean you'll be slaying dragons for the rest of your life. Once you're aware of those patterns, can connect them to your core wound, and have the mastery of being in practice, you'll be able to apply the tools you have with urgency in real time. Even though new irritations and pattern "flare-ups" will arise, none of them will ever be as loaded as your core wound. Everything is survivable after beginning to heal that.

134   LIVING IN WISDOM

Step 2: Palpate for the Wound

This is the second part of releasing. Remember, the patterns you've been noticing are merely the symptoms of your original wound. They are what you unconsciously crafted and developed in order to cope with the pain of that wound. By that logic, your pattern can tell you a lot about what that wound is.

Digging down to that wound and excavating is the core of this work because that wound has changed your behavior and your perception. It's the root of the root. There can be no lasting or sustainable healing if you don't address that. There can be no transcendence if you don't address that. This is the crevice work; it's getting deeper into the darker, tighter parts of yourself that don't want to be touched. If you don't clear those out, you cannot truly reap the benefits of this process. Even if you're finally able to manage how your coping mechanisms show up, you're still going to have friction. You're still going to find yourself spiraling every now and then—because the core need hasn't been addressed.

That said, as you'll perhaps be relieved to hear, this process is not something you're going to "solve" during these early phases of your healing. Again, this step is about the exploration. You're rappelling down with a headlamp to see what you can find. Meditating on it. Journaling about it. Creating movement around it to clear away the debris. I'll be giving you all the tools you'll eventually need to tend to the tender spots, but for now, take notes. But still challenge yourself here. God doesn't want you to be concealed in any way—meeting that directive *is* the spiritual curriculum. Anything short of that is missing the point. It is difficult work, but it is beautiful work.

I've included practices for you to trace back to your original wound on pages 137–144. Think of them as the rope and the headlamp. What these practices aim to do is help you follow a feeling and link that feeling back, back, back to what you believe to be its origin.

RELEASE AND FIND INTENTION 135

Remember, there is no hierarchy for pain. This isn't about justifying whether your wound is "enough" to have caused you to suffer. You do not need to have experienced big-*T* trauma for your wound to have triggered you into rearranging yourself as a response. I once met a man who, when sharing at a retreat, divulged to our small group that he was once separated from his mother at the beach for twenty minutes when he was young, and ever since, he's felt a deep fear of abandonment. There were others in our group who had experienced the worst that humans can do to one another, and yet, that was the root of his suffering. And it was causing him just as much pain as anything else more terrible.

Our wounds are simply the formative moment that activated pain and fear for us, and it's usually pretty distilled down to the fundamentals: a time when you were not supported or protected.

TRAVELER'S CAUTION

There are no hacks to healing, but you come close by being willing to stare your original wound in the face. It is dark and challenging work, and while it will condense your healing timeline, it is not without friction. As I said earlier, this requires examining negative thoughts and emotions that are tightly bound inside of your person. There is no way to do that without bringing those things to the surface. You can reasonably expect to feel aches and pains, physically or emotionally. You can expect to feel energetically drained and destabilized. That is why it is so important that you continue working through the steps of this process, which will ensure that you are nourishing and supporting yourself appropriately. At the very least, be sure to get adequate sleep—at least eight hours a night—and create spaces for your body to absorb all of this new understanding using the practices on pages 137–144.

136 LIVING IN WISDOM

Step 3: Find Intention

I've paired intention with release because they fit together like a puzzle. Creating space to release *is* an intention in and of itself. Finding intention—or being clear on the needs that you have to have met—is what drives your search for wisdom about your path and purpose, otherwise known as your spiritual curriculum. Knowing what to let go of and what to live in pursuit of comes back to the quest for self-study and mastery.

It's also getting *specific*. What are your cravings, your deepest desires? Simply saying, "I want to be happy," is far too general to be actionable. What does that even mean, anyway? Happiness isn't the contrasting pillar to pain. Acceptance is. Enoughness is. If it's not the deepest root, if there hasn't been an investigation into what your needs truly are, then it won't be actionable. (Explore the prompts and practices on pages 137–144 for more guidance of how to work with intention.)

Intention is also what creates space for all the things that you don't know to come online inside of you. The awarenesses that you don't have yet but are looking to experience—like putting up antennae. Leaning into intention versus calculated action is what leaves room for the unknown. And ultimately, the *only* way to heal is having access to the unknown.

I had some of the most profound realizations about how to heal myself when I finally started tapping into this universal stream of consciousness that runs through all of us and everything. Truths and suggestions would come to me in dreams, after meditation, or during a writing download. It was like a big game of connecting the dots, such as being able to see how people's past experiences were showing up in their present, which helped me experience other people with more compassion and a deeper understanding of yin and yang, shadow and light. Other times, it looked like subtle encouragement, such as my body craving bananas when it needed potassium or berries when it

RELEASE AND FIND INTENTION   137

needed antioxidant support. It then was hardly surprising when I learned that my Epsom salt baths, which I'd started taking intuitively, were actually an ancient ritual, that salt is an ancient healer and purifier that's been used in sacred rituals across many different cultures. It's believed to be cleansing and sanctifying, removing toxic energy from both your body and all the compartments of your auric field, and expanding your connection with God, leaving you feeling nourished and relaxed. I was so desperate for relief from my aching body, and I'd seen people use these baths for athletic recovery, so I picked up a couple of big bags of the salts and added both to my bathwater. After soaking in there for half an hour, I felt a hundred pounds of weight coming off me in a spiritual and emotional sense. The same happened with my fledgling movement practice and mirror work. My body simply felt called to move, but I also felt a call to gaze at myself in the mirror as I danced. At first it felt strange, but eventually it felt like learning myself. Bearing witness to myself. I eventually learned that in some belief systems, mirror work is considered to be a sacred and potent way to come into a deeper, more heightened acceptance of yourself.

How did my body know to do the things it was doing that just felt right? How did I come into awareness of these practices or prayers? It was because I'd created space to welcome something new, something other than what I had been doing for the prior ten years. I'd received a new connection to consciousness, and it will come for you, too, when you are ready.

Once you identify what your unique patterns are, once you make peace with admitting to yourself that there is, in fact, a pattern at play, and then, once you finally lock into the work of your life, your spiritual curriculum, and accept that (even if you don't necessarily like it), you'll be on your way toward clearing away the pile of pain accumulated around the original wound. You'll be on your way toward creating significant change.

138   LIVING IN WISDOM

Practices for Release and Intention

As I walked out the door toward the gate that would lead
to my freedom, I knew if I didn't leave my bitterness and
hatred behind, I'd still be in prison.

—*Nelson Mandela*

Meditation for Releasing and Finding Intention

Start by sitting in a comfortable position and taking five deep belly
breaths to ground yourself in your body and in the present moment. Set
an intention for how you would like to feel or what you would like to
release. Call forward your higher self and wisdom: *I call forward the highest guidance available to me for the highest good of all concerned.*

Now begin a body-scan meditation with your hands in your mudra of
choice. (See Mudras for Releasing and Finding Intention below.) Incrementally move your focus from the top of your head to the base of your spine
(your crown to your root), gently releasing any physical or emotional tension
points (such as in your jaw, neck, shoulders, or heart) that you may notice as
your attention travels down your body. Throughout the meditation, notice
your breath. If at any time you find yourself connecting to your thoughts,
bring your awareness back to your breath and the rise and fall of your chest.

Let your practice stretch anywhere between five and twenty-five
minutes. Allow the length of your meditation to gradually increase over
time as you feel more settled into your practice.

Mudras for Releasing and Finding Intention

Uttarabodhi Mudra. The awakening mudra is the yogic hand gesture
of enlightenment. *Uttara* means "upward" and *bodhi* means "enlightenment" or "awakening." This mudra has a positive effect on the nervous
system.

Begin with hands at heart center, elbows bent. Bring the index fingers flat against one another, and interlace the remaining fingers. Join the tips of the index fingers and extend the thumbs, pulling the index fingers away from the thumbs so the palms naturally separate slightly.

Start with this mudra at the diaphragm or the base of your lungs, your index fingers pointed downward, and then slowly raise the mudra following the centerline of your spine, or the central channel. You'll feel an instant connection with the central channel: a column of light, harnessing the energy in your body.

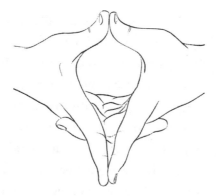

Kshepana Mudra. The Letting-Go mudra—sometimes known as the Steeple mudra—is a gesture that directs stress and negativity out of the body, making space for calm and positivity.

Begin with hands at heart center, elbows bent. Bring the index fingers flat against one another, and interlace the remaining fingers. Cross the thumbs, resting the pad of each thumb on the back of the hands. Press the index fingers together, but ensure that there is a small hollow space between the palms of the hands. Point the index fingers toward the ground. Hold for seven to fifteen slow, even breaths, focusing on lengthening the exhalation or sighing out the breath. Imagine anything you'd like to let go of being blown right out of your system and out of your fingertips. Connect to the power you feel of your other fingers being interlaced, and either hold the shape while meditating or while practicing any variation of yoga postures.

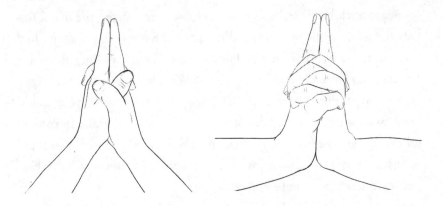

Ganesha Mudra. This mudra is named after the elephant-headed deity Ganesha, who is believed to be both the place and the remover of obstacles—like a sheepherder directing you on your path. To call on this mudra is to help build confidence, willpower, and trust in the divine order of things. It is believed to help instill in you a sense of courage and ease, in addition to a trust that any apparent roadblocks are an important part of the journey. In this way, the Ganesha mudra is considered to be energetically strengthening, physically and emotionally. This gesture can either be used to ask for obstacles to be removed or to honor the obstacles for making you stronger. By performing this mudra, you bring your attention and energy to the *anahata*, or heart, chakra, opening up your lungs and heart to the subject of your meditation. It is also considered to be a heart-opening practice.

Make two C-curve shapes with your hands, and hook the fingers together. The joined hands can rest in your lap, in front of your heart, or be held overhead with a pulling energy, which can increase strength and determination. During your meditation, inhale deeply, holding your hands in this gesture, and then pull outwardly on your hands as you exhale without unlocking your fingers. Repeat this motion up to six times, then reverse the gesture (i.e., put your right hand in front of your chest facing outward with the thumb down). Be sure to perform this mudra the same number of times in each direction to maintain the balance of the pulling act.

Essential Oils to Support Release and Intention Rituals

Geranium: The oil of release and regaining trust

Hyssop: The oil of releasing judgment of self and others

USING ESSENTIAL OILS

An easy, effective way to work with essential oils is to put them in a diffuser. They can also be applied directly to the skin. Always check to see whether the oil you're using needs to be diluted with a carrier oil or lotion. A quick way to activate the oils is to rub them on the palms of your hands, the soles of your feet, and your temples, or dab them on your chakra points—or simply take a deep inhale of them right from the bottle.

Movement for Releasing and Finding Intention

Running or other physical activities that encourage a good amount of sweat are a great way to release built-up stress and tension in the body or gunk from life.

Swimming allows the weight of gravity to slip off for a while, letting the body become light and able to make space for new intentions.

Yoga poses can be performed individually or together as part of a gentle flow:

- Cat-Cow Stretch (Marjaryasana-Bitilasana)

- Seated Forward Bend (Paschimottanasana)

- Supine Bound Angle Pose (Supta Baddha Konasana)

- Supine Twist (Supta Matsyendrasana)

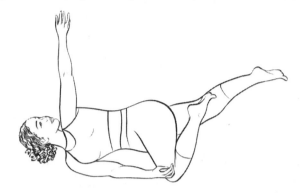

- Corpse Pose (Savasana)

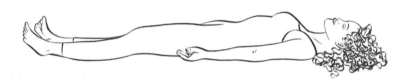

Affirmations for Releasing and Finding Intention

I am in highest remembrance of my authentic self.
I choose to release that which causes harm and suffering.
I choose to set my intentions with harmony and peace.
I release unhealthy memories, attachments, relationships, and experiences. I accept healthy and healing love in my life.
I release what blocks my path, making space for new beginnings.

Journal Prompts for Releasing and Finding Intention

What are some anger and frustrations I'm holding on to?
What's something I need to let go of?
How would I feel if _____ were released from my body and my mind?
Are there any ways that choosing not to release _____ benefits me on some level?
What do I desire my new beginning to look and feel like?

144 LIVING IN WISDOM

Creativity for Releasing and Finding Intention

Write what you wish to release this season on a piece of paper. This can be composed as a letter or a list. If you have people, situations, relationships, or anything else you'd like to release, write it out. Then:

- Read the paper, connecting with your intention to release these issues, to make space for what's to come.
- If you can, carefully burn the paper over a fire outside.
- Try doing this at night, perhaps followed by enjoying a bath or other releasing or restorative rituals.
- In the morning, write your intentions out in your journal and take one step toward those intentions that day.

Other ways to release can be less formal and more primal. Maybe it's release through dance, or stomping the feet on the ground to release excess tension in the nervous system. Soft tapping on the chest, neck, and arms can also encourage muscles to release and relax.

I am courageously standing in my brilliance, effortlessly connected to my sacred creativity as I share my God-given gifts with radiant vitality.

Chapter 14

Retreat

I have taken a moment here to rest, to steal a view of the glorious vista that surrounds me, to look back on the distance I have come. But I can rest only for a moment, for with freedom come responsibilities, and I dare not linger, for my long walk is not yet ended.

—*Nelson Mandela*

In my midtwenties, I experienced another pivotal low point. I had, by choice, just given up my successful career in New York, including my dream job in TV and radio, to get married and follow my partner to Houston. I went willingly because while that particular job was, indeed, a dream come true, it wasn't necessarily *the* dream in terms of my aspirations, and also, I'd fallen in love with this man. Shortly after moving, I began realizing that I had married someone with very little emotional capacity and a penchant for cruelty, and that the relationship was killing my soul. I couldn't feel any gratitude for anything, even though life was checking so many boxes—the big house, the nice car, the new marriage. That deep, existential unhappiness was showing up in intense stress responses in my body. I was inflamed and uncomfortable in my own skin, on the verge of chronic autoimmune disease, but I hadn't yet connected the dots between my emotional agony and my body screaming for help.

The final straw was when I was diagnosed with shingles, which causes incredibly painful rashes all over your body, but more than that, it affects your nerves in a severely painful way—and is very uncommon in people as young as I was. I was watching myself wither, and it was clear to every single cell in my body—and now me—that I needed to rest.

At this point, I had started dipping my toe into traditional medicine modalities and meditation, and I knew that I wanted to explore that more deeply in order to feel even the tiniest bit better. But this also wasn't a time when everyone was posting about their wellness retreats on Instagram (or posting on Instagram at all). So under the advice of a friend, I went online and searched "detox" then added "stressed out help." Deepak Chopra's face immediately popped up on my screen and I thought, *Oh my God, I* know *him*. It represented the miraculous nature of synchronicity—I had just gotten one of his books, *The Seven Spiritual Laws of Success*, which had already planted a life-altering seed. So I signed up for a ten-day retreat with a focus on *panchakarma*, an Ayurvedic therapy that cleanses the body, and took a leap of faith.

The retreat consisted of about thirty people, all of whom were decades older than me. The only person who was about my age was a guy from New York who had a very different background from mine. I was also one of the only people there who didn't have a yoga practice— namely because I avoided yoga since it was so triggering for me, all the ways it felt like my body was letting me down (to the point where I sneaked out of the daily yoga sessions). But I've always considered myself to be a seeker of new experiences and knowledge—and I was also spiraling, exhausted, and broken—so I decided to commit to the process.

For the following ten days, I connected for the first time in my adult life. I learned how to meditate. I ate detoxifying foods and experienced each of the six "tastes"—bitter, sweet, astringent, pungent, salty, sour— at every meal, which in the Vedic tradition is meant to enliven each of the senses and promote a satisfied, balanced feeling. I was given herbal diuretics and ghee colonics, so I was literally expelling everything my

148   LIVING IN WISDOM

body had been hoarding—the toxins, plus the emotions they informed. I received Ayurvedic body treatments meant to move energy through the body and open a higher awareness. I spent every moment of my day in these highly curated spaces, where everything from the scent to the colors to the textures to the facilitators' tone of voice was consciously chosen to facilitate our energetic balance and healing. It was all just there, subtly in the background, to support your undoing, letting go of yourself, letting it *all* go. Even though I was so disassociated and numb from my physical body and I wasn't sure whether I'd be able to get to a better place even if wanted to, the experience that the facilitators had so brilliantly constructed left my body no choice but to lead the healing and my mind no choice but to catch up.

The other powerful element of my experience was the community. Even though, at first glance, we had nothing in common, we bonded over the commonalities of our experiences. I'd always felt that my own suffering was unique, but there we all were, hurting in our own way, but each able to see the universality in that—and the hope that we'd make it out the other side. For years afterward, I stayed in touch with many of the people I'd met there. Over the next two years, I went on seven more retreats with Deepak and the Chopra Center, and then, even though I had no intention of teaching at the time, I signed up for his yearlong teacher training and meditation program. To say that that first retreat experience was transcendent and nourishing is an understatement.

The most important mindset shift you can have at this point in your healing journey is embracing retreating, or the act of removing yourself from everyday life—whether you are going on an actual organized retreat or simply creating an alternative space for yourself. It is a necessity, not a luxury. It's not necessarily a long-term solution, but it is a powerful and eye-opening way to gain knowledge and kick off the healing process.

When you step out of your usual environment and its demands and the stresses you associate with it, you create space to supercharge your

RETREAT   149

healing and transformation. You are not just retreating from everyday tasks and responsibilities; you're also retreating from the outside in and giving yourself the opportunity to fortify your internal world. You are able to glimpse your most authentic self—think about how you feel when you're on vacation. You suddenly find yourself breathing a little more deeply, expanding, seeing things as they are more clearly. Think about how much more easily you make new friends when you're traveling than when you're in your own neighborhood—it's because you're free from all of the roles you usually play. You're not wearing all the masks you put on for people. You're not being tugged in any way; you're just there to immerse yourself in the process and focus on the experience. When you are completely unencumbered, it's a lot easier to transcend the patterns and processes that have become so ingrained— and then get a bird's-eye view of them. In fact, that's one of the most powerful aspects of a retreat: the witnessing, both of yourself and of others. Retreating expands your capacity to bear witness to your own experience and the experiences of other people (if there are other people participating in your retreat)—and not trying to change *anything*. You simply sit with discomfort and explore it in real time with the luxury of space and clarity.

Retreating also gives you the opportunity to try on new ways of being. Each of the daily practices you'll experience, regardless of the type of retreat you choose, is not about making you a better person or solving your problems. The practices are meant to allow you to be your true self in all the ways that it shows up, and then be able to see what your true self looks like when it's not coming from a trauma response, when it's not a projection, when it's not a coping mechanism. Retreating allows you to experience emotional regulation and how that is the truth of you. The best of you.

For some, even the simple act of showing up, of choosing to step into an experience that is foreign with people you don't know, is scary. To be so vulnerable and raw and open with people is daunting. But it is such an incredible opportunity and an accelerator for growth to lean *all* the

150 LIVING IN WISDOM

way into the discomfort and to let the natural ease of the environment support your nervous system.

Retreats for the Practical and the Mystical

I'd like to introduce you to the concept of **Hermit Mode**. In storytelling traditions, hermits are associated with knowledge gained from deep inner reflection and solitude. In Tarot, the Hermit is the ninth card in the major arcana, nine representing the tipping point of the journey before ten, where we reach a level of completion and go back to one. The hermit has the gift of perspective gained through solitary observation, or retreat, which is why I like to think of attending a retreat as embodying your own Hermit Mode. It's allowing yourself to rebuild in seclusion. To release, renew, rejuvenate. To have the space to become something else, something more.

In that way, retreating is very similar to metamorphosis. That's when the caterpillar leaves its journey of the earthly realm, retreats to its cocoon as a womb for transformation, and emerges with the qualities, skills, and knowledge to quite literally take to the sky. In that pause and reflection, there is a physical restructuring of the body, a loss and a gain, death and rebirth.

When you think about what you gain from a "practical" perspective while retreating, this metaphor suddenly doesn't sound so esoteric. We know that when the body is allowed to rest, it naturally begins to repair itself. Our breath becomes more relaxed, signaling to the autonomic nervous system that it's time for the parasympathetic nervous system to take over for rest and digestion—the physiological opposite of fight-or-flight.

And by physically taking a trip, specifically one intended as a retreat, you may experience a change in your thoughts, emotions, and reality. This energetic shift, plus the time and space to mentally declutter, gives you the ability to release dynamics, addictions, distractions—anything—that is keeping you from your highest self.

Retreating creates the opportunity to:

- Turn inward for self-reflection and direction, and to be clear and connected to one's self, soul, gut, heart, and vision
- Receive support and guidance
- Connect with community
- Gain knowledge and wisdom
- Solve or address a problem
- Receive rest—in body, mind, and spirit
- Be seen, heard, honored, respected, challenged, and accepted

Retreating offers a massive acceleration of growth because it is essentially an incubator for the seeds that you can plant, speeding up the time between your dreams and reality. Through retreating, you can reclaim new awareness, insights, and perspectives, as well as new goals, commitments, or values. Retreating allows you to reclaim your *power* and the ability to pursue your life in a reinvigorated way. Similarly formidable is that retreating allows you to celebrate your life, your wins, your success, or just the fact that you are alive, are excited, and have gratitude. Because when you send out a vibration of "yes" into the world—*Yes, more of this, please*—the better you're attuning your biology to hold that frequency.

Retreating Does Not Replace the Work

After I went on that first retreat, something in me woke up. I went back to Houston and tried to re-create my own seasonal *panchakarma* experience (wisdom dictates that you do this when the seasons change) and even found a local Ayurvedic practitioner who would provide me with the herbs and oils needed for certain rituals. But even though I'd brought back so many tools from this experience, part of me also expected that I'd come home completely fixed, that life would be totally different after ten days. But there was a piece missing. I was not only severely depressed,

152 LIVING IN WISDOM

I also wasn't ready to meet that pain. Going deep still frightened me. I would avoid journaling exercises because I wasn't ready to see the truth of my pain on paper. Because I wasn't ready to make the choices that those truths would require me to make if I ever wanted to start healing.

I would get some relief by doing the physical practices and meditation. I was trying to heal my life, but without actually having to excavate my life—without recognizing my patterns and limitations—my hands were tied. In fact, it would be years before I was able to develop my own practice for myself to do that excavation.

As you add retreating to your healing toolbox, be mindful that you are not using your retreat experiences to bypass. Meaning, you're relying on work at the surface to avoid digging into the deeper, darker bits. It's easy to show up to a space that already feels comfortable, choose to not push yourself out of your comfort zone, and center yourself on your existing expertise—what you already know versus what you're there to learn. That is not doing the work. Nor is posting beautiful photographs of yourself in that place. If it's *comfortable*, then it is not drilling down to the parts of you that need to be examined in order to make effective, lasting shifts.

Yes, there are elements of retreating that are meant to feel lovely and nourishing, which is intended to keep you feeling supported and regulated as you ease yourself into the more uncomfortable work. Take advantage of that healing cocoon and that safety to spelunk into the abyss below.

Ensuring Your Retreat Is a Soft Space

Early in my healing process, I took a class as part of a group of about two hundred people. I was the only Black person and one of the only women under thirty years old. It was right after my very close friend had been murdered. I had been so privileged to watch his ascent from the very beginning of our relationship and to have the honor of seeing this man—a Black man in America—grow as an artist and as a person. The grief left me grappling with my own fear of showing myself, of putting my work out there; that grief was intermingling with the sleep-deprived depletion and postpartum anxiety I was experiencing as a mother of an eight-month-old. At this point in my life, I felt like I was wearing my nerves on the outside of my body. The world felt so dark and disorienting.

During this class, we received a lecture from the retreat facilitators—white, in their seventies, with a beautiful house in an affluent neighborhood and a beautiful life that was very insulated from the real world and people and experiences that looked like me or mine. I felt called to stand up at the end of their lecture and share how I was feeling. I shared with the room about how I still had so much fear inside of me, how I feared for my son's life and was scared that something was going to happen to him or to me. I shared that my friend had been murdered, and how it shook me so deeply because not only did I lose someone abruptly and violently, but the person I lost was at the pinnacle of living his purpose. It's not something we haven't seen before: Dr. Martin Luther King, Malcolm X—Black men who had been shot down for their activism. I expressed how this was creating a visceral barrier to my own work, and how that stood in the way of my call to have purpose. The messaging I had received from my friend's death was that if I offered my work to the world, then it will be time to die and leave my son.

In the wake of that confession, of laying myself completely bare in that room, there was *snickering*. People were rolling their eyes. The facilitators—who knew nothing about me, my life, or my history of raising myself, experiencing extreme loss and grief, living through my *seventh* friend dying as a result of violence, living with PTSD, and taking a stand in ways they could never fathom, particularly as a woman of color and mother of a son who will grow up to be a Black man— told me I just had to "*let it go.*" I had to simply "attune to the light." They told me I was getting in my own way. They said that I was being

154   LIVING IN WISDOM

a helicopter parent and using that as a cop-out for living my truth. One woman, who approached me after the session was over—against the number one rule of the program, that you don't talk to anyone about what they've shared unless they invite you to—had the audacity to suggest that I look up the term *codependence* as it relates to my relationship with my son.

At that time, we were still another year or so away from Black men and women making the national news for their murders at the hands of police (even though many communities had been watching and experiencing this for decades). There hadn't been mainstream willingness to better understand the systemic dynamics that affect every element of life as a person of color living in America. But this was also indicative of a potential retreat pitfall for anyone who has experienced trauma or who lives with PTSD or CPTSD. Because not everyone is equipped to navigate those experiences, and that can, of course, be a barrier to healing—not to mention incredibly hurtful and triggering in the moment with the ability to shame you back into your suffering.

After I had that experience, I felt confused and angry for a long time. Then it continued to linger in my thoughts for *years*. It took me a while to sift through all the layers of it and process all the ways it was wrong; ultimately, I understood that I had to find a community that suited me better. I also took the experience as a personal imperative to expand my understanding of the work beyond my own experience in order to create a soft space for others who seek out my help. As a teacher, that unsafe space made me better equipped to offer a lifeline to others with complex lived experiences who require and deserve something suited perfectly for them.

Finding the Right Retreat Experience for You

If you identify with my story in any way and you want to participate in an organized retreat, I highly recommend looking for one led by

trauma-informed facilitators. In my opinion, they don't necessarily have to be certified because, while there is a certification process, it doesn't mean that someone can't be proficient without it. When signing up for a program, ask questions: What does your demographic tend to look like? Have you done any work with people who have had traumatic experiences? Could you give me information about who is facilitating? What is their training or field of study? Will there be opportunities for me to have open-ended alone time to integrate this experience?

This experience also taught me how to navigate feeling activated in a personal share situation—which, no matter how well you choose to retreat, you may encounter. I advise you to get clear about whether you need people's approval to do what you need to do to heal. And then, after finding a safe-feeling space, investigate your response and use it as an opportunity for practice.

When seeking out a retreat, get centered and think about what kind of experience would be meaningful to you, where your spirit is most likely to want to come alive, and what environment is going to be the most nourishing for you. Ask yourself:

- *Do I want to challenge myself, meet new people, and do hard things together?*
- *Do I want to learn and grow through intentional deep study? Or through optional lectures and ceremonies?*
- *Do I want to be deep or light?*
- *Do I want to allow myself to rest and relax, to receive in luxury and abundance?*
- *Do I want to experience a fabulous lifestyle or a spiritually seeking experience?*
- *Am I going here to escape my problems or to become more aware of them?*
- *Where do I want to be? A beach, the mountains, the forest, under waterfalls?*

156   LIVING IN WISDOM

- *Do I want to be around people who share the same gender identity as me?*
- *Am I going here to experience solitude or togetherness?*
- *Do I want to be told what to do, or have the freedom and flexibility of choice?*
- *Do I want to learn or deepen a specific practice, such as meditation or yoga?*
- *Am I going here to change my life or celebrate my life?*
- *Am I here to question my beliefs or reaffirm them?*
- *Am I here to create change or deepen the changes and commitments I've already made?*
- *Am I going here for active or passive healing?*
- *Am I guiding this choice, or is God guiding this choice?* (Neither is wrong, just something to consider.)
- *What does my body need?*
- *What does my mind need?*
- *What does my nervous system need?*
- *What does my heart need?*
- *What does my womb need?*
- *What does my soul need?*

Types of Retreats: There's Something for Everyone

- Holistic healing retreats
- Darkness retreats
- Breathwork retreats
- Yoga retreats
- Sleep retreats
- Fitness retreats
  - o Pilates retreats
  - o CrossFit retreats
  - o Training camps
- Nutrition or culinary retreats

- Spa retreats
  - Massage, acupressure, acupuncture
  - Cryotherapy, infrared saunas, mud baths
  - Head spas, Korean spas
- Luxury retreats
- Nature retreats
  - Forest bathing / waterfall bathing
  - Kayaking
  - Hiking
  - Mindful marathon running
  - Guided foraging
- Adventure retreats
  - Sport or "endorphin tourism"
- Sound healing retreats

How to Maximize Your Time During Retreat

One of the most powerful influences of a retreat is how it trains you into new habits and practices that you can take with you. Private students sometimes stay at my home, or at another location, so we can run process all day. Part of that is so I can be in service of their spiritual surgery, but it's also about being there to reinforce every facet of their practices throughout the day through both my presence and the repetition. We're building a comfort and consistency with these practices, and it's training my students to translate these practices to their life at home. From how they breathe, to how they move, to how they eat, to how they prepare for sleep—that's woven into the experience so that it becomes more innate. These things are essential to the healing process, and it's really hard to start new practices at home by yourself. There's just too much self-doubt or irritation that creeps in when you're on your own. Unfortunately, these newer habits are often the first to be lost the moment anything else comes up. Leaning into the innate nature of a retreat is the antidote to this.

You could show up at a retreat with only the clothes on your back and zero preparedness and still have a transcendent experience. But also, taking the time and resources to send yourself on retreat is sacred, and something I've learned over the years is how to really wring every last drop of nourishment from the experience.

A retreat is a time to fortify each of my existing practices. The natural structure of a retreat, even if you've chosen a program that's a little more open-ended, lends itself to disciplined devotional energy. You don't have the constraints of real life; there are no distractions. This makes it a great time to focus on supercharging your existing practices or to start a new practice that you want to reinforce as part of your every day. Perhaps it's a new supplement you want to try, or a health regimen, or a book you've been meaning to read. Commit yourself to doing any homework that's assigned, such as journaling exercises. Commit to following a set sleep protocol, dimming the lights an hour before bed, and giving yourself at least eight hours to rest. Do all the things that are too difficult with all the demands of home but that you know are part of your "best life"—stretch, floss, pray. Use this time to gain repetition in all the things that make you feel restored; it'll be easier to maintain consistency after you leave. And definitely challenge the urge to turn on the television, if there's one in your room.

Stretching the Retreat Experience

I strongly suggest, after you come out of a retreat experience, you *do not* plunge headfirst back into your normal life. Remember, a retreat is not the final word on the work. You will not emerge fully healed. And if you don't continue to do the work, then no matter how incredible you feel after coming home, you will most likely be stress spiraling again at some point. There's a reason why people, myself included at one point, live from retreat to retreat.

RETREAT   159

That said, you will resurface from your retreat with a lot of new wisdom in your pocket and momentum at your back. And if you build a post-retreat plan, you can harness that feeling and channel it into your work. Reflect on the touches that made the retreat special. Was there a particular scent you loved? A blanket you'd use for meditation? A song that would play during yoga? A tea or elixir you enjoyed? A quote you found particularly resonant? A meal you can't stop thinking about? You can bring any and all of these details home with you and weave them into your daily devotion. It doesn't even need to be every day. In fact, choose just one day to light that candle or make that dish or play that song and move your body as it's called to do. All of these touches will help you bottle the afterglow of your experience just a little bit longer.

You can also create your own container for retreat at home, which is something I will do from time to time and is great if you don't have the time or resources to go somewhere else (see page 164).

Practices for Retreating

> There is a life force within your soul, seek that life. There is a gem in the mountain of your body, seek that mine. O traveler, if you are in search of that, don't look outside, look inside yourself and seek that.
>
> —*Rumi*

Meditation for Retreating

Start by sitting in a comfortable position and taking five deep belly breaths to ground yourself in your body and in the present moment. Set an intention for how you would like to feel or what you would like to release. Call forward your higher self and wisdom: *I call forward the highest guidance available to me for the highest good of all concerned.*

Now begin a body-scan meditation with your hands in your mudra of choice (see Mudras for Retreating below). Incrementally move your

160 LIVING IN WISDOM

focus from the top of your head to the base of your spine (your crown to your root), gently releasing any physical or emotional tension points (such as in your jaw, neck, shoulders, or heart) that you may notice as your attention travels down your body. Throughout the meditation, notice your breath. If at any time you find yourself connecting to your thoughts, bring your awareness back to your breath and the rise and fall of your chest.

Let your practice stretch anywhere between five and twenty-five minutes. Allow the length of your meditation to gradually increase over time as you feel more settled into your practice.

Mudras for Retreating

Dharmachakra Mudra. This mudra is about tapping into cosmic law and order. *Dharma* means "divine law" and *chakra* means "wheel," so the combination of the two translates to "wheel of divine law." Think of it as going back to basics or that which is within the space of retreat. It is also connecting to the role of teacher, particularly inner teacher. In this mudra, you form a wheel with each hand. The wheel formed with the right hand symbolizes the beginning of life, and the wheel formed with the left symbolizes the transition from this life to the next. Just like yin and yang, the interconnection of these wheels represents the continuous flow of energy mutually arising from and transforming into birth and rebirth. Three fingers on each hand are extended beyond the rings you're creating with your thumb and index fingers. These fingers of the right hand symbolize the three important teachings of the Buddha: The middle finger signifies the one who is listening to those teachings; the ring finger signifies the "lone buddha" or "private buddha," meaning each of us is a Buddha; and the little finger signifies the Mahayana or "great vehicle" that will carry the suffering of this world to another world. The fingers on the left hand symbolize the three jewels of Buddhism: the dharma (universal truth), the Buddha (the awakened), and the sangha (the community).

To practice, join the thumbs and index fingers of both of your hands to make two rings, extending the middle, ring, and pinkie fingers. With the left palm facing the body—the heart—and the right palm facing outward, kiss together the thumbs and index fingers of both hands. You can chant, "*Om mani padme hum*" ("the jewel is in the lotus" or "praise to the jewel in the lotus"). *Om* is the primordial sound of all creation. *Mani* means "jewel," with *ma* to dissolve jealousy and the attachment to fleeting pleasures while cultivating ethical behavior and *ni* to dissolve our attachments to desire and passion while cultivating our ability to be patient with ourselves and others. *Padme*, or "lotus," represents wisdom. *Pad* dissolves our attachments to the many prejudices and judgmental notions we have while cultivating the quality of perseverance, and *me* dissolves our attachments to being possessive while also cultivating our powers of concentration. *Hum* indicates that which cannot be disturbed by anything. In short, we work to dissolve our attachments to aggression and hatred, and instead cultivate our own innate wisdom.

Hakini Mudra. *Hakini* is Sanskrit for "power" or "rule" and is believed to give the practitioner power over their own mind (which is why it's sometimes called "mudra for the mind"). It also cultivates one's connection with the third-eye chakra, thereby promoting intuition and insight. Hakini mudra is particularly useful to counter the effects of stress, fatigue, and anxiety. Other benefits include:

- Boosting memory power
- Increasing concentration

- Energizing the brain
- Promoting a calm mind
- Improving academic performance
- Enhancing clarity
- Developing creativity

To practice this gesture, first bring the palms to face one another a few inches apart. Bring the fingertips and thumbs of both hands together, allowing them to maintain light contact. The hands can then be raised to the level of the third-eye chakra, in the center of the forehead.

In order to enhance the benefits of this mudra, the *drishti* (gaze) should be lifted toward the third eye. While breathing through the nostrils, the tongue should be placed against the roof of the mouth with each inhalation, and relaxed with each exhalation. Hakini mudra can be practiced for up to thirty minutes daily, either in one go or broken down into three ten-minute practices. Although this gesture can be practiced at any time of day, ideally it should be performed during sunrise.

Dhyana Mudra. This mudra is shared across several Eastern meditation disciplines, and the Buddha is often pictured doing this gesture.

Its root terms are *dhi* and *yana*, *dhi* being the process of thinking or perceiving and *yana* as the vehicle or practice of moving. *Dhyana* simply means "the practice of properly thinking or perceiving." The significance of this mudra is to bring you into deeper, more profound concentration. This gesture can also help bring you tranquility and inner peace. In the Buddhist perspective, the triangle formed by joining thumb tips in Dhyana mudra represents the three jewels of Buddhism: dharma, Buddha, and sangha. The right hand signifies knowledge, wisdom, and awareness, and the left hand represents the fantasy of existence in this world. When the right hand is placed over the left, it represents the dominance of knowledge and awareness over the illusions created by the world. It also indicates the balance of dualities (solar and lunar energy, hot and cold, masculine and feminine energies) in the body. The complete gesture signifies the balance of all the elements and soul.

Sit with your hands facing upward, right hand resting on top of your left palm. Bring the tips of your thumbs to touch.

Essential Oils to Support Retreating Rituals

Sandalwood: The oil of calming and lowering anxiety
Cypress: The oil of emotional cleansing

For more information on how to use these oils, see page 141.

Movement for Retreating

Retreating could be taking a walk in nature, getting lost in the wilderness for a while, taking slow, deep breaths, like that of forest bathing. Child's pose (Balasana) can also support your other retreat rituals (see page 189).

Affirmations for Retreating

When I retreat, I give myself the space to surrender to and connect with the truth.

Retreating is my sacred act of nourishing and healing my body, mind, and soul.

I retreat to receive.

I retreat to expand my brilliance so I may return with enhanced clarity and purpose.

I retreat to connect to my innate wisdom, receiving gifts and guidance that are just for me.

Journal Prompts for Retreating

- *What does retreating mean to me?*
- *Do I need to retreat? What kind of retreat do I need?*
- *How can I make space for retreat in my life? Does this look like a small trip, a full-scale experience, or daily rituals that help me now?*
- *Do I carry any guilt or shame around taking time for myself?*
- *How would I like to feel when this experience ends? Who will I be?*

Creativity for Retreating

Take yourself on a retreat. Retreat into nature if you can, taking a weekend to yourself to be in a landscape you enjoy. Relax, rest, turn off your phone, and connect with yourself. Bring things like books or personal projects but nothing demanding of your time, and allow for boredom to bring you new information, ideas, and inspiration. If you don't have time for a full-scale retreat, try treating yourself to a nourishing experience. Perhaps it's a massage or a community event like a sharing circle. Or have your own retreat at home by making a mug of your favorite tea or cacao and having a personal ceremony (page 205). Put on healing sounds and take an Epsom salt bath (page 207).

I am trusting and savoring the experiences of my life, joyfully surrendering to spirit, and effortlessly expanding my heart to all that is.

Chapter 15

Heal and Accept

Making your unknown known is the important thing.
—*Georgia O'Keeffe*

It may feel surprising that we're well into this book and only now moving into a chapter specifically devoted to healing. After all, this entire book is about healing. Well, this is the part of the process when you can take a look back at the milestones you've traversed and see how you've been slowly and steadily building the infrastructure you needed in order to fully commit to this pivotal step. It's almost as though you've been preparing for the final exam: acknowledging the necessity of grief and embracing that life is and will be uncomfortable, identifying your patterns of behavior, locating your spiritual curriculum and giving your process a compass, connecting with intention and asking yourself, *Who do I want to become?* You've created containers for this process through your practices and retreat. You've been living in the flow of integrity and devotion, proving to yourself that you're worthy of your commitment to yourself. You've unlocked higher awareness. You've excavated; you've studied; you've collected data. Now is the time when you put the pieces together, figure out what it all means...and then begin to make peace.

168   LIVING IN WISDOM

You've been removing the larger sediment to catch glimpses of what lies beneath. The crevices are probably still a little gunked up, and that's to be expected. You cannot yet vacuum out the in between if you haven't taken out the big bits first. Heal and Accept is when you lift back the last few strata between you and the core.

This specific part of your journey lies at the crossroads I described in part 2, introducing the daily practices. It's also where so many people stall out, because awareness, or the intellectual understanding of who you are and what challenges you, is a far cry from consciousness, or the *embodied wisdom* of those same ideas. The former is where you've essentially been up until now—learning, naming. Now is when you aim for integration: taking the lessons you're learning and applying them to other obstacles or points of discomfort. Walking in and with that knowledge, actively practicing it, living in wisdom.

I once went to a teacher of mine, Dr. Ron Hulnick, in a state of despair. I had hit a wall in my own process and was feeling burnt out. I told him how I'd spent ten years trying to heal and process, and yet there I was, crying again. In pain again. I asked him why it still felt so new. "I thought I had healed this," I said. To which he responded, "You did. And because you did, now you have an opportunity to look at another layer of it and from another perspective. You *get* to go deeper." I understood then how some wounds require healing over and over again. But you're never starting from scratch. Every time you hold something up for examination, you're bringing a new understanding. You'll relate to it differently. Until one day, instead of telling that story from a place of pain or even overcoming, you'll tell it simply from a place of observation—which is when it becomes wisdom for others.

This calls to mind the Taoist parable "Sāi Wēng Lost His Horse." In the story, a farmer's horse runs away. His neighbors offer him their condolences, saying, "This is most unfortunate." To which the farmer responds, "Maybe." The next day, the farmer's horse returns, bringing seven wild horses back with it. The neighbors celebrate the event as lucky, but the farmer says again, "Maybe." The day after that, the farmer's son tries to break one of the horses, is thrown off, and injures his leg. The neighbors express how that is such a shame, and the farmer responds with "Maybe." The next morning, conscription officers come to draft all eligible men to fight in the army. The farmer's son is rejected because of his injury, and the neighbors once again celebrate his luck. "Maybe," he says.

This is exactly what Ron was describing. We should strive to meet any experiences that arise in this process—without judgment. Without labeling it as "good" or "bad." Without expectations. Just seeing to see and not allowing our judgment of it to be the final word about ourselves and our lives, whether it's a charged interaction or a new, exciting opportunity. One does not preclude the other. One does not mean the other will not happen. And so we hold both as equal contributors, equal forces in our education.

I felt so free knowing that that *is* what the work looks like. You're standing in this exact place now, ready to receive a new set of tools with which you can examine your experiences.

Note, though—you will be applying a powerful salve to your core wound through this process, and for most if not all of us, there's no turning back the clock to meet and change our childhood selves. That version of us in our particular experience will forever exist. What we can do, however, is break the chain of generational trauma. Many wisdom traditions hold a belief that if you intend to heal something in your family lineage, you have an opportunity to extend that healing seven generations behind you and seven generations ahead of you. I say this not to add pressure to your undertakings—this is not you having to show up as the warrior, arriving with the trauma of your forebears on your back and the martyred mission of devoting your life to forever reversing it. That's too much pressure for one person. I believe that we are all here to do our part, and sometimes our part is to just *inch* it forward. So instead, ask yourself, *What is possible for me to heal in this life?*

I have been devoting daily attention to healing certain patterns with my mom for the past six years, and I've seen miracles occur. That doesn't

170 LIVING IN WISDOM

mean perfection. It doesn't mean I've rewritten my own history and childhood, much less my mom's history and childhood. It just means that I see more of her, and she sees me. We see our restrictions and are able to reach for patience. This has healed our relationship, our past, and what is possible between us. And while I may not have been able to have everything she now can offer my son, watching her give to my son selflessly and with joy heals me. It also heals the pain she's carried from the experience she had with her mother, which is compounded by watching her own daughter mother in a way that was not available to her, which in turn heals my son and every child that comes from him. As I said, it is nothing short of miraculous. The love and gratitude I feel for her is vast.

At this point, you know you need to heal and that you want to do it. The question to now ask is: How can you build a *supporting structure* for the healing you need to do? To do that, you'll first need to reference your blueprint: know where the wound is, what the resistance to self is. So now you can reverse engineer to see which tools in your toolbox will be in service of that. For me, my starting point was being emotionally and mentally abused in my marriage. That was the tippy top of pain, the penthouse. I then needed to construct the supportive scaffolding around that building in order to make my way to the top from the outside so that I could take control of my experience, rewire it, and transcend it. The healing modalities are the scaffolding, which I've curated to suit the specific structure of my building. And then, through devotion to them and the practices I've amassed, by choosing to be in participation with that pain, I'm supporting myself in that climb, transmutation, and transcendence.

And then, when you've moved through your biggest pain points in this lifetime and slayed the biggest dragons, you're free to undergo this same scaffolding process for all the smaller irritations as you notice them. Even if that pattern isn't rooted in trauma, you can still look at it and say, *Okay, I gotta do something about this because it's on my nerves.* (Ever think about that expression and the actual activation of the *nervous system*? Ding! Ding! Ding!) You locate what is upsetting you, you map out the blueprint, you make the plan, and you build those structures. It's the same formula for the macro and the micro.

Want to know what comes of building these structures with time and care and consciousness over and over again with delicate refinements each time? Speed, skill, efficiency. Mastery. Suddenly, the smaller irritations dissipate more quickly. The pain doesn't land as hard. You've now freed up a whole lot more room for letting in the joy and the good stuff. And you've now invited in a whole new layer of magnetism and auspiciousness into your life.

Acceptance

Not everything that is faced can be changed, but nothing can be changed until it is faced.

—*James Baldwin*

There is an understanding in the healing community that trauma does not become rooted and stored in the body automatically. It's only when that experience is *denied* that it insinuates itself somatically. For example, when a child is sexually abused and they're not believed or they're not supportively held and they're just expected to move forward—a scenario I've heard far too often from my students—that trauma registers as part of their personality and identity that they wear their entire lives. They internalize it as *I'm bad, I deserved that*, or *there is something wrong with me.* Conversely, as I've learned from talking with my friend Dr. Sheila Marie Campbell, a Traditional Chinese Medicine doctor who specializes in treating women who have been sexually abused, particularly in childhood, if you are able to work with a child immediately after they've been abused and get them into a treatment protocol, you can actually hit the reset button before these new neural pathways form, before they translate that experience as meaning something about who they are.

172 LIVING IN WISDOM

We can't meet our childhood selves with the compassion and acknowledgment that we needed in our pain, but we can meet our core debilitating experiences with love and support; we can look them in the eye and accept them as truth. With the desire to change the perception of what happened, these traumas needn't become the most encompassing, definitive part of our human experience. You can't transcend anything until you accept that something did or does exist. But I'd like to first clear something up—acceptance is not simply settling for less or allowing mistreatment. Acceptance is seeing the truth of something, to be in observation of the actual reality, and then coming into choice with how you'll interact with it. It doesn't mean it needs to stay; it doesn't mean you need to enjoy it. It just means that you need to acknowledge that it's true.

Acceptance is one of the most powerful vehicles for healing, if not the most powerful. When you take responsibility for your perception and the way you're interpreting or making meaning out of the situations you find yourself in, you can begin to respond in choice. When you accept something rather than resist it, you are able to get closer to receive new insights and information. You gain the ability to transform your relationship to the experience. Acceptance gives you agency and power while releasing you into the fluid flow of life. It imbues you with flexibility—of mind, body, heart, and soul—which reinforces the structural integrity of your container and your sense of self. This also creates space for new life by both releasing excess tension, blockages, and entanglements, as well as making room for new, healthier truths.

Acceptance is flexible yet strong, consistently calling you back into balance, harmony, and your innate power to be the change you need in your life. It is the portal that transforms pain and grief into pleasure and joy. It is what allows you to access that transformation and ease the resistance of movement between the two ends of the spectrum. It is at the root of improved emotional regulation, better coping skills, the capacity to stay within your window of tolerance (i.e., the ability to regulate your nervous system), improved psychological well-being, better

HEAL AND ACCEPT   173

communication skills, healthier relationships with others, and the ability to accept that life can be both painful and worth living.

In Buddhism, acceptance is referred to as "the middle way" or the transformation out of the wheel of samsara, or the mundane existence of simply cycling between birth and death. It is the yin and yang in cohesive harmony rather than opposition. It is physiological regulation and coherency between brain, heart, gut, and womb. It is the light of consciousness embracing the shadow of unconsciousness, and it is what allows liberation through the paradox of transformation. Through acceptance, possibility arises; and from possibility, potentiality; and from potential, power; and with power, choice; and with choice, presence; and with presence, action.

Simply put, **what we resist persists; what we accept, we access**.

Acceptance requires you to embrace emotions, thoughts, and circumstances that are unchangeable and out of your control—even when that reality includes pain or discomfort. For those who are just coming to terms with their awareness, acceptance can feel triggering, particularly individuals with CPTSD or PTSD. This is why acceptance is not the first step of the process, but that's not to say that it loses its charge by the time you find yourself there. If that is the case for you, begin with self-compassion. Compassion, for many, is the key to opening up to the beauty of the healing journey and can make acceptance easier to access. Specifically, it gives rise to nonjudgment, an essential ingredient when moving into acceptance.

Whatever your path looks like, acceptance is a nonnegotiable element of the formula. That said, this is not the "you gotta get over it and get over it fast" party line that our society operates with. That's how we ended up with tools of avoidance that have been passed down generationally, especially evident in the Silent Generation and their refusal to acknowledge pain or suffering, their belief that talking about something will somehow make it worse. I'll always remember asking my mom why she never checked on me about something painful that had

174   LIVING IN WISDOM

happened in my life and her saying, "If I said something, it would bring it up. It would be upsetting." In her mind, she believed that keeping me comfortable was the most healing thing for me. It's the common belief that people who have been given few if any tools about grieving hold: avoiding the feeling at all costs is what will make that feeling go away. That you can *choose* another emotion. That crying about something is causing harm to that process versus *being the process*. Because one must cry about something in order to stop crying about it. That's the whole thing—people avoid the work because they're afraid it's going to hurt, but it's going to hurt anyway. It's the difference between ensuring that there's an ending to the pain versus existing with it your entire life because you just keep avoiding it.

This process is requiring that you *do* express that pain. It's coercing you to acknowledge it, accept it, process it. It's saying to you, "I am here to support you, but you also have to dive into your work fully, because then there will most likely not be a reason to continue to bring it up with such a charged feeling." When you can do that in a safe, supported way, there is no longer a need to cling to the pain and constantly bring it up for review. The process is demanding acceptance in the name of transcendence. Because the only way out is through.

Holistic psychotherapist Dr. Edward Tick echoes this idea in his work surrounding reintegrating soldiers into society after being in active combat. Having studied warrior cultures across 5,600 years of recorded history, he identified "storytelling and confession" as being an essential part of the process for reentering everyday life. As he writes in his book *Warrior's Return*, "Stories release emotion, reveal secrets, educate, organize our lives into coherent narratives, point toward meaning. In the story, we transform from victims to heroes and heroines."[1] What Tick is identifying is that when we tell the story of our pain, when we allow ourselves to unpack the details of our narrative, we are no longer allowing these things to fester, or become what Tick describes as "inner poison." We are claiming ownership of them so that we may let them go.

THE FORMULA FOR HEALING

1. Accepting that whatever happened did, in fact, happen
2. Grieving that truth with space for sadness and rage
3. Surrendering to that truth
4. Acknowledging that you need support for metabolizing that truth
5. Making space for the new energy that emerges
6. Bringing forth creation with that new energy
7. Transcending into higher consciousness

Excavating the Authentic Self

Making your unknown known is the important thing.

—*Georgia O'Keeffe*

Necessary to this work is to clearly see the difference between your two innermost selves: the **cultural self** and the **authentic self**. The cultural self is built from the outside in with stories we're told by society, relationships, family systems, the collective consciousness. The **authentic self** is built from the inside out. It's the version of us that allows for our individual autonomy and creativity, as well as the understanding that we have our own unique plan within the greater plan. We're having our own personal experience within the greater shared experience—and that we are in observation of *all* of it.

Social scientists developed the idea of the "culturally created self" to describe the belief system we hold informed by forces external to ourselves. It is the version of ourselves shaped by our family of origin and generational experiences, shaped further by the societal measuring sticks of who we should be, how we should act, and what we should be doing based on what is popular and acceptable at that moment. In its most extreme

176   LIVING IN WISDOM

manifestation, this self is basically who we would be if we were to walk through the world completely unconscious, absorbing the values, wants, and needs that we were told we should have by everyone around us.

That version of us does serve a purpose, and it creates a foundation for how to be in this human experience. But there inevitably comes a time when we begin to feel friction with this version of self. It happens whenever we question the status quo. Whenever we want autonomy or want more for ourselves. Because we know, even if we don't fully understand, that there is another version of ourselves tucked in a deeper, more authentic part of us, and it wants to be nourished. It wants to feel whole and good. That is the "authentic self."

The authentic self is the version of us that makes the highest choices for us from a place rooted in wisdom, protecting those choices with firm boundaries, and standing in the confidence of that. It is steeped in mental, physical, emotional, and spiritual well-being; and it is aligned with our higher purpose.

Problems arise, however, when the two selves are in opposition to one another, which they frequently are. The cultural self is an alluring promise of homogeneity, inclusion, and majority. As opposed to the daily work required of maintaining the authentic self, the cultural self needs only to be lazily spoon-fed by just walking out of the door in the morning. So many of us stay in that version of self because it is the easiest. It's what we've always done—wake up, go to work, come home, watch trash TV, crash, and then do it all over again the next day and the day after that. There's no room for creativity of any kind. No expression that ever allows us to expand and transcend.

In fact, you cannot transcend if you remain in your culturally created self. When you take up residence there, that friction between selves only festers. Social scientists call this in-between space our "dormant self." It is the gray, shadowy part of ourselves where suppressed, unexpressed feelings churn. The more you struggle against your authentic self and the beliefs and practices that truly serve you, the more you

HEAL AND ACCEPT 177

ignore misaligned beliefs, the more you refuse to acknowledge wounds and harmful experiences, the more you stuff and stuff and stuff it all down, the more prominent your dormant self becomes. This manifests as suffering, whether that's depression or physical disease. It is, to be blunt, a miserable existence.

You cannot move beyond the cultural self if you haven't examined it. You have to evaluate those belief systems. Why do you hold a particular belief to be true? What do you actually know about that belief? How did it become a belief? *I noticed my initial response is X, but I know I don't actually believe that, so let me not do that now and see what happens.* This is part of the shadow or crevice work. You really are getting into the constellation of teeny-tiny spaces that have existed at your core since birth. You have to observe where those biases show up. You have to activate your curiosity—because you can't sustain growth or change without curiosity. Get curious about your own reactions and behavior and other people's reactions and behavior. Get curious about the world at large. We will often be required to surrender to other people's choices or be at the mercy of the collective consciousness until a future civilization learns to see things differently. So for now, observe. Learn. Make space for new functions, thoughts, and practices.

That is when you can fully inhabit your authentic self. It's when all the facets of you, light *and* shadow, are in harmony. In your authentic self, you are beautifully steeped in your highest choices, navigating life in effortless ease and grace. You have a sense of being in the right zone. You're not triggered by the unresolved parts of other people. The ability to experience maximum joy and gratitude, worthiness, goodness, enoughness is part of our highest self.

Being our most authentic, best, highest self doesn't mean being the most ideal or even perfect. Think of your highest self as the best vantage point, the best seat in the house. From there, you have the clearest view of the bigger picture. Which brings you into choice, and gives you the power to transform, both yourself and the world around you.

178   LIVING IN WISDOM

Why Healing Is Hard

I couldn't in good conscience send you further down this path without acknowledging that what you're doing is *hard*. It's awful and it's exhausting, and I'm so sorry that you're the one left to have to do it for yourself. Because we weren't meant to heal on our own. Healing has traditionally been a collective initiative in many cultures since the beginning of time. A great example is the Zulu Nation Tribes of South Africa. Zulu culture includes the deep belief that ancestors, or Amadlozi, are the mediators between God and humanity. They are seen as guides who can be appealed to for assistance with releasing or bringing certain things, such as forgiveness, or healing conflict with someone who has passed. Bert Hellinger brought this idea of "family constellation therapy" to the West in the 1980s, and it has since become a modality for revealing the unconscious dynamics of a family system and bringing it back into balance or harmony, resolving patterns inherited from both the family and broader historical, social, and cultural systems that negatively affect the quality of life of the descendants. (Hellinger is a controversial figure, but we can at least credit him with this.)

What's at play is the recognition that from a cultural view, everyone plays a role in everyone else's trauma. We carry the pain of everyone who came before us, and so it makes sense that we would need help from our ancestors to unwind those patterns, whether it's our physical living relatives or our ancestors in a spiritual sense. That dynamic is not currently the norm in our family structures, particularly in the non-white experience. At the very least, we could use an acknowledgment of the pain that we're expected to carry, whether it's isolated to trauma experienced in our immediate families or trauma at the hands of society at large. Collectively as a civilization, that recognition, that simplest of simple "I see you in your pain" is missing because everyone is dealing with their own unfinished business. The vibe is "I can't take on the weight of your experience because no one's helping me with mine."

In conversation with Shaka Senghor, a criminal justice reform activist who came up in this life with a lot of hardship and challenges, he shared that when he was a teen, he was sentenced to prison for twenty-six years for killing someone in self-defense. As we discussed his path to enlightenment while incarcerated, he said that of those years, he spent ten of them in solitary confinement. That is not something the human brain is equipped to process. It is not a silent retreat, especially when not by choice. Irreparable harm is done to the psyche after just one week in solitary, let alone ten years.

Shaka and I were talking about how even when formerly incarcerated people come out of prison, they're expected to atone for everything they did wrong. And then they're indentured to society, pariahs, always seen as having to make up the deficit because of a bad decision they once made. It occurred to me how absolutely impossible it would be for real transformation to happen in that environment. Because society would never be able to acknowledge how, for so many of these individuals, the game was rigged from the jump.

The bottom line is that for many of us, the setup is real. Without being given the proper tools or support or acknowledgment, it is very difficult to transform, to transcend, and to heal. But it *can* be done. You were built to do this.

Also, the healing modalities that I'm describing below are designed to see you where you need to be seen and hold you where you need to be held. This outsourcing of healing is a normal, if not essential part of the process, especially as we move farther away from community systems and their emotional safety nets. Your task now is to tune in to what would feel good to you and how you can care for yourself on all levels of your being.

How to Heal

This chapter is not about telling you how exactly to go and heal; you need to do the fact-finding and blueprint drafting. I am not educated in your pain the way you are becoming the definitive expert. And besides,

180 LIVING IN WISDOM

there are numerous ways the healing journey can look depending on you, your experiences, and your needs. But I can show you all the tools and the formula with which to use them.

Below I've included a list of modalities, which you can look at as your menu for healing. While they each look quite a bit different from the others, they are each uniquely designed to create energetic shifts, bring forward wisdom, and connect you with your authentic self.

Pick and choose according to your intuition and preferences. Also consider the pillars of healing—mind, body, heart, and spirit—and be mindful that each is being fed. Be sure to do something that is for each of these facets; oftentimes these modalities intertwine. But you cannot *not* meet one of those needs. That's why many people don't see full transcendence—they go to therapy and believe that's enough, but that's only feeding the mind; it's not connecting you with spiritual, emotional, or physical input. The role of being human means filtering our experiences through all four of these elements, and so we need to nurture them accordingly. We need to learn not just how to think about things, but how to feel them and understand what it means for the greater arc of our soul's path. Gifting yourself the unique cracking open that these modalities offer is like supercharging your healing experience, particularly if you find yourself avoiding dropping down into your body or surrendering to more esoteric, spiritual work. Plus, you'll not only be accelerating your progress, you'll also be connecting with the beauty, pleasure, and joy of healing.

Healing Modality Road Map

This is by no means an exhaustive list of healing approaches, nor is it more than a fraction of the volumes of data that support these methods' efficacy. My intention is to expose you to just some of the vast number of paths to healing, and my hope is that you'll spend time with the entries, research those that resonate with you, and follow your curiosity to find classes and practitioners in your area.

HEAL AND ACCEPT 181

- **Trauma-focused therapy (mind, body, heart spirit):** Processing feelings about a traumatic event with the goal of changing one's perspective around what happened. Trauma-informed psychotherapy approaches—or practices that recognize the impact of trauma on an individual's development and aim to avoid re-traumatization—include:
  - Eye movement desensitization and reprocessing (EMDR)
  - Progressive counting
  - Somatic experiencing
  - Biofeedback
  - Internal Family Systems therapy
  - Sensorimotor psychotherapy
  - Emotional freedom technique (EFT)
  - Cognitive processing therapy (CPT)
  - Solution-focused brief therapy (SFBT)

- **Cognitive behavioral therapy (CBT; mind, body, heart):** A form of psychotherapy focusing on modifying dysfunctional emotions, behaviors, and thoughts by investigating and disrupting negative/irrational beliefs. CBT is based on the idea that thoughts and perceptions influence behavior.
  - Dialectical behavior therapy: A type of CBT that is designed to provide skills for managing intense emotions and navigating relationships.

- **Animal-assisted therapy (heart):** Integrates animals such as dogs and horses to amplify emotional and mental health techniques.
- **Sound therapy (mind, heart):** Combines sound and music with self-reflective techniques to improve health and well-being, whether it's listening to music, singing, moving to music, meditating, or playing an instrument.
- **Art therapy (heart):** A form of psychotherapy that encourages self-expression through painting, drawing, or sculpting. Guided

182   LIVING IN WISDOM

by a specialized therapist, patients use art to explore and understand emotions and conflicts, then find resolution.

- **Color therapy (heart):** Also known as chromotherapy, this is based on the understanding that each color has a unique wavelength and frequency that produces electrical impulses. These frequencies are believed to enter the body and affect our mental, emotional, and physical well-being.
- **Horticulture therapy (mind):** Calls for passively or actively interacting with the healing and rehabilitating elements of nature, whether you're cultivating your own garden or spending time in thoughtfully planted spaces with the guidance of a trained therapist.
- **Forest bathing (mind, body):** Also called *shinrin-yoku* in Japanese. A research-based therapy for tuning in to the senses while spending time in nature. Formalized in Japan in the 1980s, forest bathing has been used to improve both mental and physical health and yet requires spending as little as ten to fifteen minutes observing nature's details.
- **Somatics (body):** Uses physical movement and exercises to reinforce the mind-body connection and observe the body from within. The objective is to tune in to signals about pain, discomfort, or imbalance.
- **Yoga (body, spirit):** Uses physical postures, breath, and meditation to integrate mind, body, soul, and spirit. This practice has been described as a "spiritual discipline of the subtle experience."
- **Compassionate/intentional touch or bodywork (body, heart, spirit):** An evidence-informed approach that combines skilled touch (e.g., massage) with compassionate presence. This can help build trust, particularly around physical contact.
- **Myofascial release therapy (body):** An advanced form of sports or medical massage that can reduce tension and pain in the body by releasing trigger points across muscular systems. (Fair warning: this is *not* a relaxing massage, but it can work wonders!)

HEAL AND ACCEPT 183

- **Energy healing (mind, body, heart, spirit):** Based on the belief that vital energy flows through the human body and that healing occurs when that energy is brought into balance, which positively affects the physiological systems of the body. This can be used to reduce stress and anxiety, recover from surgery, reduce the side effects of physical ailments, process grief, boost the immune system, and generally improve one's quality of life.
- **Traditional Chinese Medicine and acupuncture (mind, body, heart, spirit):** Like energy healing, Traditional Chinese Medicine (TCM) is based on the idea that the body has vital energy called qi that flows through meridians, or channels. Imbalances in qi are believed to be the root cause of illness. TCM aims to remove blockages of qi, as well as balance the natural opposing forces in the body (yin and yang). One common method for doing so is acupuncture (see more below), as well as acupressure, moxibustion, cupping, meditation, and *gua sha*, among others.
  - ○ Acupuncture: Translates to "needle penetration." By placing tiny needles into specific acupoints, a TCM practitioner can open and move qi through the body's meridians. Manual pressure, electrical stimulation, laser, heat, and ultrasound can also be used to stimulate qi in this way.

- **Ayurvedic medicine (mind, body, heart, spirit):** A healing tradition and Indian medical system thousands of years old that uses a holistic approach to health and wealth. It is literally the marriage of life (*ayur*) and science (*veda*). Ayurveda believes that disease is caused by imbalance; therefore, its goal is to restore balance to the body, mind, and spirit. Ayurvedic treatments can include diet recommendations, herbal remedies, meditation and mantra, breathwork, massage, and yoga.
- **Journey Breathwork (heart, spirit):** Deeply healing breath sequences that can get to the root of the root of whatever it is that you are exploring. Unlike the breathwork that's part of your

184 LIVING IN WISDOM

Pillar Practices, I suggest seeking out a trained guide or practitioner for them, as they will know how to ease you in and out of the practice and the type of support you may need should you have a strong reaction. There are many types of practices that fall under this category, but those that I have experienced, enjoy, and recommend include:

- o Holotropic breathing: Guided breathing at a fast rate for a set amount of time in order to bring about an altered state of consciousness. The experience is like being inside of an ultrasonic machine that shakes loose emotions and trauma, giving you greater access to your subconscious and internalized past experiences.

- o Rebirthing Breathwork: Intended to support emotional release and remove triggers from subconscious thoughts and feelings. This breath pattern focuses on continuous circular breathing, or breathing without pause, in and out—not unlike the sound of a woman in labor. This stimulates a process that removes you from control as you wait for realization to arise—as though you are birthing yourself into the world as the full truth of who and what you are. This can be incredibly powerful for people who have experienced childhood trauma, allowing them to come back to a state of original innocence and control over their experiences moving forward.

- **Sauna therapy (body):** Exposing the body to high, dry heat in an enclosed space in order to increase the body's temperature. This is believed to contribute to relaxation, improved circulation detoxification and immune health, skin purification, and physical healing.

- **Cold plunge (mind, body):** Also called cold water immersion, cold plunging is the practice of submerging yourself (partially or fully) in water that is typically between 55 and 69 degrees Fahrenheit. Traditionally used by athletes to help sore muscles recover after a workout, cold plunges are also believed to reduce inflammation and symptoms of chronic pain, boost metabolism, reduce stress, improve resilience and sleep, increase dopamine, and regulate mood.

- **Infrared therapy (body):** A light-based treatment using infrared radiation, a type of electromagnetic wave that's just beyond the red side of the visible light spectrum. Because red light is believed to penetrate deep layers of the skin and promote cell repair and the circulation of oxygen-rich blood, it's used to relieve pain, increase circulation in specific areas of the body, and ease inflammation. Unlike ultraviolet light, which can damage skin and tissues, infrared is considered safe and can be administered using lamps, heating pads, hot water bottles, or entire infrared chambers.

- **Food and supplements (mind, body):** What we eat and drink has an enormous effect on our body's systems and their ability to operate efficiently and harmoniously. When any of the body's systems are out of balance, that has an effect not only on your physical well-being, but also on your emotional and mental health. Working with a nutritional expert, particularly one who has the ability to assess how your body is using essential nutrients (and where they might be lacking), can create a foundation of wellness on which you can continue to build.

- **Psychedelics (spirit, heart):** An ancient healing tradition that spans cultures across the world and uses psychedelic medicine to alter the perception of reality in order to arrive at new levels of clarity, creativity, and healing. Examples include psilocybin (from mushrooms), ayahuasca, 5-Me0-DMT (toad venom), cannabis, and ibogaine. These naturally occurring psychedelics have been used for centuries as part of sacred rituals and ceremonies, and they continue to be available as part of a healing protocol through the use of a shaman, guide, or therapist. Because of the varying legality of such things, I cannot tell you to go try mushrooms or ayahuasca or cannabis. I can, however, tell you about my experiences with them. In short, these things changed my life. They made my healing process so much faster and easier as someone who is always in my brain, as someone whose "monkey mind"—perpetually thinking and overthinking—had always been my biggest hindrance to getting out of the same old loops. Cannabis is what finally got me into the soma, the body. My experience with psilocybin mushrooms has been one of the most faith-building relationships I've had with medicine, purging old pain and expanding the way I relate to earth, how much I appreciate its beauty and greater connectivity. I consider mushrooms to be a God activator. It also helped me get into my body, appreciate my body, and be able to be in peace and gratitude in my body. Every psychedelic medicine offers its own unique gifts. For example, ayahuasca is considered to be the champion of shadow work because it triggers the purge response, inspires visions, and enables awareness from a state of surrender. It's also referred to as a grandmother medicine because of its ability to transcend the timelines of our lifetimes and place us in suppressed memories that we'd otherwise have no way of accessing.

These modalities are not for everyone, but they effectively open the portals to mind, body, heart, and spirit. If this is something that speaks to you, I suggest you find an expert to help guide you in your psychedelic medicine journey and not attempt to navigate it on your own.

Practices for Healing and Acceptance

Meditation for Healing and Acceptance

Start by sitting in a comfortable position and taking five deep belly breaths to ground yourself in your body and in the present moment. Set an intention for how you would like to feel or what you would like to release. Call forward your higher self and wisdom: *I call forward the highest guidance available to me for the highest good of all concerned.*

Now begin a body-scan meditation with your hands in your mudra of choice (see Mudras for Healing and Acceptance below). Incrementally move your focus from the top of your head to the base of your spine (your crown to your root), gently releasing any physical or emotional tension points (such as in your jaw, neck, shoulders, or heart) that you may notice as your attention travels down your body. Throughout the meditation, notice your breath. If at any time you find yourself connecting to your thoughts, bring your awareness back to your breath and the rise and fall of your chest. To enhance your concentration, you can chant the *bija* mantra *ram* (pronounced "rahm") or visualize a bright yellow light at the solar plexus, the area associated with the Manipura chakra.

Let your practice stretch anywhere between five and twenty-five minutes. Allow the length of your meditation to gradually increase over time as you feel more settled into your practice.

Mudras for Healing and Acceptance

Rudra Mudra. This mudra is also known as "the gesture of inner strength and vitality." *Rudra* translates to "lord" in Sanskrit, which is fitting for this gesture, because it benefits your personal power center, the solar plexus, and is often associated with the Hindu deity Shiva because it applies to your internal transformative abilities, healing, and empowerment. This mudra is believed to improve clarity and concentration of thought, and it is also prescribed for those suffering from dizziness, exhaustion, and chronic tension in their body. Use this mudra to energize your physical body and empower you to reach your highest-potential goals.

To form this mudra, bring your thumb to meet your index and ring fingers while keeping your other two fingers as straight as you can. Rest your hand on your knee or thigh with your palm facing upward.

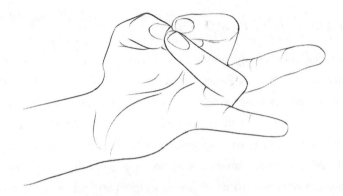

Prithvi Mudra. Also called the Earth mudra, Prithvi is Sanskrit for "the vast one," which is the term also used for the earth element in Ayurveda. This mudra fosters a sense of calm and security, can alleviate feelings of anxiety and restlessness, and promotes grounding, stability, and physical health by creating healing and spiritual balance in the body. These qualities can be a valuable addition to practices meant to enhance physical strength or emotional balance.

To form this mudra, touch the tip of your ring finger to the tip of the thumb. Keep the other fingers extended, relaxed, and slightly apart. Rest your hand on your knee or thigh with your palm facing upward.

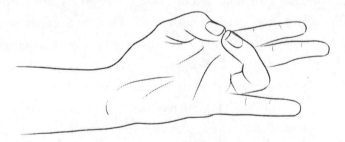

Essential Oils to Support Healing and Acceptance Rituals

Thyme: The oil of releasing and forgiving
Clary Sage: The oil of clarity and vision

For more information on how to use essential oils, see page 141.

Movement for Healing and Acceptance

Try these restorative yoga poses:

Balasana or Child's Pose: Come down to the floor on hands and knees, then gently bring your hips back to your heels, extending your arms, and lowering your third eye to the ground.

Variation 1: Keep your knees together to restore the spine and lower back. Gently rock your head back and forth to stimulate and release the third eye, then bring your hands to frame your feet, palms up, to release and receive. Try gently pressing your hands to the bottom of the feet to further release and stimulate the feet, which is where the nervous system ends and we meet the earth.

Variation 2: Keep your knees apart to open the hips, a place where we store a lot of our emotions. Take deep belly breaths as you stretch your arms forward, palms facing down, and play with stretching the hands, perhaps lifting the torso. Walk your hands to the right, encouraging a stretch in the side body. Repeat on the left, and then return to center to relax. Experiment with gently rocking the pelvis forward and back, like cat-cow, to furthur stimulate the release.

Gentle Cat–Cow: Begin in a tabletop position on hands and knees. Gently begin to articulate your spine from crown to tail, pressing through the palms, bringing the head upward, pulling the chest forward and the tail up to create a Cow. Gently rock in the opposite direction, moving from head to tail, lifting the spine up, curving and arching into Cat pose. Move through these two postures five to ten times, or until you feel complete, inhaling through Cow and exhaling through Cat. Begin inviting circular motions, perhaps shifting through the shoulders and down to the hips. Allow your body to guide you and work with any spots that feel sticky or sensitive, breathing into the sensations.

Supported Legs up the Wall: Sit with one side of your hips nestled against a wall with a block, folded blanket, or other support within arm's reach. As you lie down, gently shift to bring your legs up the wall together, feet above your hips. Place any support beneath your hips that feels good. The pose will feel effortless when you find alignment. Breathe as your blood circulates down through the body, pelvis, and womb. After settling in and taking several rounds of deep belly breaths, begin to let your legs slowly separate into a gentle straddle stretch for the inner thighs. Our thighs are deeply important for our ability to move and take action in this world.

Shavasana or Corpse Pose: This pose is for deep rest and rejuvenation. Lie on your back with your arms at your side and palms facing up. If it is comfortable for you, close your eyes. Breathe.

HEAL AND ACCEPT 191

Bolsters, Blocks, and Support Pillows: All of these props are available to make any of your yoga postures more comfortable. Simply straddling a bolster on your knees and sitting in supported stillness can feel therapeutic.

Affirmations for Healing and Acceptance

I honor my wounds, for I know it is where the light enters.
I respect the healing process and give myself grace through this experience.
I have compassion for my human soul throughout this healing process.
I love and respect myself.
I accept and surrender to the truth of my life.

Journal Prompts for Healing and Acceptance

What are some of the lessons I've learned from my healing so far?
If any are present, where do I hold fear around healing and acceptance?

192   LIVING IN WISDOM

When will I feel more complete in my healing journey?
What has my pain taught me?
What are some of the unexpected gifts this season of healing has given me?

Creativity for Healing and Acceptance

Art can always be therapeutic, as it encourages the release of reality and welcomes deep focus on a project for the pure being of it.

- Some things to try:
  - Writing poetry, to allow the healing to take its own form through words
  - Creating a mandala, whether by drawing, painting, or going outside in nature and making one with a stick in sand or dirt
  - Finger painting for the sensation of freedom or abstract art
  - Using watercolors to paint whatever catches your eye

Chapter 16

Self-Care and Devotion

I want to start from the jump and acknowledge the response you might have to the term *self-care*. Almost universally, I've noticed that people have such an aversion to the idea. And not just self-care at the level of meditation, breathwork, and the other pillars of practice; I'm talking about some of the most basic ways that we tend to our needs. Putting ourselves to bed at a time that ensures we're rested, eating foods that make us feel energized and nourished versus depleted and inflamed, moving on a regular basis, honoring commitments to ourselves and to others. And sometimes it goes deeper, making doctor's appointments for ourselves or tending to ourselves when pain is present.

Self-care can be innately challenging. Especially if your needs weren't met in childhood and you never had any assistance growing up, you might have a real aversion to feeling "forced" to do it all yourself or struggle with a sense of worthlessness. Many of us, regardless of whether we've experienced trauma, struggle with the idea of worthiness. And as you get older, when you get closer to thirty-five or forty and the enthusiasm of youth begins to fade along with the sense of hope and possibility and potential as you leave behind the glowing apex of your twenties and early thirties, when you're most likely not in community with as many people as you used to be, getting positive feedback and care, it can get more difficult to suppress those feelings of hopelessness.

193

194   LIVING IN WISDOM

Many people hear "self-care," and it immediately triggers avoidant, manipulative tactics we reach for to appear more righteous. Particularly for women, the idea of self-care activates a feeling of martyrdom; the *lack* of self-care being the honorable thing. Selfless. "I don't have time for that because I'm too busy taking care of everybody else." By enveloping ourselves in the care of others, we take that on as our complete identity, but it's really disassociation. The reality is that we don't know how to meet our own needs, and we've never slowed down enough to know ourselves.

I get it; it took me *years* to develop a self-care routine—because I actively disliked it. As I've told you before, there's nothing I've shared with you in this book that I haven't resented myself, sometimes deeply and violently. It wasn't until there was literally no other choice that I started to examine how I could get that elevator to start moving down from my head into my heart. Even then, it took me years of slow, methodical investigation and discovery to be in practice with self-care. What caused this radical shift wasn't realizing that there was something I wanted to achieve; it was understanding that what I felt was something missing, and I was curious how else I could feel.

When I first started teaching, self-care—outside of meditation—was really how I honed my chops, because I had to really work to understand why everyone, including me, was so against it. I wanted to figure out how to make self-care more interesting to my students. It wasn't as simple as sharing the amazing benefits self-care provided and telling people they needed to go and do it. I once gave a talk to a corporate group, and what happens so often in those environments containing a majority of older men and just a handful of women is that the women start reaching for more "masculine" care practices—aggressive exercise, intermittent fasting—which aren't necessarily supportive of their physiology and the unique nature of what they carry as women. Oftentimes as an adaptive response to the environment they must navigate, they are feeding the masculine element of the masculine-feminine energy that

SELF-CARE AND DEVOTION 195

we all carry because they don't want to come across as frivolous or silly or woo-woo. So the entire group starts to tilt toward a very rigid, unreceptive type of energy.

At this particular talk, I was speaking to all the ways self-care can level up everyone's leadership and how they show up for their teams. I could see that no one wanted to do any of the practices I was describing—breathwork, self-massage, or Epsom salt baths. No one was responding to the idea of going home and dedicating thirty minutes to that protocol. So I stopped. I looked around the room and said, "Let me ask you this: How worthy or valuable do you consider yourself to be *of your own attention?*" For whatever reason, this stirred everyone. I saw hands raised in the air, people sitting up a little straighter in their chairs. To these individuals, self-care went from being a frivolous, selfish thing to being deeply valuable. It led them to ask the question, *How worthy or valuable do I consider myself to be?*

Over the course of investigating blockages around self-care, what I found was most effective was not to first educate people about what practices they could embrace or give them any sort of directive; instead, I'd have to guide them to see what was missing from their lives, their heart, their general sense of being, and then ignite their curiosity about how else they could feel.

Eventually I honed this lesson, which I would open by leading a body-scan meditation, prompting everyone to incrementally visualize their entire body, from the top of their head to the tips of their toes. I'd ask them to notice all the different compartments of their physical body, and offer them the opportunity to release areas that were holding any tension. Then we'd settle into a light meditation practice, and I'd ask everyone, "By this time next year, how do you want to feel in your physical body? By this time next year, how do you want to feel in spirit? In mind?"

Ultimately, I would show people—as I learned through my own experience—that healing and self-care go hand in hand. Self-care isn't

196   LIVING IN WISDOM

just what assists that process, it provides the supportive structure that holds up every single part of it—your life's work, your wisdom, your purpose, who you are. It's what makes the healing sustainable. Without self-care, healing would collapse. You would be prevented from reaching all the way down into the depths and cleaning out all the nooks and crannies. The lack of self-care is one of the most significant barriers to getting the job done.

Leveling Up

As essential as self-care is to your process, though, there's a reason why this chapter falls here, as we near the end. To put it bluntly, you wouldn't have been ready. You'd most likely have rejected it outright. And that's okay; it hasn't yet been time for this particular milestone. Just as healing requires constantly bringing things up for reexamination and re-circuiting as you peel back the layers, you're now, in a way, bringing your Pillar Practices back up for reexamination and re-circuiting.

When I first introduced you to your Pillar Practices, it was just to get you to start *somewhere*. It was triage. Popping an Advil to help take the edge off the pain. You didn't have to intrinsically understand how or why these things work in the body to reap their benefits; practicing them didn't require you to have to make substantial decisions. It maybe was a little ugly and a little awkward because you were just getting started, but by tending to your practice every day, sitting in your sacred space every day, you started noticing muscles that you didn't even know you had, like going to physical therapy and working on the tiny supportive muscles in your shoulder or wrist. Over time, you most likely started developing a relationship with these practices, noticing the nuances and shifts you were feeling, maybe even having a sense of pride. Eventually, you perhaps started to believe you're worthy of this nice treatment. That you were worthy of having less pain in your day-to-day life.

SELF-CARE AND DEVOTION 197

Well, this is the upleveling of that experience. If I had asked you from the beginning to spend tender time with yourself, you might have found some frustration, agitation, or even pain around the idea. But now you've started to sink deeper into your awareness; you have a better inner inventory of where things are; and you've begun experimenting with letting the joy in. Part of mastery is constant refinement and getting creative with passionate dedication—this is that moment. Taking that urgent care model and making it sustainable, enjoyable, and beautiful.

Now these actionable habits in your life can start to take up more space and take up residence, seamlessly, in all the facets of your life, from the moment you wake up until you crawl into bed at night. Think of this as expanding your sacred space, widening the container so that it cradles not just your life, but your life*style*. Self-care is bringing your lifestyle into alignment with your healing. Because a self-care protocol naturally turns into an innate wisdom that resides inside of you to meet your needs in real time. It's recognizing that you're feeling a little sleepy today, and that maybe you need to reach for energizing yoga poses and mudras to jump-start your energy. If you're feeling stuck or closed off, it's sipping cacao before your meditation to open your heart. It's taking a moment for tea at the end of the day to bring your systems back into regulation and calm the body for sleep. Or it's reaching for something simply because it feels good, transforming Pillar Practices into rituals, ceremonies, making sacred the day-to-day. Ringing a gong or sound bowl because you're passing through a space and it calls to you, pausing to admire a flower in salutation to the sun, reading things that expand your consciousness like poetry. It is the opportunity to create consistency. It is repetition that allows the nuances of refinement to enrich your life. It is building strength, compassion, and acceptance for overcoming mistakes, facing challenges, and realizing truths. It expands your capacity to cultivate and grow yourself. It is living in your wisdom, constantly in the call-and-response, ebb and flow of life.

198   LIVING IN WISDOM

★ ★ ★

When I was being wrung out by lived experience—grieving the end of my marriage, grieving people I loved and lost, meeting my father for the first time and grieving the emptiness he created in my childhood as a result of his megalomaniacal emotional unavailability—I spent *two years* developing my self-care protocol. Starting at the top of the pandemic, for the entirety of twenty-four months, I created a very specific system for myself to heal from what I was going through. I didn't want to invite anyone else's thoughts on anything, so I avoided television, movies, and books. I needed to turn down the volume on everyone else so I could tune in to my own inner wisdom.

At the foundation of my practice were the fundamentals: meditation, breathwork, journaling, movement. Mind, body, heart, spirit. That gave me the freedom to have faith in myself to create a constellation of self-care protocols I could use to self-soothe and meet my needs. This approach of mixing and matching to suit what called to me, making it experimental and playful, staying with it for a length of time so my body could learn to sink into it and respond to it—that's what made me understand how to unlock the wisdom that is stored in the body. My intuition came online in a way that it never had before, and I could finally identify what my needs were—as though it were an informed dialogue between two trusting, loving partners. I learned how to treat myself with more dignity and respect. I learned the true power of devotion.

Devotion and Self-Care, Self-Care and Devotion

Devotion is at the bedrock of the healing process, but that is never more evident than when examining self-care. Like many of the big ideas woven throughout this book, we first visited with devotion when getting a feel for the necessary ingredients for this journey. And, like all of the other elements you've been discovering along the way, I'd like to bring it up for reexamination.

When I think of what devotion means in a nonreligious sense,

SELF-CARE AND DEVOTION 199

particularly through the lens of self-care, it comes down to these three ideas:

Devotion is loyalty, love, and care for someone or something. Often when we hear the word *devoted* in this context, it's the "devoted mother." A woman who is so giving of herself, who fiercely commits to the stewardship of her children, and who always makes the highest choice for them. A devoted mother is not just a "good mom"; she is conjuring this love and care from deep within and never turning it off. Within the context of self-care, we become the devoted mother to ourselves. We place the needs and well-being of our own souls and purpose first. It is owning that allegiance to our own human experience with the same righteous conviction and commitment we give to another person or cause. What could be more deserving?

The second idea is **the act of dedicating something to a cause or activity.** Meaning being devoted to a larger narrative or theme that is for the greater good. That could be devotion to family, devotion to students, or devotion to a cause, whether that's through volunteering or philanthropic contributions.

And the third is **the state of being *ardently* dedicated and loyal.** This represents the opposite of what we're actually doing when we're trying not to let self-care practices in or let people care for us or are unwilling to make changes in our lives that are supportive. In the state of hypervigilance, which is how we react to repeated mistreatment, harm, or neglect, we are in the mode of ardent *protection* of self. It's a sort of stagnant warrior energy. When you're in *devotion* to yourself, you have the same depth of strength, but it's in service to you, which keeps you open. So devotion is the idea of being ardently dedicated and loyal to your spiritual and human experience, and all of your potential within that.

In the context of all of the above, it's easy to see why I believe self-care has a layer of romance and self-courtship. Just as I told you when you started easing into the pillars of practice that you were essentially beginning the dating and discovery process of yourself with yourself, this is

200 LIVING IN WISDOM

the continuation of that conversation. Think of this part of the process as moving in together. This deepening of a relationship with self is something I discovered in my own practice; I realized I could feel pleased and pleasured by something as small as appreciating a hummingbird that flew by my face. Not only was that enough, it was remarkable. A treat. A gift.

It's possible you are not quite ready to receive true joy and pleasure right now, and that's okay. You'll get there eventually, but for now, see what you can begin to connect with on a small scale, the little details that make up the truly miraculous texture of everyday life, things you can touch and feel. I like to call these **tiny joys** (a concept I coined and began teaching in 2020 and talk more about on page 247). Sit in the grass and take deep breaths. Reach for a Pillar Practice like abhyanga (see page 101) and really pay attention to the type of touch that you like from yourself to yourself. Notice the feeling of your arm on your fingers and your fingers on your arm. The sensation you get from the type of pressure you enjoy and what it's releasing for you. Show yourself that you care, and see how special you can learn to make yourself feel— lighting candles for your yoga practice, scattering flower petals on the breakfast table, making yourself a devotional playlist.

As we talked about earlier, meeting your own needs on this level and not having to rely on someone else to do so is extremely empowering. It also alleviates loneliness, particularly for people who have complex lived experiences and tend to hold the idea of romance at arm's length until it takes away the ability to feel presence or joy in the body. Although, most of us experience loneliness, especially those of us on the path to mastery and growth, which can also be lonely, regardless of whether or not you're partnered. Self-care presents the opportunity to be in a committed relationship with ourselves.

Creating Your Self-Care Road Map

Just as you drafted a blueprint to assist with plugging in the right healing modalities, crafting a self-care practice is like creating a road

SELF-CARE AND DEVOTION   201

map—each point on the map being an approach or concept that feels organic to you and what you respond to. What speaks to your creative desire? Then plug a healing practice into each of the pillars of healing categories—mind, body, heart, spirit—which is what will ultimately add up to your **Self-Care Road Map**.

Start by asking yourself, *What do I enjoy? Music or quiet? Movement or stillness? Dynamic movement or slowness?*

From there, I also highly recommend tailoring your protocol to your own innate rhythms that are attuned to your natural design of being. For example, consult an Ayurvedic expert to determine your *dosha* type. Doshas are the elements that exist in all bodies in a unique balance that makes up your disposition. They include *kapha* (earth and water), *vata* (air and ether or space), and *pitta* (fire). Take an enneagram assessment, a personality-typing system based on one's core motivations and desires. Take a human design assessment, which incorporates traditional systems such as astrology, I Ching, Hindu chakra teachings, and Kabbalah, and can give you insight into what moves you and how you process information. Have an astrologer create a birth chart for you to see where Venus resides, which gives you ample information about how you experience love and romance, in addition to what feels best to you.

My Venus is in Taurus, which represents sensuality and decadence— being *invoked* in a way that calls to and stirs my entire being. It's why I feel best enveloping myself with things that feel pleasing, smell pleasing, taste pleasing, sound pleasing. It's why, if I'm going to slather myself in oil, it's going to be high-quality and luxurious. It's about aesthetic enhancement and beauty, as well as slowness and going at my own pace. Feeling like I can pause at any moment to take a breath. That completely tracks with my experience and what I respond to.

When you build a self-care protocol in alignment with yourself on a deep, bio-spiritual level, you will notice that every element of your life will click into place. You'll have more energy, better sleep, fewer bouts of illness, and fewer aches and pains. You'll experience more balanced

202   LIVING IN WISDOM

moods, a more even keel, more ease. It's as though you're surfing in synchronicity with the Universe.

To illustrate this point even more clearly, let's look at what happens when you're living *out* of sync with your environment. Dr. Frank Lipman, whose background is in both Traditional Chinese Medicine (TCM) and Western medicine, describes this as "cultural arrhythmia," something he has described seeing in almost every single patient who walks into his practice. He compares cultural arrhythmia to jet lag—think about how you feel when you've just gotten off a long plane ride and you land in another time zone. You're drained, dragging, and foggy. You maybe have digestive issues; your body aches. You fall out of sync with your rhythm when you—among other things—don't eat foods that properly nourish your body, are perpetually stressed, don't get enough natural light or fresh air, don't get enough sleep, and are generally operating on a wavelength that's not attuned to your needs.

The idea of natural rhythm is at the foundation of many traditional healing systems and has been regarded as the gold standard of well-being for thousands of years. In TCM, that looks like the "body clock," in which each organ and physical system corresponds to a time of day when it's at its peak function. As qi, or energy/life force, moves through each of these systems, it's important to adjust your daily rhythm accordingly to be working with your qi and not against it. For example, your stomach's optimal window is between 7:00 a.m. and 9:00 a.m., which is when it's advisable to have your first meal of the day and harness that digestive energy. Between 11:00 a.m. and 1:00 p.m., your heart qi activates, which traditionally characterizes peacefulness, making it important to find a restful moment during this window.

Ayurveda describes a twenty-four-hour cycle that follows doshic energy. For example, the hours between 6:00 a.m. and 10:00 a.m. fall in kapha's realm, which is earthy and stabilizing. It's the ideal time to wake, exercise, and gently begin to bring more energy to all of your body's systems, which creates a slow, gentle build for pitta to take over with its heat and fire to stoke your digestion and prepare your body for its first meal around 10:00 a.m. Vata then kicks in around 2:00 p.m. to support movement, creativity, and flow, making this a great time to shift from your analytical work to more imaginative tasks. It's also a gentle, transitional energy that extends until about 6:00 p.m. and calls for welcoming in winding down for the evening with a return to kapha.

Even Western medicine's understanding of the body is aligned with this ancient wisdom. Scientists discovered that within the hypothalamus resides the suprachiasmatic nucleus (SCN). It takes in information from our environment to ensure that all of our body's systems are synced up on a twenty-four-hour cycle. And the way it does that is by using light-detecting cells in your eyes (yes, even when they're closed) and sending out hormones and neurotransmitters, like the conductor of a body-wide symphony. For example, when your SCN first detects the light of morning, it signals to get your metabolism up and running, your body temperature rising, your muscles warmed up for movement, and your active brain function to boot up and come online. Conversely, when the SCN senses light waning in the evening, it sends word that the body should start cooling down and digestion should start to slow. Which is, by the way, a great case for exposing yourself to natural sunlight as soon as you wake and being extra mindful of any light, including from screens, that you're exposing yourself to in the evening. Even artificial light can throw off the SCN.

The other powerful bit of wisdom that we can glean from TCM and Ayurveda is that you have to be an *active participant* in your healing, and that's exactly what self-care is—being in active support of your systems and tending to their wants and needs in real time. In Western medicine, the norm is to receive medication or surgery to address most issues—both passive modalities that don't require you to make any substantive changes to your lifestyle. Some doctors say "it might be nice" if you

204 LIVING IN WISDOM

made X or Y change, but ultimately, you could just go back for more medicine and more surgery. The same thing goes for reading a book about healing or listening to a podcast about mindfulness, which is not taking an active role in any actual processes. You're only in the audience, you're not on the stage. In stark contrast, Ayurveda and TCM rely primarily on healing practices that you administer yourself. That could be eating a wider variety of foods that serve different physiological functions in the body and address doshic imbalances; or practicing self-massage, which moves lymphatic fluid around the body, a key ingredient in preserving your health; or drinking certain herbs that stimulate wellness—and lovingly preparing them in a slow, gentle way. The bottom line is, the only way to grow and change and heal is to choose to participate. Self-care is the ability to care for oneself through awareness, self-control, and self-reliance in order to achieve, maintain, or promote optimal health and well-being.

What then becomes so life-changing about actively participating and living in sync with the day through your self-care protocol—which in and of itself *is* self-care—is that you'll notice when your body clicks into rhythm. You'll find that your digestion feels better, your body feels better, your moods feel more stable. You'll be in active conversation with your body, being able to sense when you're getting sick, sense where you are in your menstrual cycle, which often starts to attune to the moon cycle. Because that, too, is universal design. You'll start to naturally embody the elemental flow of the seasons too. At every moment, you'll have more clarity about what your body wants and needs, from how you're moving to what you're eating. Your body will also have gained more wisdom about how it can support you back, such as the vagus nerve and your central nervous system coming into a space of calm regulation and being able to maintain that baseline automatically. These things all begin to happen naturally when you get into the devotional level of your practice and protocol.

Self-care is about creating something that supports and benefits your entire life. It is what makes life and all the work that it requires sustainable, maybe even pleasurable. It is, quite simply, living in devotion to yourself.

You are the offering. Your life is the altar.

Your Menu for Self-Care

Below is just a small sampling of some of my favorite self-care practices. Experiment and play, and then sink all the way in.

- **Mindful movement:** Yoga, Pilates, tai chi, martial arts (things that involve breath, concentration, connection, strength, stretching, integration, and relaxation).
- **Diet:** Not only what and when you eat, but *why* you are eating something—in what energy are you eating? With gratitude and respect? And the way in which you or others prepare the food, from the picking to the cleaning to the cooking—can it be done with love, joy, and kindness?
- **Practices that improve digestion:** Tongue scraping (see below), oil pulling (see below), drinking warm water, intermittent fasting, cooking with spices (especially coriander, cumin, and fennel), walking after meals, eating seasonally.
- **Practices that sync you with a daily rhythm:** Waking and sleeping with your circadian rhythms, eating your largest meal at lunchtime when your digestion is most robust, and reducing activity in the evening to prepare for sleep (especially screen time).
- **Practices that calm the mind:** Meditation (see chapter 6), restorative yoga, and pranayama (see chapter 7).
- **Abhyanga massage:** See page 101.
- **Aromatherapy:** To relax or revitalize. Humans have used aromatherapy for thousands of years as part of rituals in China, India, and Egypt using plant resins, balms, and oils. Diffuse high-quality

(i.e., non-synthetic) essential oils to create shifts in mind and body, including peppermint for clearing congestion, soothing headaches, and enhancing concentration; frankincense to reduce inflammation and to create a sanctified space for meditation; lavender for promoting calm; and eucalyptus to encourage circulation to the brain and support the respiratory system.

- **Tea as ritual:** Teas and herbal infusions have also been used for centuries as part of sacred rituals—from their harvesting, to their brewing, to their preparation, to their enjoyment. A gesture as simple as making and sipping a cup of tea with complete presence of mind can be incredibly powerful. Feel free to work with teas that speak to you for their flavor and aroma, such as chamomile, ginger, peppermint, echinacea, sage, rose hip, green, or mint. Imbibe with closed eyes and bring your focus to the moment.
- **Cacao as a heart opener:** Cacao was used by the Mayans and Aztecs as a ceremonial beverage. Cacao is known to be a powerful key for opening the heart chakra, giving people a grounded yet energized feeling. Scientifically, we now know that cacao contains theobromine, which is known as a "sister molecule" to caffeine. It has a gently stimulating effect that enhances blood flow, concentration, sensuality, and mood. To invite this energy into your day, mix a tablespoon or two of good-quality cacao (not to be confused with cocoa powder) into hot water. Sip with complete presence of mind, body, and heart.
- **Reading:** Enjoying inspiring or centering text in the morning (or "morning pages") can set the tone for the day, while reading in the evening is an excellent way to prepare for sleep without the overstimulation of watching television or scrolling through social media. Reading Scripture and connecting with God energy at any point of the day is another way to shift frequency as desired.
- **Journal:** See chapter 8.
- **Breathwork** See chapter 7.

- **Periodic detox:** Particularly during seasonal change and times of stress, to clear the system of accumulated toxins and boost the digestion.
- **Epsom salt baths:** This is one of my very favorite practices and has been a part of my self-care regimen from almost the very beginning of my healing journey. Just like tea, sometimes your body, mind, and soul need some time to steep. Sometimes that's to release all the toxins and stimulate circulation, and other times it's simply to have a moment to reflect, integrate, and connect to intuition. Regardless, it's a time to relax and just receive.

  Epsom salt breaks down into magnesium and sulfate, which are absorbed through the skin and help loosen tight muscles and stiff joints, as well as soothe swelling and inflammation. Magnesium is also an important mineral for a number of processes in the body, including regulating muscle and nerve function, blood sugar levels, and blood pressure, in addition to making protein, bone matter, and DNA. Epsom salt is also believed to be a spiritually detoxifying agent, and bathing in it is thought to be helpful for purifying the spirit and clearing the aura field.

  To prepare an Epsom salt bath, fill your bath with warm to hot water. Add one to two three-pound bags of Epsom salt or Epsom salt with magnesium flakes. Gently circulate the water to encourage the salt to disintegrate. Soak for at least thirty minutes, at least once a week. I enjoy this as much as three times a week.
- **Tongue scraping:** This is another of my go-to practices. It's so simple and seamless because you can do it when you brush your teeth in the morning and evening, and yet it delivers so many powerful benefits.

  In Ayurveda, the mouth is seen as the entryway between the mind-body and the outer world, making it essential to practice good hygiene. The tongue is also the first point of contact with nutrients from food, so it's important to keep healthy. Scraping the tongue with a copper tongue scraper in the morning and evening

208   LIVING IN WISDOM

removes bad bacteria, refreshes the palate to be more available and sensitive to what you consume (encouraging you to perhaps consume less salt and sugar), and increases your satisfaction with your meals. It also makes the tongue more receptive to identifying beneficial phytonutrients in your food and making that connection with body-signaling molecules, making your food more nutritionally available and your digestion more effective. Because you're removing bacteria from this primary passageway in the body, you're also relieving a burden from the immune system.

To practice tongue scraping, find a tool made just for this ritual, ideally made of copper because it's believed to aid healthy enzymes and is toxic to unhealthy bacteria. You can also find them made of stainless steel. Use the tool to gently scrape the entire surface of your tongue from back to front, seven to fourteen times, rinsing between each scrape. Repeat in the morning and evening.

- **Oil pulling:** Oil pulling is an Ayurvedic practice that involves swishing the mouth with oil to bind with fat-soluble plaque and bacteria, allowing you to purify the mouth once you spit the mixture out. It's also believed to whiten teeth and promote gum health, and it has been used as a treatment for arthritis, blood disease, headaches, gum disease, toothaches, lung and liver conditions, eczema, ulcers, and intestinal disorders.

  To incorporate oil pulling into your practice, place one tablespoon of coconut or sesame oil in your mouth after tongue scraping, swish for five minutes (working up to ten), and do not swallow. The oil will turn thin and milky. Spit out in a trash can or outside so you don't clog the sink, then rinse with warm water (some use salt water), and brush your teeth as you usually would.

- **Neti and nasya:** These are the Ayurvedic practices for both clearing and "oiling" the nasal pathways using a traditional spouted pot called a neti. These two practices are often used together to open

SELF-CARE AND DEVOTION 209

the sinuses, reduce respiratory allergies, promote mental clarity, and enhance the proper absorption of prana or breath.

To practice neti, combine one-quarter teaspoon of salt in a half cup of warm filtered water in a neti pot. (You can find these in most drugstores these days.) Stand in front of your sink and place the tip of the pot's spout in one nostril. Tilt your head to the opposite side and gently pour the solution so that it enters the nasal passage and flows out the other nostril. Keep your mouth open and your head tilted in such a way that the water does not come into the back of the throat. If the solution stings, you can decrease the amount of salt. Repeat on the other side, then blow your nose with a tissue to expel any remaining mucus and water.

If practicing *nasya* daily, place one to two drops of nasya oil (sesame oil infused with herbs) or sesame oil on a clean fingertip and apply in each nostril. For weekly practice, tilt your head backward and apply three to five drops of oil into one nostril, inhale deeply, and repeat on the opposite side.

TURNING RESPONSIBILITIES INTO RITUALS

The tools of self-care aren't relegated to candles and incense and singing bowls—I deeply love each of these, but self-care can also feel more "practical," specifically in turning rote, everyday responsibilities into something slow, intentional, and meaningful. In this context, my mind goes to cultures where women spend a lot of time on their hair, particularly Black women. I'm talking about Wash Day, the day when, depending on your hair type, you know you're going to be sitting at the kitchen counter all day so your hair can be washed, dried, and detangled. Think about how beautiful and devotional that act of service becomes when you sit

210   LIVING IN WISDOM

in present silence with yourself, having your hands in your hair and scalp, or creating that space with a child or grandchild.

You can apply this same layer of ritual and devotion to any household task. We all have required duties, or those that we choose to do, which can be reframed with joy and tenderness and care of intention.

Practices for Self-Care and Devotion

You yourself are your own obstacle, rise above yourself.

—*Hāfez*

Meditation for Self-Care and Devotion

Start by sitting in a comfortable position and taking five deep belly breaths to ground yourself in your body and in the present moment. Set an intention for how you would like to feel or what you would like to release. Call forward your higher self and wisdom: "I call forward the highest guidance available to me for the highest good of all concerned."

Now begin a body-scan meditation with your hands in your mudra of choice (see Mudras for Self-Love and Devotion below; note that both Chin and Jnana mudras are used to receive the energy of the sun— Jnana during the day and Chin after sunset). Incrementally move your focus from the top of your head to the base of your spine (your crown to your root), gently releasing any physical or emotional tension points (such as in your jaw, neck, shoulders, or heart) that you may notice as your attention travels down your body. Throughout the meditation, notice your breath. If at any time you find yourself connecting to your thoughts, bring your awareness back to your breath and the rise and fall of your chest.

Let your practice stretch anywhere between five and twenty-five minutes. Allow the length of your meditation to gradually increase over time as you feel more settled into your practice.

Mudras for Self-Love and Devotion

Chin Mudra. Also known as Gyan mudra, this is the mudra of awareness, clarity, and mindfulness. (*Gyan* is Sanskrit for "knowledge" or "wisdom.") It also symbolizes the union of self with the Universe. The thumb represents supreme consciousness, while the index finger represents your individual soul. The bringing together of these two realities is fundamental to the yogic philosophy of evolving from ignorance to wisdom and from darkness to enlightenment. It is, in many ways, a seal of consciousness and can be used to improve the quality of the mind, to analyze, to heal, to focus, and to find calmness and peace.

Sit in a comfortable position with a straight spine. Touch the tip of each of your thumbs and index fingers together, forming a circle. Keep the other three fingers straight and relaxed, slightly apart. Place the hands on your knees or thighs with palms facing downward (for grounding). Relax the shoulders and maintain a natural breath.

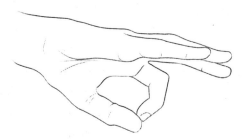

Jnana Mudra. This is the gesture of knowledge. It, too, is used to promote mental clarity, spiritual enlightenment, and wisdom.

Sit in a comfortable position with a straight spine. Touch the tips of your thumbs and index fingers together, forming a circle. Keep the other three fingers straight and relaxed. Rest your hands on your knees or thighs with palms facing upward. Keep the shoulders relaxed and maintain a natural breath.

Vitarka Mudra. This is a variation of the Dharmachakra mudra (page 160) and is a symbol of wisdom. In Sanskrit, *vitarka* means "reasoning," "consideration," or "deliberation." To use this mudra is to be in search of knowledge and enlightenment. It is believed to activate specific energy points in the body, promoting mental clarity and alertness. And like the Dharmachakra mudra, the circle formed by the index finger and thumb symbolizes the flow of information, energy, and ideas.

Form a circle with each hand by touching together the tips of your thumbs with the tips of your index fingers. Rest your left hand on your lap with the palm facing upward. Hold the right hand at shoulder height with the palm facing outward.

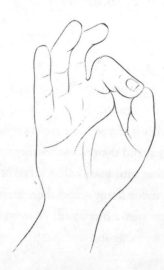

Essential Oils to Support Self-Love and Devotion Rituals

Frankincense: The oil of uplifting, healing, and promoting inner peace

Myrrh: The oil of spiritual awakening

For more information on how to use essential oils, see page 141.

Movement for Self-Love and Devotion

FORWARD FOLD AND WIDE-LEGGED FORWARD FOLD

For both of these, try getting your head below your heart, encouraging action and decisions to be heart led.

Forward Fold:
Bring the feet together or hip-width distance, then gently fold your upper body toward your lower body, bending the knees to encourage the upper and lower body to meet. Relax here, perhaps grabbing for opposite elbows, allowing gravity to do the rest. From here you can begin gently rocking back and forth, bouncing (known as ballistic stretching), and straightening into the legs.

Wide-Legged Forward Fold:
Stand in a wide-legged position. You can find this distance by moving from a warrior or lunge stance about double hip's width apart, then turning so your feet are parallel. Place your hands on the hips or extend them up to the sky. Gently fold your body forward, bending into your knees as needed. Allow your hands to rest gently on the floor, grab for opposite elbows, enjoy twists to either side, or take a headstand. (Inversions such as headstands require a level of focus and discipline; do not practice if you have

214 LIVING IN WISDOM

not been taught by a professional.) When you're ready to come out, engage your core, rise with a flat back, circle the hands high, and then bring them to heart's center.

SUN SALUTATIONS

This series of poses is known as a way of greeting the day and to practice devotion, self-care, and cultivating balance within and without.

1. Begin with feet together, palms resting at your sides.
2. Open with Mountain pose, feet separated to hip-width distance, palms facing forward, pelvis engaged, crown high. Bring your palms to heart center, gently pressing them together.
3. Keeping your hands together, raise them above your head, engaging the abdomen, pressing the feet into the ground, encouraging a slight backbend.
4. Bring your hands to meet the floor in a brief forward bend, and then step the right foot back into a low lunge.
5. From here, move into a plank position. Bend your elbows, stopping at 90 degrees so that your chest is hovering above the floor. (Feel free to move to knees here.) Shift your weight forward, rolling over your toes to come up in Upward-Facing Dog or Low Cobra. Pressing into the top of your feet and palms of your hands, reach your shoulders away from your ears and the crown of your head to the sky as you engage your lower back and neutralize your pelvis.
6. Now, in a wave-like motion, roll over your toes to push up and back into Downward Dog. Stretch here as needed. Then extend your right leg behind you before bringing it into your chest and placing your right foot by your right hand in a low lunge. Bring your left foot to meet the right in a forward fold.
7. Rise to stand, reverse swan diving the hands together above your head with a slight backbend, and then bring the hands back to the

SELF-CARE AND DEVOTION 215

heart before releasing into Mountain pose and repeating on the left side.

Other self-care movements can be as simple as going for a walk in the morning or doing a gentle mobility routine to ensure longevity and harmony in the body. Light exercises like qigong or tai chi are great for stimulating the body and balancing qi. Try also committing to running, biking, or hiking once a week as a cardio exercise or time to be in nature.

Affirmations for Self-Care and Devotion

I am devoted to the practices that heal and nourish my spirit.
I prioritize self-care as an act of deep reverence for my life.
When I take care of myself, I am able to be a vessel for my purpose.
My devotion to myself makes my life more beautiful.
My self-respect is fueled by my self-care. I am in alignment when I am devoted to my daily practices.

Journal Prompts for Self-Care and Devotion

- *How can I incorporate more self-care into my life? What does that look like? Feel like?*
- *What do I see as self-care? And how do I feel about self-care? Do I have any shadow work that needs to be addressed to be in harmony with self-care?*
- *What am I devoted to? Is this devotion in harmony for the life I desire to live?*
- *What am I devoting myself to in this season of my life? For the next three months?*
- *Who am I in practice to be, who am I becoming, and what am I committed to?*

Creativity for Self-Care and Devotion

- Daily self-care:
  - Get creative with what you eat; try out a new recipe or two.
  - Get creative with your movement, change up your routine, try a new exercise or practice, try a new posture in class. You can be devoted to your practice and still stagnate if you don't continually invite new experiences in.

- Try a self-care Sunday:
  - Deep condition or oil your hair during the day.
  - Prep a delicious meal for your body, or order something you love.

SELF-CARE AND DEVOTION   217

- Meditate, journal, pray.
- Have a personal tea or cacao ceremony while watching or being in nature.
- Put on some healing music.
- Dry brush the body.
- Light a candle.
- Sink into an Epsom salt bath with essential oils.
- Finish with oiling the body and self-massage.

*I am residing in the radiance of my holiness,
enlivening all whom I encounter with Divine love
and joyfully embodying my majesty.*

Chapter 17

Set Boundaries, Live in Choice

You and I are essentially infinite choice-makers. In every moment of our existence, we are in that field of all possibilities where we have access to an infinity of choices.

—*Dr. Deepak Chopra*

As you move on from your exploration of self-care and devotion, it is only fitting that you begin to contemplate boundaries and the role they play in your growing consciousness. First of all, setting boundaries— or having a no-entry policy toward energies and relationships that are not in service of your peace, well-being, or evolution—*is* an act of self-devotion. It is a way for you to identify your needs and how your needs are met. How you want to show up in your integrity.

As you are tapping into your devotional practice and working to transcend the patterns and ways of being that tether you to limiting beliefs, you'll begin to recognize what the nonnegotiable necessities are for your life. You're going to start noticing the structure you're building—through choice, through creation—around yourself in order to support your higher ideals. Enforcing boundaries in service of that structure, in service of ensuring you receive those necessities, is vital— because those boundaries *keep you in choice*. They keep you on the path of your spiritual curriculum, your highest good, and self-mastery.

This is also a natural place in your healing journey to begin exploring boundaries, because you've begun to acquire some self-knowledge of

219

220 LIVING IN WISDOM

where you're going and what you need to get there. You have awareness of what those patterns and limiting beliefs are, and you have more clarity about what you are now in pursuit of in the form of your spiritual curriculum. So putting boundaries in place at this point is, in many ways, putting your money where your mouth is. Walking the walk. Even if it scares you. Even if it triggers all of your abandonment wounds, insecurities, and impostor syndrome (and it will, but we're getting to that).

It is not a coincidence that this is the part of the process where, in my experience, most people want to check out. It's ground zero for spiritual bypass. It is the kryptonite for those espousing toxic positivity, or trying to keep everyone on an emotional wavelength that keeps you feeling comfortable—which, by the way, is just another form of control. Also, putting boundaries in place is *hard*. It requires proving to yourself that you have self-respect and self-trust. Boundaries require you to be in service of that love and trust in order to recognize where you're sacrificing your own integrity and to *do* something about it. Boundaries push you to make your inner work outwardly real. Because none of this is real until you enact boundaries. Every book you've read doesn't mean anything until you physically stand up for yourself and physically create what I like to call a "pristine" environment for you to be yourself. You can't be in alignment if you're letting people constantly push into you or compromise your integrity. You can't be in alignment if you're not actively in choice, actively creating your new structures in the image of your highest pursuits.

But one step at a time. We're getting there.

What Boundaries Are—and Aren't

> The message I'm sending to myself—I can't change the world until I change myself first.
>
> —*Kendrick Lamar*

When most people think about boundaries, I find that their minds go directly to this idea of putting up walls that shut people or things *out*.

SET BOUNDARIES, LIVE IN CHOICE   221

And, yes, boundaries can be protective. But the purpose of this process isn't to insulate yourself from pain. It's not so you'll never be triggered again. You need that kind of input in order to investigate it, hold it, and incorporate it into your own process so that its effect is lessened over time. You can't do that if you're isolating yourself from it. That's not how life, or this work, works.

I'd also like you to let go of the idea that a boundary is individualized. *I have a boundary against my mother because of X. I have a boundary against my ex because of Y.* Your boundaries should extend to *all* people and *all* circumstances. Because boundaries are *not* meant to simply bypass difficult conversations and relationships. Instead, they are meant to be protective of larger, more universal needs in your life. *I don't want to be put in a position where I find myself being responsible for people and activating my desire to please. I don't want to be spoken to in a way that diminishes me. I only want to participate in conversations that involve deep listening and empathy.*

So putting boundaries in place is less about what you're keeping from interfering with your inner peace, and more about the structure you're building around you to support your higher ideas. To create more space for you to explore and evolve. Boundaries offer you the opportunity to choose that which serves you and then devote yourself to it. In the yin-yang order of things, when you work, when you choose, when you give—you also receive. When you choose your boundary, you receive in accordance with that choice.

Boundaries are also not just in service of self. They allow all of us to harness the powers we collectively hold owing to free will. When you hold boundaries that are in service of your highest self, you hold boundaries that are in service of the greater good.

A great example of this is the way millennials and Gen Z are putting boundaries in place surrounding workplace values. They are not being satisfactorily incentivized to go above and beyond, and so they have come into a collective conversation about workplace expectations from both management and employees, as well as demanding a livable wage and pay transparency. The collective whole benefits when we each

222 LIVING IN WISDOM

recognize and defend our individual needs on a physical, emotional, and mental level.

Every moment you have the opportunity to choose the immediate gratification of adhering to a pattern that no longer serves you versus the delayed gratification of the hard or uncomfortable choice made out of self-respect and honor. Every moment you have the opportunity to choose darkness or light, chaos or harmony, liberation or suffering.

Boundaries Support Self-Mastery

Through almost every ancient healing tradition, there are examples of boundaries as a necessity. In Ayurveda and Traditional Chinese Medicine, boundaries provide balance and harmony within and without. They serve as a container, gateway, channel, and funnel to hold and use energy so that the whole can function optimally. Boundaries are believed to be the interplay between yin and yang, dual energies that at once contradict and reinforce one another. Limits and spaciousness, distance and proximity, resoluteness and flexibility. Balance and harmony are not the clear division of opposites, but the equilibrium of them. In Buddhism, metamorphosis requires the depths of the dark to be alchemized, metabolized, and transformed so that the lotus of the highest spiritual attainment and self-mastery can reach toward the light and receive the gifts of the sun with greater intensity. The symbol of the lotus also teaches that we can learn from the opposite end of the spectrum—that one cannot truly know the magnitude of light without experiencing the depths of the dark.

Boundaries are, undeniably, natural law.

When I think about self-mastery, I think of peak performance, being in a flow state of being at one's best, lit up by life, ready, and radiant. This is the result of coming into consciousness about what's serving you and what you serve, and it's also largely because of the tangible pursuit of and devotion to keeping that path clear. Or when obstacles do cross that path, such as someone pushing up against your boundaries, choosing to

SET BOUNDARIES, LIVE IN CHOICE 223

use that information as another opportunity to transform, to surrender even more deeply to your boundary.

This transcendence happens when you are in practice of holding boundaries because:

- Boundaries create a sense of stability and safety. They allow you to walk through the world knowing that in uncertainty you are protected because you are going to choose what is best for you.
- Boundaries maintain a healthy sense of self and a clear energy field not entangled with others, be that people, work, careers, habits, routines, thought forms, etc.
- Boundaries naturally help loosen the grip of ego in favor of a more human, spiritual, natural, innate, or authentic operating system or perspective. As one's perspective becomes more conscious, naturally so too do their values and boundaries. Think as within, so above.
- Boundaries help us know our edges, especially which edges we'd like to push for our growth and which ones need to be fortified for our growth.
- Boundaries from the perspective of growth, rather than fear, will always be the most supportive way to understand what changes need to take place in order to maintain and create a healthy, thriving life.
- Boundaries enhance honesty and communication. They hold you accountable to your word, your power, your integrity, your commitment to consistently choosing that which serves and your integrity and the ability to respond and receive response.
- Boundaries keep you focused and connected to your purpose, to the moment, to your life.
- Boundaries teach yourself and others how to treat you, what you will and will not allow, and what you value.

Boundaries also create the opportunity for what I like to call **role modeling,** as in showing up as your highest self even when it's not

224 LIVING IN WISDOM

reciprocated—but not in a martyred or self-righteous way, rather as the creation of space for someone else to tap into their capacity for change. Oftentimes the people we wish would change haven't had the authentic experience that would inspire them to change. But as you're on your journey and you're being your authentic self in highest choice, you innately become the fertile soil for other people to grow. You don't have to tend to them, but you can give them the chance of taking root.

It's also important to note that boundaries do not apply just to relationships. You can have boundaries surrounding your health, such as protecting the time you require for rituals and routines in the morning and evening, or having boundaries around what you eat or do not eat. Bedtime boundaries, or ensuring that your sleep-related needs are met, is another big one. You can have boundaries at work, such as making sure that there's a balance between your generosity and the reciprocity of those transactions. Or getting clear on the kinds of clients or work you're willing to make space for. There are also bigger-picture boundaries, such as simply your time and energy. Remember, where attention goes, energy flows. What are you growing or investing in?

What Keeps Us from Setting Boundaries

There are a large number of reasons why many of us feel hesitant to set boundaries, if not completely paralyzed by the idea. For some, it's simply lack of awareness—without which, the need of a boundary has not yet registered. Or it could be lack of will or willingness. It might feel too uncomfortable, take too much effort, or rock the boat too much. This might be where your pattern shows up, perhaps in relationship dynamics and wanting to please people or struggling with codependency. It could be unconscious self-sabotaging. It could be because of an imbalanced power dynamic owing to any of the "isms"—racism, sexism, classism, ageism. It could be owing to difficulty accessing resources that would allow you to make more informed choices, such as books, podcasts, education, or therapy.

And then there are all the reasons that stem more significantly from a core wound sending mixed signals. These might be:

- Fear of rejection or abandonment when one's needs are expressed
- High tolerance for disrespect or pain after being accustomed to not having one's needs met
- Guilt or shame for asking for something one needs
- A bias to seek comfort in a way that is controlling of one's experiences
- Neurological pathway lag as a result of building new habits or ways or being
- Unconscious or conscious patterns such as addiction (avoidance, escapism, numbing, abusing) or manipulation (lack of self-control or a desire to control others)
- Inability to take responsibility
- Anger as a barrier to taking action
- Anxious-avoidant attachment style
- Functioning from a state of dysregulation owing to CPTSD, PTSD, anxiety, depression, stress, or energy fatigue and constantly operating out of fight, flight, freeze, fawn, or a combination thereof

In many of these cases, it's difficult to even know your needs let alone set boundaries around them. For some, moving beyond this obstacle will "just" take commitment to practice and higher consciousness. For others, you may require assistance from a professional (see page 34).

I Am Not Available for Anything That Is Not Mutually Beneficial: Learning How to Navigate Boundaries

In 2021, I did a fireside chat with my dear friend Angela Rye; a clip from that conversation went viral, getting *three million* hits in just a couple of days. I'd said, "I'm not available for anything that is not mutually beneficial." In every interaction, there has to be an open exchange, an energetic flow of giving and receiving. If in a relationship—work, marriage, family, friendship—someone is running all over you in all kinds of ways or you're giving, giving, giving and not getting anything in return—that goes against cosmic law. To be in community requires a reciprocal exchange of energy. So if you are not in that dance with someone or something, you need to ask yourself: *Why does it have a hold on me? Why am I required to stay here if I'm not receiving anything in return?*

But also, get clear on what is being exchanged when you give and feel as though you don't receive in return. Receiving in return is not always tit-for-tat. Sometimes receiving gratitude can be reciprocal. Sometimes someone just being present to the experience and sharing good energy is enough—because it feels nice and pleasurable. But if none of that is happening, then you're just leaking your own energy. You're exerting in a way that is not in alignment with your life. You deserve to have reciprocal relationships.

The only exception to this is someone who is not able to reciprocate. Maybe it's because of their own emotional limitations, unresolved wounds, or lack of self-awareness. You might feel called to help—and that can be fine. It can be your charity, your way of giving selflessly without the expectation of anything back. *But it cannot be your only relationship.*

Something I realized during the pandemic was how much I needed to overhaul my friendships. Since I've worked in industries that have a lot of networking elements involved, in addition to living in three states, my life is *filled* with people—more people than is actually practical for me to nurture relationships with and still be the kind of mother I want to be or have the quality of life that I want to live. Especially because I frequently found myself giving so much more than I got in return.

I had to, in a non-egoic way—look at what I brought to the table and what I was taking away. When I reflected on myself, the work I've done on myself, and my natural gifts, I realized *I bring a fucking lot to the table.* Goddamn. I'm an exceptional friend; I live in integrity; I give people the dignity of their own process; I give people experiences in ways that can be upleveling. I had to be honest about that with myself. But more importantly, I had to recognize that up until now, I was doing a whole lot of bringing myself down to the level of whoever it was that I was with. I was so used to thinking I was too much or hearing the voice of my past trauma that *I can't shine when you're around*, because my light was too bright. So I'd limit my own magnetism and power. I'd undershare.

But then it occurred to me that if I'm in community with people I need to do that for, I've chosen to be in a community that is too small for me. It's a container I shouldn't be existing in. I didn't want to be a big fish in a small pond; I wanted to be a small fish in a big pond. Or better yet, in a nice, equitably sized pond. So I started putting some boundaries in place.

I realized first that I really wanted to clean house regarding the amount of people I knew. So I unfollowed every single person I had been following on Instagram. I wanted to let myself be present with this false construct we've been living in for the past fifteen years and what it means to have followers, as well as to follow other people. I wanted to examine whether we're actually in relationship with one another or just have access. At the time I was following close to two thousand people, and in looking at that list, I could so clearly see many of the chapters of my life where following that individual after meeting them one time felt like it might lead to something—a relationship, a collaboration. We usually never talked or met again, and yet I kept that connection intact. But I knew at this point in my life that if God wants me to work on a project with someone, I'll work on a project with someone. I needed to have enough trust in my skills to accept that I didn't need to follow someone to be in relationship if we're not meant to be in relationship.

I also realized how unhealthy it was and how much time it took to be so attuned to the nuance of the day-to-day of someone's life when you don't know them that well—what they're eating, what they're

228 LIVING IN WISDOM

reading, what's happening with their kids. *I met you once twelve years ago at a party and don't know anything about you, yet I know everything about you.* It's exhausting with all the projections and assumptions you're making based on that surface-level glimpse of their life, and it's actually quite confusing. It is not an actual relationship that we have.

I also started recognizing where people were taking more than they were giving. One of the clearest examples was a woman whom I'd met one time at a dinner for someone else I didn't know, and ever since she'd gotten sucked into the parasocial construct of social media—as though, just because she liked my posts meant that somehow, she'd have unlimited access to my time, that we were in reciprocal relationship. Every couple of months, she'd hit me up and ask for things from me—to be connected with someone I knew, to help promote an event for personal gain—but never once offered me so much as a kind word or inquired how I was. And she certainly never took the time to ask how she could support me.

Finally, I said to her, "I need for you to look at the structure of this relationship. Scroll up in the text thread and notice how many withdrawals you've made versus deposits. You ask me for a lot of things, but I don't see one 'happy birthday' here or asking how my son is or recognizing the time it takes—time away from my child, away from my own life—to do the things you've asked of me. So I cannot move forward continuing to help you."

She got pretty pissed, but she stopped reaching out. And I got my time back.

Recognizing that I didn't have—or need to have—the space in my brain for so many thoughts about other people whom I'm not actually in intimate connection with or working with felt amazing. So for a couple of months, I kept it that way, following nobody. Then, if someone naturally came into my consciousness, I'd follow them. But I was still in my process, noticing whether it was reciprocal energy for me to be present in someone's life even though I was glimpsing it from afar.

I had prepared myself for the discomfort that my commitment

would cause, for myself and for others, and I saw it as a phenomenal opportunity to practice staying the course of my own integrity, as well as investigating my own triggers. The worry that if I unfollowed, say, a celebrity—what if they one day wanted to work with me and saw I didn't follow them? But I figured if they were really interested in me and my work, they'd ask anyway. There was also the worry about whether someone would be upset with me or talk trash about me. To which I came to realize *I will live*. And then there was holding space for the people who were triggered by my choice. One woman hit me up and said, "Hey, I want to know why you unfollowed me. I thought we were good; did I do something wrong?"

She was a friend of a friend whom I'd hung out with on and off for about fifteen years, always just making small talk, never in each other's texts or call log. Nothing. So I said to her, "Hey, I just want to let you know that in no way is this personal or a reflection of your worth or how I view you as a person. I was becoming overwhelmed by social media and the amount of information that I was always feeling required to interact with, so I've decided to unfollow people I don't have a daily relationship with, even though I think you're so dope and love running into you." She did not get it. People can only meet you as deeply as they've met themselves. They're only going to hear what they're going to hear.

If you have a similar relationship with social media, this is a great place to start. Notice any page that makes you feel bad about yourself. Don't necessarily unfollow that account because it makes you feel a certain way; that gives away your control and creates the false belief that you're being *made* to feel bad. Although, you have complete license to unfollow whomever and whatever you like. But do notice why you're triggered and investigate why that feeling comes up for you when looking at the life of someone you barely know. And why you felt called to follow them in the first place.

After my social media cleanup, I took a deep inventory of the people in my life. For me, that was prompted by having been in relationship

230 LIVING IN WISDOM

with someone with extreme narcissistic tendencies, the most insidious experience that truly almost killed me. Experts say if you've had one someone like that in your life, you've likely had many. So I wanted to investigate all of the relationships in all of the categories of my life where that dynamic might exist. There's so much we don't know about people with these personality traits, in large part because many psychologists won't take them on as clients because change can be so intensive and challenging to achieve, so I didn't have extensive criteria to draw from. But what I did have that was more powerful was the patterns of behavior that I knew showed up in my life when I was around that type of person—the pleasing, the making myself smaller, dimming my light.

I wanted to undergo this process with surgical precision, so I got out my journal and wrote lists:

On the first page, I made a list of the most active relationships in my life at the time, the people I talk to the most or see the most or hold up as influential in my life.

On the second page was a list of casual friendships, people I had good conversations with or had known for a length of time but only really had nostalgia keeping us connected.

The third page was a list of acquaintances.

For each list, I went through and took note of what I created in the relationship and what they created, what my need was for our connection, and what I received. I asked myself if there was anyone who needed to be elevated to another category of friendship, and whether there was anyone who was requiring too much of me or taking too much time in comparison to what they gave. I also crossed out any names I was done with and knew the sentiment would be mutual without needing to discuss it further.

During this time, I also made a list of the villains in my life, people who had betrayed me in significant ways or were massive catalysts for pain points. I'd meditate on each of their names, holding them without judgment or charge, and notice what role they played in my life and my spiritual curriculum, as well as what role I played in theirs. I'd look at the fibers of what built these connections between us and how those betrayals were allowed to happen. I'd ask myself, *What did I miss? How did I let them get this close? In what areas was I perhaps naïve or people pleasing or frozen?* Then I'd allow myself to visualize them as their childhood versions and take a moment to come into compassion for whatever unmet needs contributed to their becoming the person that they had. I'd soften my heart toward them by looking at their experience that predated the experience that we shared, and I'd begin to zoom out from my own perspective and consider that perhaps that person didn't serve the villain role in someone else's life. That perhaps in their other relationships, they served goodness. I'd also honor the fact that karma is always at play, so perhaps this dynamic was present because it was I who had wronged them in another lifetime. So I would pray for them and myself and say to their highest self, "I'm sorry for any harm I've caused you in any life we've shared. Please forgive me. I'm sorry, and I forgive you." I'd cross out their name, burn the paper, and let that experience leave me.

In addition to that list, I made a—thankfully short—list of people whom *I* caused harm. I did a loving-kindness meditation on these individuals and said a prayer for each of them. I apologized for all of the ways I've harmed them in this lifetime or other lifetimes, asked for forgiveness, and granted forgiveness in return.

And then there were those individuals who were trickier. People whose friendship meant a lot to me in the past but didn't as much now, and the feelings were most likely not mutual. I put these individuals in their own separate category and gave myself a year to study the purpose of the relationships in my life. I took that time to observe through a devotional lens. I became a spiritual scientist, studying my interactions. Under a new moon—a potent moment for setting intentions for new beginnings—I would reflect on where I was overperforming or giving too much. Where was someone possibly doing that for me? Where had I gotten a little lazy in reciprocating and showing up? It got me clear not only on who I needed and wanted to be in my life, but also on the kind of friend I wanted to be.

Throughout that year, I kept little notes. I noticed when someone was

232 LIVING IN WISDOM

able to show up for me, especially if I was in crisis. And if they didn't, was that because they didn't have the capacity but tried to do it in a way that was more natural for them, making up for their lack of emotional intelligence with the best of their gifts or abilities? Or were they just not there because they didn't want to be, or because they were undervaluing me?

I remember going to visit my friend Ella just after finding out that my ex-husband had had two children with two other women while we were married. One of whom I, too, had known, who had been in my home. One of whom I had trusted with my body as my rehabilitation therapist and who had supported me throughout my pregnancy with my son. But also, these were two women whom he was not in deep relationship or even communication with either. They had been disposable to him. They had been completely disregarded after these affairs. He took a sledgehammer to our marriage in the name of nothing. But beyond that, he also set into motion a multigenerational rupture that these children and their children and their children's children will have to cope with. There were no winners here. Every single one of us was a casualty.

Pause for breath.

I was in the throes of self-flagellation for how this relationship affected my son and our family and was navigating deep and difficult self-forgiveness. I told her everything about what had happened, and how I was just trying to show up with joy and enthusiasm for my child. In that moment, I just needed someone to *hold* me. To hug me. To help hold my pain, if only for a moment. Instead, she tried to distract me with small talk and food. I left feeling empty and unseen and neglected, and it triggered all my emotional wounds from childhood.

This person had at one time been one of the most important people in my world, but because of the work I was doing around setting boundaries— because of the importance I knew that work was to my healing—I knew that I was ready to let go. I knew that I'd love her from afar, but in no way did I want to hold up this friendship, because I wasn't supported by it.

I'm not going to tell you it was that straightforward or simple. I ultimately gave her another chance. About a year had gone by, and I was once again in a really bad place, feeling like I would never feel safe in love again. I felt so sad for myself. I was dealing with the divorce, with the realities of being a single mother—both of which also limited my possibilities for finding a partner, despite the fact that I was a successful woman. I wanted desperately for her to really hear me and greet me with tenderness and compassion. But she just kept cracking jokes without acknowledging what I was saying. She said, "Girl, don't worry; you're gonna find another man!" At that point I decided that I'd miss her and grieve her, but I was done.

But I didn't want to just cut her off. So I promised myself that I'd have a conversation with her to say goodbye, along with all the other individuals whom I didn't want to be in relationship with anymore at this point in my life. I called them and had conversations to help me determine whether I wanted to continue our relationship based on how they responded. If not, I'd gently let them know how I'd felt let down and how, because of their actions, I couldn't prioritize spending time with them. It was, as you can imagine, excruciatingly difficult. But whenever someone's response to this laid-bare truth felt unsatisfactory, I felt even more resolved about my decision.

Some people acted casually or bypassed with humor. Some blamed me instead. Some said they'd change their behavior and never did. In all of these cases, I knew that as soon as I stopped feeding that relationship, it would wither and die. And that could be beautiful in its own way. I no longer needed to maintain active expectations of who they could be for me.

I said goodbye to about thirty people over that time, a mix of close friends, casual companions, and acquaintances. And in that space I had *space*. I was able to give more to the smaller groups of people who meant the most to me and who were the most worthy investment of my time. Or I could devote that space to my son and me and the new things that I couldn't even imagine but knew would emerge.

But there were also people who surprised me.

That same friend who could only meet my despair with jokes and snacks started crying and immediately told me she'd been waiting for

234 LIVING IN WISDOM

me to bring this up. She said she felt like such a coward after those experiences; she was anxious because she had a hard time finding the right thing to say. As I listened to her so fervently but lovingly trying to help me understand where she was coming from, I was reminded of how she had been there for me at such a high level over the years. She'd always supported me professionally and could be counted on to show up on a moment's notice to physically be present with me. After I moved to Houston, she'd made me a scrapbook of my best moments in LA with photos and drawings and sent it to me. This presented the opportunity for a reset in our relationship, for me to internalize the value of it in my life, but also an opportunity for me to explicitly express my needs if we were going to move forward. I told her that in no way did I expect for her to always have the right words or even solutions. I just wanted someone who was going to hug me and bear witness to my sadness. She said, "I can do that. I'm going to work on that. And work on us."

I suggested we ease back into our relationship and see what our capacity for friendship could be. I told her that I wanted to move slowly and that I didn't have a lot to give right now. She said absolutely, and she meant it. She went out of her way to invite me out and practiced her active deep listening. Now, a couple of years later, not only is she beyond valuable in my life, but we've been able to deepen our connection in really special ways. I'm so grateful that I had the guts to have that conversation instead of writing her off.

In the time since I began implementing boundaries and being in choice, I've grown new acquaintances and friendships that are more in alignment with where I am now and worthy of what I need. They support the version of me that I've become instead of feeling threatened by it. They also allow me the space and energy to tend to the things that matter most: my son, myself, and the practices I need to feel grounded and well.

The spiritual teacher and bestselling author Caroline Myss said, "If you want to know for sure that you are on the right path, here's your clue: You're not put in a position where you feel like you have to negotiate your sense of integrity, which is an act of betrayal. You don't feel like you have to compromise who you are."

Nothing truer could be said about a life defined and nourished by informed boundaries. And then, when you are ready for liftoff, you'll be able to reach for the next delicious rung of the ladder: joy.

"I WILL" VERSUS "I WON'T"

Although there are multiple creative ways to go about setting boundaries, I think the simplest way to understand them is **I will versus I won't**. Or a simple "yes-no" structure.

We do this with our bodies; we can *feel* what a yes is and what a no is. Typically, a yes feels enlightening, exciting, radiant, and enlivening. It pulls us forward. It feels good.

A no, on the other hand, feels like anxiety, upset, dislike, or unpleasantness. Like something pushing us away, the opposite of magnetic attraction.

People who have cultivated a connection with their body and intuition can flow through life according to their internal GPS— the nervous system—and set up boundaries that are supportive to their using this simple yes-no inquiry.

For those who need to cultivate that awareness, we'll go back to the "I will versus I won't" structure.

I like to think of this boundary-making exercise as "progress and protection." It asks you to use your language to take responsibility for your behavior, using positive "I will" statements in support of progress you'd like to make (much like an affirmation) and "I won't" statements as a means of protection. For example:

- **I will** do things that are supportive of my growth, even if they appear to be uncomfortable.
- **I won't** engage in activities that are harmful or unhealthy for my mental, emotional, physical, or spiritual well-being.

LIVING IN WISDOM

Depending on your current level of self-mastery, it might be more helpful in the beginning to view things from the positive perspective. Because many people struggle with the concept of limitation, such as "I won't eat sugar anymore," it can be more productive to work with boundaries that engage in a positive trajectory or reward. In this case, "I will have sugar only in my coffee or tea." It's a nice little psychological trick that signals to us that we're receiving rather than having something being taken away.

Practices for Setting Boundaries and Being in Choice

I've learned that you shouldn't go through life with a catcher's mitt on both hands; you need to be able to throw something back.

—*Maya Angelou*

Meditation for Setting Boundaries and Being in Choice

Start by sitting in a comfortable position and taking five deep belly breaths to ground yourself in your body and in the present moment. Set an intention for how you would like to feel or what you would like to release. Call forward your higher self and wisdom: "I call forward the highest guidance available to me for the highest good of all concerned."

Now begin a body-scan meditation with your hands in your mudra of choice (see Mudras for Setting Boundaries and Being in Choice below). Incrementally move your focus from the top of your head to the base of your spine (your crown to your root), gently releasing any physical or emotional tension points (such as in your jaw, neck, shoulders, or heart) that you may notice as your attention travels down your body.

Throughout the meditation, notice your breath. If at any time you find yourself connecting to your thoughts, bring your awareness back to your breath and the rise and fall of your chest.

Let your practice stretch anywhere between five and twenty-five minutes. Allow the length of your meditation to gradually increase over time as you feel more settled into your practice.

Mudras for Setting Boundaries and Being in Choice

Kali Mudra. This is the gesture of purification. It invokes inner strength and courage; aids in releasing fear and negative emotions; encourages transformation and personal growth; energizes the body and mind; inspires transformation, inner strength, and fearlessness; and can be empowering, particularly in challenging situations.

Firmly interlace your fingers. Extend the index fingers together, pointing straight, resembling a sword. Hold this gesture in front of your heart or above your head, keeping the spine straight and the shoulders relaxed. Breathe deeply and focus on the intention of the mudra.

Vajra Mudra. This is the gesture of fiery thunderbolt. It is a mudra for transforming ignorance into wisdom. *Vajra* means "diamond," and this mudra directs breath and energy into the third chakra, which is called Manipura, aka the "city of gems." Vajra is said to have the quality of both diamond-like indestructibility and thunderbolt-like irresistible force. Another meaning for *vajra* is "firmness of spirituality." This mudra stimulates blood circulation, which can reduce restlessness and dizziness.

Form a fist with your right hand around your left index finger. Form a fist with the remaining fingers on your left hand, below your right hand. Raise both hands so they are in front of the heart chakra.

Bhutadamara Mudra. This mudra serves as a shield to keep negative energies away while maintaining a calm and peaceful state.

Face your palms away from the body. Cross your wrists and extend your ring fingers down toward your thumbs.

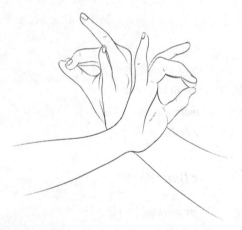

Essential Oils for Supporting Boundaries and Choice Rituals

Cardamom: The oil for strong body awareness

Dill: The oil for tense relationships, handling triggers

SET BOUNDARIES, LIVE IN CHOICE 239

For more information on how to use essential oils, see page 141.

Movement for Setting Boundaries and Being in Choice

- Weightlifting or mentally active forms of movement like boxing or Pilates can be a great way of encouraging fortitude and flexibility.
- For softer, more energy-oriented practices that teach about the distribution of energy, prana, or chi, yoga, qigong, and tai chi can bring you into balance in a different way.
- Warrior 2, Cobra, and Bow poses are great for cultivating and expressing fortified yet breathable boundaries, as the goal of the poses is to be engaged and strong yet relaxed and centered.
- If you are already someone who incorporates movement into their day, try experimenting with new time, rep, or weight boundaries to enhance your practice this season.

Affirmations for Boundaries and Choice

I honor my boundaries, and my boundaries honor me.
My boundaries are a way of cultivating healing and growth in my life.
I respect my boundaries, and I respect the boundaries of others.
My boundaries allow me to be in alignment with my purpose.
I observe, refine, and maintain my boundaries as I grow, making sure I am in alignment with the desires of my heart.

Journal Prompts for Boundaries and Choice

- *What boundaries are working for me?*
- *What boundaries feel challenging to maintain?*
- *What purpose do my boundaries serve? How do they nourish me?*
- *What boundaries do I need to embrace in this season of my life to evolve and transform?*
- *How do I honor and participate with the boundaries of other people in my life?*

240 LIVING IN WISDOM

Creativity for Boundaries and Choice

- Practice drawing your boundaries: Some spiritual traditions understand the power of spirals as a way to represent and connect with the spiral nature of the Universe, the cosmic order. A spiral can be seen as the pathway to transformation or the spiral staircase toward our unfolding. Begin by standing in the middle of your spiral space, and continue to walk outward, taking larger steps. When you feel complete, you can finish with an affirmation.
- Other ways to work with boundaries can be experimenting with a new boundary for the week, speaking more honestly, waking up earlier, or clocking out on time. There are ways to play with creating boundaries without the be-all and end-all mentality. Encouraging your boundaries to grow in a satisfying and sustainable way is what's important.
- If the concept of boundaries is newer to you, explore the topic. See what's out there around the psychology and practicality of boundaries, listen to podcasts, read books, or find people whom you can gain wisdom from, as to what boundaries you might benefit from.

I am maximizing the energetic potential of each moment for the highest good of all concerned.

Chapter 18

Experience Joy

Check in with your heart today.
Check in with your breath today.
Check in with your gut today.
Check in with your anger today.
Check in with your joy today.

—Me

It is my belief that during our time in this life, we are meant to experience the entire spectrum of human emotion, from grief to joy and back again. We've spent a good amount of time talking about this already, but it bears repeating: Both of these experiences aren't just necessary for our understanding of and connection with higher purpose—they are the entire point of existing. Grief and joy and the ability to be with them, embrace them, and embody them unlocks all of the obstacles to feeling a deep sense of harmony and completeness.

The only obstacle—and one that most people find surprising—is that these two polar but complementary opposites are equally uncomfortable to inhabit. *It is just as difficult for us to sit with joy as it is to sit with grief.* We are impressively good at shutting it down, being suspicious of it, or rationalizing it away. But to turn your back on joy is to turn your back on life's deepest sweetness. This is your permission to let joy in. It is your invitation to recognize the important and challenging work you've been doing to metabolize grief and face potentially painful truths. Here is the balm, the release, the reward.

In its fullest spiritual meaning, joy is the expression of God's goodness. It is a deep-rooted, inspired bliss that brings with it great pleasure. It is our alleviation from suffering and the powerful reminder that not all of life will hurt. I experience joy as peace and celebration in one. Unlike happiness, which requires some sort of catalyst to make it appear, joy has a deep embodiment built from surrender and trust. Joy isn't necessarily happiness. It is an experience we can radiate outwardly in a way that inspires others. Just as grief usually begins externally before we bring it internally, joy must be internal before it can be external.

So joy is the point. It is the foundation of happiness and the fuel for purpose. Attuning to joy is sacred work and requires just as much mastery as healing grief.

For me, connecting with personal joy is what gave me a reverence for life and for God during my hardest moments. It's also what made me realize that my joy is solely my responsibility—and something that I could do for myself, which felt like such an exciting challenge. I'd ask myself, *How are you going to make yourself smile today?* It was such a powerful reframing because at the time, I felt as if someone else were shaping my feelings. This also relates to how we're socialized, particularly how women are programmed to be more attuned to other people's feelings than their own. I had to let that go and relearn all the ways that *I* make myself whole and complete and able to meet my needs for joy and romance without anyone else.

I remember sitting in the bathtub, almost catatonic from the sheer overwhelm of my life at the time. I was staring at my reflection in the drain, and the first concrete thought that came to mind was *You'll know you're healed when you get to Paris.*

Twenty-four months later, I got to Paris.

It was my first time leaving my son for more than a couple of days,

244 LIVING IN WISDOM

but I knew how important it was to go alone. I had made no plans other than doing things that felt right and good in the moment. Every morning, I woke up, asked myself, *What shall we do today?* and walked for miles around the city, admiring all of the beauty and smelling the flowers. I took mushrooms at the park and listened to children playing and had visions of Mary Magdalene. I met a man who said he wanted to take me around the city on his Vespa and take my photograph. And I let him. I realized all of the joy and romance I experienced in those moments wasn't because of Paris or the gardens or this beautiful man. It was because I'd been able to cultivate it first, and then I shared the overflow. I learned that in that way, joy is completely intertwined with our most authentic or higher self. And that joy begins with me.

Joy is also essential to understanding your spiritual curriculum. Because joy really just represents desire—for something else, something unknown. A desire to feel and to be open inside. And what is required for the presence of joy is a real connection with and observation of yourself.

However, if you have not cleared out the space to do that or do not have the tolerance or the practice, you start reaching for the external sources of joy. Performative joy. But that kind of joy will not nourish you on a cellular level; it doesn't fuel your experience. It feels hollow and leaves you feeling like a fraud. So instead, let's connect with real, true joy.

Recognizing Your Barriers to Joy

To truly embody joy, you're going to need to confront what your own barriers to embracing joy look like. There are many, many to choose from.

One of the most common ways we all reject joy is when we can't receive compliments, positive feedback, or kindness. Many of us have a desire to either deflect praise entirely or downplay ourselves in false humility, or we try to pay the compliment back immediately. Sometimes that's because we feel like we're being duped into feeling safe or grateful because at any point that can be taken away. Some people are insecure about not being able to repay that person at the level they assume they want to receive something back, and so it's a loaded exchange. But when we're looking at the minute-to-minute aspects of life, this is a significant way you're robbing yourself of joy. You're denying yourself the experience of receiving—specifically of receiving joy. A great practice is to slow the exchange *way* down. When someone compliments you, try to hold on to every single word, even if you have to watch their lips move. Take deep breaths, put your hand on your heart, and let that person get their full thought out before you say anything. If you don't know how to respond, simply say, "I really receive that. Thank you." It's a way to train your body to be more receptive to joy.

Similarly, we might shun the experience of joy because it feels so brief. We may fear the impermanence of joy. When you understand joy as something that comes only from outside of yourself, over which you have no agency and that can be given and taken, this fear makes sense. In that case, it feels a lot safer to reject joy—because who would want to be attached to something that might be snatched away without warning? But that, too, leads to the deprivation of joy.

I've seen this in action. When an elder in my extended family came to visit us in California, she had been chronically ill for years and was wheelchair-bound, and she had really burrowed into that pain. She made pain her identity, had completely committed to misery. Yet I always got the sense she wanted more for her life. We would often talk about the ocean and how, living in Oklahoma, she never got to see the water she loved so much. So, during this particular visit, I took her on a long drive down the Pacific Coast Highway, which hugs the Pacific Ocean and has some of the most incredible views. The entire drive, she refused to look out the window at the beach. Refused. "Mm-hmm that's nice," she said. In that moment, I could see her fear of what she believed to be the impermanence of joy. If she saw the ocean now and allowed herself to feel that flood of positive emotions, it would all just go away

246 LIVING IN WISDOM

the moment she left. And in closing herself off from that moment, she'd closed herself off from joy completely.

When we do that, we're never open to what might feel good or beautiful or fulfill a wish or desire, period. We're closed off from *any* joy at any moment. However, when you are open to experiencing the entire spectrum of feeling, the fear of happiness fades because joy is regenerative. It's a well that doesn't run dry. It simply requires your awareness and intention to connect to it.

Another significant barrier to joy is how triggering it can be when everything goes right. Especially if you've had a life experience where that is very much not the case. Joy can then feel as disruptive to your system as abuse and toxicity, and is the reason why you may run from happy things.

I saw that for myself when I started seeing someone after my divorce. I'd met him on an app and was feeling sort of whatever about the whole dating experience, but he was familiar with me and my work. Not only that, he'd clearly been doing his own work to broaden his capacity for high-level conversations about feelings. Very quickly, we were able to engage in what seemed like an advanced, deeply connected way and with a lot of excitement too. It was the first time I was able to share real-time enthusiasm with someone without worrying about needing to play the game or hold back.

He lived on the East Coast, and I was staying in Mexico at the time, so he ended up flying out to take me on our very first date. We were able to have the same deeply synced experiences in person and on a significant physical level, which for me served as an awakening to emotional intimacy. I'd never been so free and so clear. However, even though I'd been working on increasing my capacity to receive love, it still created so much fear inside of my body that I didn't initially understand. I was triggered in the same way I would have been by my ex's emotionally abusive behavior but in response to good, positive things someone was feeling for me. I was triggered by how easy I was to love because I'd never felt that ease. I'd always assumed it was really hard to love me.

EXPERIENCE JOY   247

In response to this man with whom I felt completely safe holding or kissing me or making all the plans for us so I didn't have to think about a thing, my body would be in fight-or-flight mode. These beautiful things were so foreign to my experience that, on a deep core level, I wanted to reject them.

Luckily, in that moment I could recognize that pushing this away wasn't a choice that served me. I knew I had to keep nudging myself beyond that upper limit and easing my way past that initial resistance. I needed to slow down and build my capacity for feeling safe and feeling good. And so even though this individual wasn't the right person for long-term connection, I was still grateful for the experience and the wisdom it brought me.

I realized our experiences with each other are a sum of our experiences with ourselves—and that we're often just trying to protect our own hearts. My friend Resmaa Menakem speaks beautifully to this dynamic and asserts that when you get scared in love because of the vulnerability required of you, the first thing that leaves the relationship is sweetness. The joy you have together gets wiped out, and very often it never comes back. This is not isolated to romantic relationships; this can happen in friendships, families, or experiences—which is why it's so important to always be evaluating the barriers you might have with joy and to make the space for what I like to call **Big Joy**, or the larger, more significant moments beyond the fleeting daily instants that bring us pleasure. And that oftentimes means starting small (i.e., mastering the tiny joys).

Tiny Joys: The Pathway to Big Joy

I love teaching the concept of tiny joys, because it's based on the years I spent cultivating my own practice for joy and expanding my capacity for it. I wanted to train myself to let go of the anticipation that the other shoe could drop at any moment, and so I decided to start with the smallest, almost imperceptible ways that I experienced joy. I started with the tiniest fleeting moments possible—going outside and noticing

248 LIVING IN WISDOM

the changing nature of the sun's light. Or appreciating how the quality of light shifted in my home from month to month, falling in love with those all-to-brief moments when it would rest just right on a piece of artwork or an accidental still life of items on the kitchen counter. I would choose to be very present in that moment, taking three deep breaths, and allowing a smile to spread across my face. Anytime I'd pass something beautiful—a butterfly, flowers in my neighbor's garden, a bird in a tree—I'd breathe deeply and appreciate whatever it was. And it would fill my body with so much joy, which, over time, gave me the ability to feel gratitude for whatever joy—large or small—was present while it was present. It allowed me to quickly detach and release the grip of the need for something to stay.

And then, when joy did arise itself, I would soak. It. Up. Every last bit of it. Such as when a friend sent me flowers just because, an incredible, completely over-the-top bouquet just to say, "I'm grateful for you." I separated some of the flowers so that I could see those blooms everywhere I went—I scattered them on my dining room table; I put some in a vase in my bathroom; I put some by my bed. And every time they caught my eye, I'd stop, smile at them, take a deep inhale, and smell the petals. I'd allow myself to drink up the complete sensory experience of those flowers and to receive all the gifts that my friend intended with them. It was both the practice of receiving joy and stoking that fire inside of me that radiates joy.

This is what building a relationship with joy looks like. It's how you learn to trust that joy is not finite, and that opening yourself to joy doesn't lead to pain and disappointment, but rather more expansive awareness of and deeper gratitude for the joy that exists. In other words, more joy.

When We Resist Joy, We Resist Community

When you experience something that may have given you joy but choose to not radiate it out and share it, for one thing, that joy cannot bloom.

When you suppress joy, you cut off the natural energetic exchange we're meant to have with the world and with other people and with God at all times.

Take Cleo, a former corporate client. She had created a cavern for herself to hide in but so desperately wanted community. In her relationships, she often positioned herself "above" others, as if they were the ones in constant need of help or advice and she was the only one to give it. She did often have to play that role in other people's lives, but it was a dynamic that made it very difficult for her to be vulnerable or risk having things "taken away." When her friends did extend gestures of kindness, she would roll her eyes. Or she would dismiss it as the friend just trying to "please people." I so often wanted to say, "Maybe they aren't only giving you things in order to manipulate you and then take it all away once they get what they need, the way a parent did." Especially after I called her to see if she'd received the gift I sent her and all she said was "Yeah, it came a couple of days ago; I haven't opened it yet."

A couple of years ago, I brought her with me on a mini-retreat. I treated us to bodywork, took her out to beautiful meals. She was just so shell-shocked and irritated. Finally, a few days in, she started to dissolve. I saw a smile I'd never seen before, this childlike smile. I'd happened to glance at her and sort of caught her in the act, and it was jarring for her, but little by little, she settled in. However, expressing gratitude for the experience, even simply saying, "Thank you," was clearly challenging for her.

Now, I didn't do any of that for the thank-you. But there are certain ways you behave in society, saying *thank you* being one of them—no matter what your hang-ups are. But then, two years later, out of nowhere, she sent me a text that read, "I want you to know how much that trip meant to me. It changed my life. I'd never been treated that well before." She told me about how when she got into the car that took her to the airport, she cried the entire way. She didn't know where to put those feelings or what those feelings even were. She thanked me profusely.

What this experience reinforced for me was twofold:

1. That it can take time, sometimes years, to build the capacity to process certain experiences
2. How much confusion we can cause other people without intending to because of our barriers to joy

When you shut down your outward expression of joy, you're robbing someone else of experiencing that. When you reject joy, you reject others too.

Conversely, when you learn how to receive joy, you're also in selfless service of community, which then creates a positive loop of trusting that your needs can be met so that you can surrender completely to whatever your experience is. It makes you realize how powerful it is to have that level of care during childhood—or any other point of your life—and how fortifying it is. And how difficult, if not impossible, it is to reach the full possibility of your life without it. But it is never too late to begin cultivating it.

About five years ago, I was completing a three-year program in spiritual psychology. Every year involved a weeklong practicum experience where all the students would be in class together every day for more than ten hours a day, and you could not miss any days of practicum or you'd have to start back at the beginning the following year.

The morning of the first session of this practicum, I started feeling extremely ill—cold sweats, full-body chills, dry heaving, eventually throwing up. I knew that I had to make it to that evening's five-hour class, and I had no one to help me process what was happening, which was almost more overwhelming than any physical ailment.

When I arrived, I told the teachers what was going on, and they suggested that if I'd like to, I could just sit in the back of class. They also let me know that they'd seen this before, that it wasn't uncommon in practicum for students to purge, an aversion that looked like illness. What I heard was that they thought I was making up an excuse, and I rejected that idea. So I sat in the back, listening to the lecture with my eyes closed, rocking myself in pain, and moaning. I was resolved to sit there and get credit for this class.

The next morning I was still feeling awful. I got to class, sat in the back, quietly weeping and suffering. Eventually, I decided I was going to try to take a nap while lying on the floor. One of the teachers, Dr. Steve, started talking to me while my eyes were closed because I couldn't open them. I felt so vulnerable and scared having someone witness me in so much pain. And I felt a sudden wave of deep sadness as I realized how vigilant and responsible for myself I'd had to be my whole life, how terrified I was that I couldn't help myself at this moment, and how much I did not want to receive help from another person.

I ended up letting him take me to the emergency room, and for six hours, he waited outside my room. I kept coming out to apologize to him for wasting his time, to beg him to go home. It was stirring memories of breaking various limbs when I was younger and having my mom show up at school to come get me, always so frustrated. She had the significant challenge of being the sole adult caretaker for a child while navigating the patriarchal-capitalist hamster wheel and having to leave the office when others could depend on significant others or nannies, spend over an hour in traffic, and contend with the survival-compromising reality of losing wages or opportunities for advancement. But for me, I'd sense that frustration and fear and resentment of a system setting her up for failure and internalize it as it being my fault. That only mildly being hurt wasn't good enough. Or that if I was hurt, I should keep it to myself. That it was a burden. That I was a burden.

All of this had reanimated the minute I let someone take care of me.

Finally, Dr. Steve looked at me and said gently, "Can you please stop? You're robbing me of the opportunity to serve, to give something to you. Can you please just receive this? I'm here. I'm reading a book. It's okay." I realized that selfless service was not martyred service. And that I didn't need to heal myself all the time or have all the answers or be stoic and unyielding. That I didn't need to perform or be considered worthy to be deserving of care. That someone doesn't need to know me, much less love me, to give me that care. And for me to receive that would be a profound gift to them.

That relative stranger at the hospital taught me some of the most vital truths I was eventually going to need to confront head-on, beginning with being deserving of receiving care. Receiving love. Receiving joy.

Finding Joy by Romancing the Self

As I said earlier, we are responsible for the joy that we feel. The way we cultivate that joy and keep it supple and nourished is through romance. Romance is the perfect trifecta of intention, beauty, and intimate connection. Every single area of our lives can be fed by that energy, not just our personal and sexual relationships. Romancing oneself is an opportunity to sink into the practice of devotion to your own intention—a practice of the highest mindfulness of the highest expression of your highest self—and then alchemizing that intention into beautiful creation. In other words, acting on your desire to pursue experiences and things that you find pleasing, calming, regulating, stirring. And in that way, when you invite romance into your life and treat your longings with the respect they deserve, you can receive a powerful catalyst for change and growth, particularly for cultivating self-love.

Practices for Experiencing Joy

Nothing is worth more than laughter. It is strength to
laugh and to abandon oneself, to be light.

—Frida Kahlo

Meditation for Experiencing Joy

Start by sitting in a comfortable position and taking five deep belly
breaths to ground yourself in your body and in the present moment.
Set an intention for how you would like to feel or what you would
like to release. Call forward your higher self and wisdom: "I call for-
ward the highest guidance available to me for the highest good of all
concerned."

Now begin a body-scan meditation with your hands in your mudra
of choice (see Mudras for Experiencing Joy below). Incrementally move
your focus from the top of your head to the base of your spine (your
crown to your root), gently releasing any physical or emotional ten-
sion points (such as in your jaw, neck, shoulders, or heart) that you may
notice as your attention travels down your body. Throughout the med-
itation, notice your breath. If at any time you find yourself connecting
to your thoughts, bring your awareness back to your breath and the rise
and fall of your chest.

Let your practice stretch anywhere between five and twenty-five
minutes. Allow the length of your meditation to gradually increase over
time as you feel more settled into your practice.

Mudras for Experiencing Joy

Ushas Mudra. This mudra is named after the goddess of the dawn,
Ushas, who as the daughter of heaven and sister of night is known for

bringing the sun into the sky every morning on her golden chariot. Just as the goddess Ushas provides us a new opportunity every day to conquer the previous dark phase, so does the Ushas mudra. The symbolic representation of this gesture is bringing life changes and resolutions. It also helps spark creativity, is a great catalyst for new projects, and is believed to enliven sexuality.

For female energy: Interlace your fingers with palms facing upward. Encircle your right thumb between left thumb and index fingers.

For male energy: Interlace your fingers with the palms facing upward. Rest your right thumb on top of the left with gentle pressure.

Place your hands as such on your lap, and visualize the serenity and calm of the dawn with the rising sun. Shift your awareness toward positive changes that you are going to make in your life. Enhance the practice by chanting, *"Om Ushase Namaha,"* silently or loudly.

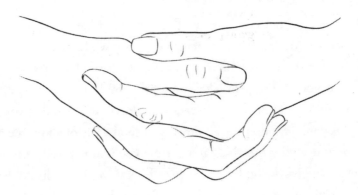

Prana Mudra. This is the gesture of life force, otherwise known as the Life Force or Happiness mudra. It is a simple gesture that harnesses the positive flow of life force energy and increases vitality and enthusiasm for life. If you feel fatigued or worn out, this mudra can boost your energy and immune response.

Bring the tips of your ring and little fingers together with the thumb. Gently press your pointer and middle fingers together, like a closed-up peace sign. Try holding your hands in Prana mudra while taking several deep breaths in yoga "power poses," such as Goddess or Warrior 2.

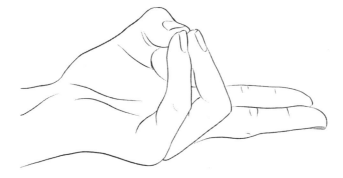

Surya Mudra. This is the gesture of the sun (*surya* is Sanskrit for sun), and, like the sun, it is believed to boost energy and metabolism. By gently resting your thumbs on your ring fingers in this gesture, the earth element of the ring fingers is eliminated, and the fire element of the thumbs is increased.

Bend your ring fingers and place them on the tips of the bases of your thumbs. Then gently place your thumbs on top of the ring fingers.

Essential Oils for Supporting Joy Rituals

Lavender: The oil of balance
Neroli: The oil of de-stressing (releasing serotonin and reducing cortisol)

For more information about how to use essential oils, see page 141.

Movement for Experiencing Joy

Simply choose anything that brings you joy—dance, social sports, competitions with friends. Dance can be particularly fun for this, as you allow your body and heart to listen to the beat and move from the soul.

Yoga Postures for Joy:

- **Sun Salutation** (see page 214)
- **Happy Baby Pose**
    - Lying on your back, bring your legs into your chest.
    - Bend your knees to allow your hands to grab for your big toes, feet, ankles, or pant legs.
    - Try to keep your lower back connected to the ground, and relax your body.
    - You can gently rock back and forth, perhaps stretching one leg and then the other, or both together.

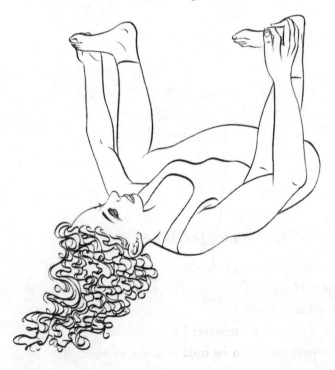

- **Dancer's Pose**
    - Bring your feet together or stand with them at hip-width distance, hands at your sides, palms facing inward.
    - Allow your arms to reach up over your head.
    - Bend your right leg behind you. Turn your right palm to face out, away from the body, bringing the hand down behind you to meet the inside of your ankle.
    - Once you have your grip, gently kick into the hand with your right leg, allowing that extension to begin elongating the pose, tipping you forward, left hand leading the way to provide balance.
    - Remain grounded in your left leg, bending if you need further stability.
    - When done, slowly release the pose, and repeat on the other side.

- **Half Bow Pose**
    - This pose is considered to be a warm-up for Over the Moon pose, or it can be used as a variation for those who are not

ready for Over the Moon or who are not able to balance in that way. Both poses stretch the same muscles (namely the hip flexors) and are considered heart openers.

- Begin in a tabletop position with your hands on the floor in line with your shoulders and the knees in line with the hips.
- Shift your weight into the right hand and the left knee and toes.
- Extend your left arm in front of you and your right leg behind you so that they are parallel to the floor.
- Slowly reach for your foot or ankle with your left hand, continuing to press the right hand and left knee and toes into the floor to find stability.
- Gently kick your right foot into your left hand to create space, stretching the hip and opening the heart. Stay here for three to five breaths.
- Slowly release and come into Child's pose.
- Repeat on the other side.

- **Over the Moon Pose**
  - Start standing with your feet together or hip-width apart.
  - Shift your weight to your right foot, then slowly bend your upper body toward the floor to rest your right hand either on

the floor or a block directly beneath your shoulder. You can leave your left hand on the floor for stability as well, if needed.
- Find your balance as you begin to lift your left leg behind you, flexing your foot and pointing your toes down. You're aiming to create a straight line from crown to foot. Push into your right foot and hand for stability.
- Slowly begin to open your body to the left, bringing your left hand up toward the sky. Your chest, hips, and toes should now all be open to the left. (This is Half Moon pose.)

- Once stable here, you may bend your left knee so that your foot is now behind you. Use your left hand to grab for your left foot or ankle and gently kick into that hand. Breathe here for three to five breaths before gently releasing the pose, coming out of it the way you entered.
- Bring your left foot to meet the right, then relax into your forward fold.
- Repeat the process on the other side.

Affirmations for Experiencing Joy

My body, mind, and soul are joyful and free.
Joy has a home within me.
I give and receive joy with ease.
My joy is contagious, helping others to expand and heal.
I choose joy, I choose to be joyful, I am joyful, I am full of joy.

Journal Prompts for Experiencing Joy

- *I create more room for joy in my life when _____.*
- *What is a tiny or big joy I experienced today?*
- *What brings joy to little me, my child self, that I can do more often?*
- *What does joy feel like in my body? Where do I feel joy in my body?*
- *What is my unique joy frequency?*

Creativity for Experiencing Joy

Joy is personal yet universal. Like a gratitude practice, try a joy practice. Learning to tap into the frequency of joy and cultivate a relationship

EXPERIENCE JOY   261

with that energy allows you to have more of it. Think of yourself like a receiver; as you expand your connection with joy, you expand your capacity, your charge, and what you are able to hold. Practice sitting with joy in meditation, closing the eyes and entering the heart, connecting with a rhythmic breath, and connecting with the sensations of joy. Where do you feel them in your body? What does it feel like? Is it easy for you, or more difficult? Notice what you are experiencing: Does joy turn into light, a color, an object, a memory, or a smell?

Notice how your body reacts to joy and how you respond to it. Are you having thoughts? Is the mind busy? Or is it a pure, connected experience? Either way, everything is okay; this is about getting to know what joy is like for you. Practice this for a week and notice what you're noticing, perhaps writing it down in your journal to see your results.

- Other options:
  - Do something that brings joy to your inner child, seven years old.
  - Do something that brings joy to your teenage self, fourteen years old.
  - Do something that brings joy to your young adult self, twenty-one years old. (These are pivotal years in psychology and spirituality; connecting with these ages can reveal a lot about the parts of you that you may have forgotten.)
  - Do something that brings the current you joy.

*I attract, experience, and receive the highest version of
each being whom I encounter.*

Chapter 19

Self-Love as Divine Love

If I am not good to myself, how can I expect anyone else to be good to me?

—Maya Angelou

Even though it might seem as though learning how to accept, generate, and radiate joy would be the final step of this journey, it—most miraculously—is not. It is one more beautiful, satisfying rung bringing you closer to the healing that you seek, and a necessary one for unlocking higher and higher heights of wisdom. And it has brought you here, to the doorstep of exploring self-love. The root of the root and the bud of the bud.

A moment like this is bittersweet. On one hand, it is a momentous arrival to know that you have completed or are in the process of completing the chain reaction of the work—slowly and steadfastly navigating your way through grieving, identifying your patterns, connecting with your spiritual curriculum, and consistently holding space for all of the above. Because that is what creates the clarity and fertile soil to create self-love. But it is also a stark reminder that without that work, that kind of vital devotion and understanding—the closest thing we get to the love of God—is elusive.

Cultivating self-love is similar to cultivating joy in that it requires us to investigate what we've been relying on others to give us versus the

263

264   LIVING IN WISDOM

essential nature of what we give ourselves. As in, knowing what exactly our needs are and that we can meet them—which will be more charged for some than others, and which we'll talk about in a moment.

This part of the process is about letting go of the misaligned belief that we need others to fill in this blank for us. In society, self-love has been contorted into meaning ego or self-aggrandizement, but this is not that. It's fewer declarative statements and more quiet, slow curiosity. It's about the remembering of one's own worthiness through self-study. Over time, self-love creates a ripple effect of expanding your natural magnetism and receiving the best possible love from another person.

Self-love is the reservoir that allows you to weather the inevitable chaos and struggle of life. People are going to disappoint you. Outcomes will not be what you imagined they would be. Sadness and grief are unavoidable. As we've spent time unpacking, this isn't a "bad" thing. It is simply more information for building and reinforcing your unique spiritual curriculum. But self-love is what fortifies you. It is the epicenter of that experience, and it informs how you go on to embody that experience.

Then, just as with joy, once you embody that internal love, you radiate it out. You *live in service* of love. You can begin to witness the effect that loving yourself has on other people and the ease and freedom that gives people without having to say a word. That is God's intended path—to embody love as a verb.

Self-love shapes your view of the world, which then shapes the way you interact with the world, and the way you allow yourself to receive from the world and the Universe. There is no love without self-love. To increase your capacity for self-love is to increase the love you are able to see and experience, including the love from God. So, in its essence, self-love *is* Divine love.

The intertwined, inseparable nature of self-love and Divine love has

SELF-LOVE AS DIVINE LOVE 265

been the topic of study for theologians and artists for centuries. Consider this poem by Rumi, the Sufi mystic:

> *I desire you*
> *more than food*
> *and drink*
> *My body*
> *my senses*
> *my mind*
> *hunger for your taste*
> *I can sense your presence*
> *in my heart*
> *although you belong*
> *to all the world*
> *I wait*
> *with silent passion*
> *for one gesture*
> *one glance*
> *from you*

That is some hot, sensually charged energy. It is deep, carnal craving for connection. And yet it is not romantic love that Rumi is describing but rather the agony and the ecstasy of loving God. Of hungering for that love. That love is revealed to us only when we open the portal through self-love, and so in many ways, it is also a desire for self.

Similarly, in Vedic tradition, there is a story about Radha and Krishna, two deities who are so madly in love with one another, so passionately entangled in their twin-flame romance, that you typically say their names as one word: Radha-Krishna. The tale has it that they meet only once, then go on to spend their entire lives longing for one another—even though theirs is a love that's never been manifested in physical form. It is believed to be the definition of love: a devotion to

266   LIVING IN WISDOM

something you cannot see, a deep belief in and a dedication to something that doesn't exist in the physical world. That certainly describes our relationship with God. But it also describes our relationship with self.

The way you touch the seemingly untouchable is through practice. Through process. In terms of understanding self-love in the context of your journey so far, it is the outgrowth of self-care. Self-care is the nourishment required to grow self-love. It is how you can actively support that love and encourage it to expand. Self-love is the essence of how you're able to be yourself. It is the ability to feel the highest expression of this human experience and how you're able to then serve and inspire other people. And so this path of releasing and living with intention and devotion to self that you have been on is the necessary precursor to this moment. Because those are the practices necessary to uphold and feed that love and make it an effortless experience.

Recognizing Your Barriers to Self-Love

There are, not surprisingly, many barriers standing between us and love. It's often a potent combination stemming from how love was modeled for us, whether it was ever weaponized against us or used to manipulate, and sometimes even our understanding of what exactly love is—and what it means to be loved.

The leading barrier to love is a product of your personal experience with love. Not so much in the sense of whether or not you were actually loved, but whether the love you received was based on the other person observing you and loving you in the way you needed to be loved in order to feel safe. Did you receive that kind of love in your family? From your friends? How was love modeled for you? If healthy love wasn't demonstrated by your parents, then it's likely you and your siblings didn't have practice exchanging love.

I experienced this with my previous partner, for whom love was so ensnared in pain and fear. He wasn't shown the kind of love that he needed; he wasn't given better himself, and so for him, there was no

SELF-LOVE AS DIVINE LOVE 267

other way to love. What he gave me was the highest capacity and absolute best of what he was capable of giving as that version of himself. As I processed our marriage after it ended, I eventually realized our relationship wasn't all fraudulent. It was ill-fated because we were unequally yoked in how we gave and received love. His love felt terrible to me— and for my own well-being, I often felt as though I had to reject it—but I was also having to face my programming around love and my misunderstandings of it. The roles that I would take on, as many of us do, to dip down into the despair of his trauma or his toxicity or to feel like I needed to fix him or earn something for him to love me. I still needed to learn that none of those seeds will ever, ever bear fruit and that they go against the cosmic law of giving and receiving.

Eventually, I was able to heal around love—in a way that felt preordained. I had a reading with an astrologer in 2014, and she said, so nonchalantly, "Right around the age of thirty-two, you might start investigating your relationship to love. You might notice that you have a new awareness of your thoughts on marriage, your connection with your partner, and your relationship." It was very casual and seemingly open-ended—as though it were up to me to interpret it in whatever way I wanted to. For a long time, I took it to mean that I should stay in the relationship and fight for it because my sense of what real love looked like was so off the mark. But after getting divorced, I had a reading with Dr. Suhas Kshirsagar, an expert in Vedic astrology. He took one look at my chart and said, without any knowledge of my personal life, "You're set to be having a divorce this year—has it happened?" He said it so easily, so frankly, and with absolutely no judgment. That alone was so healing because I finally saw that my divorce wasn't an enormous failure; it was just another choice that I was making in a long line of choices. It was so freeing that I started laughing, then confirmed it had already happened a few months prior. The astrologer said, "Okay, perfect. That's the intended path. Let's start thinking about the next five years." Just like that, he took away all the charge of the relationship failing. It didn't have to be the defining scenario in my life. It's one of many, many, many stories and experiences.

268   **LIVING IN WISDOM**

Since making peace with that, I was no longer as triggered by my ex. I realized I didn't need to win him over. I wasn't at his mercy anymore. When that shifted, he didn't manifest as a predator in my life. I was able to recognize that he is the way he is because of the trauma he's experienced, and I didn't need to have any expectation for him to be anything other than what he is. And that I was safe and happy. So even if he did still have the desire to suppress me, I didn't have to take that personally and play by those rules. As a result, we could begin to function as co-parents and have casual conversations with ease. And I know this is something we are both grateful for.

But this life-altering moment of clarity could only arise once I was able to understand what love even is in the first place—clarity that I'd received once I had dedicated myself to self-devotion. Commitment to the process, to practice, and to showing up for myself had also healed another major barrier I had with love: distrust. Distrust of other people, of life, and as a result, of myself. Learning that I could count on me to show up for myself in the exact ways I needed to be shown up for alleviated so much disappointment and cynicism. I accepted that everyone has a unique way of showing their love and that no love is any less valuable just because it's not in the form you expect—particularly when you're starting from a place of a very full self-love cup. But most powerfully, my devotion to myself showed me what I was worthy of.

Particularly if you are coming to this process from a place of trauma, it may be difficult at first to find ease around the idea of self-love. It is likely more comfortable to reject it—but resisting self-love is not the stand you want to take. Only self-love can move you forward.

Let Your Myth Unfold

I want you to think about nurturing self-love the way you'd think about dating someone—or nurturing a relationship with another person. You must court the self, get to know what your likes and dislikes are. What feels good in and to your body, and what does not? What are your hopes and dreams for yourself? How do you want to be in a long-term relationship with yourself? We so rarely think about how we relate to ourselves in that way. I mean, we rarely even think about how we relate to our *friends* in that way. The only time we tend to be hyperfocused on commitment and staying power is when we're thinking about romantic love. But not only do you have to do that for yourself, you *get* to do that for yourself. And experience how exciting and beautiful it is to treat yourself with that same level of intention and romance.

Once you reach that level of relationship with self, you get to start taking up a little bit more space, ascending to a higher plane of self-consideration. Because self-love is not just about butterflies and stolen kisses. This is an all-consuming kind of love rooted deeply in respect, reverence, and exaltation. There is an innate trust, admiration, and awe. It is your own ascendance in your mind's eye. Bringing this devotional love to yourself unlocks new levels of wisdom and sets your purpose alight.

So create beauty.
Live the art.
Trust the way God uses you.
Surrender to the mystery.
Make room for the synchronicity.
And let your myth unfold.

Practices for Self-Love

Your task is not to seek for love, but merely to seek and find all the barriers within yourself that you have built against it.

—Rumi

270 LIVING IN WISDOM

Meditation for Self-Love

Start by sitting in a comfortable position and taking five deep belly breaths to ground yourself in your body and in the present moment. Set an intention for how you would like to feel or what you would like to release. Call forward your higher self and wisdom: "I call forward the highest guidance available to me for the highest good of all concerned."

Now begin a body-scan meditation with your hands in your mudra of choice (see Mudras for Self-Love below). Incrementally move your focus from the top of your head to the base of your spine (your crown to your root), gently releasing any physical or emotional tension points (such as in your jaw, neck, shoulders, or heart) that you may notice as your attention travels down your body. Throughout the meditation, notice your breath. If at any time you find yourself connecting to your thoughts, bring your awareness back to your breath and the rise and fall of your chest.

Let your practice stretch anywhere between five and twenty-five minutes. Allow the length of your meditation to gradually increase over time as you feel more settled into your practice.

Mudras for Self-Love

Lotus Mudra. Also known as Padma mudra, this is a mudra for compassion. It helps anchor your awareness back to your heart. In fact, it is believed to enhance the virtues of the heart, which are compassion, kindness, generosity, and connection. When we practice Lotus mudra, we give ourselves the gift of loving-kindness.

Take a steady breath in and a steady breath out. Bring your palms to touch at the center of your chest in Anjali mudra (page 122). Keep your thumb and pinkie fingers touching and slowly begin to open the middle three fingers, as if your fingers were the petals of a lotus flower blossoming. Stay here for about a minute, and, if it is comfortable for you, close your eyes, noticing where you feel expansiveness in your body. Allow your awareness to rest in the space at the center of the chest, feeling a sense of luminosity there. Stay for as long as you like, bathing in your own radiance.

When you are ready, slowly float your hands down with the palms facing up so that the backs of your hands rest on your thighs. Gently float your eyes open and notice any shifts you feel here. Keep this sense of softness with you as you move throughout your day, remembering that, just like the lotus flower, you, too, can experience growth in the muddy waters. You always have the potential to move toward the light and realize your fullest potential.

Citta Mudra. This mudra is a gesture of tranquility. It is believed to bring mental clarity, stress relief, and balance.

Sit in a comfortable position with a straight spine. Press your palms together in front of your heart in Anjali mudra. Touch the pads of your index fingers to the tips of your thumbs on the same hand. Keep the middle, ring, and little fingers extended straight out. Relax your shoulders, pulling them back and down, with the elbows held away from the body.

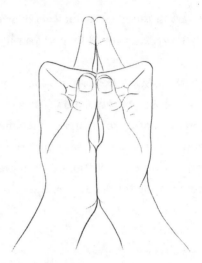

Dhyana Mudra. See page 162.

Essential Oils to Support Self-Love Rituals

Myrtle: The oil of energetic truth
Jasmine: The oil of support
Bergamot: The oil of self-acceptance and self-love
Geranium: The oil of love and trust
Rose: The oil of Divine love

For more information about how to use essential oils, see page 141.

Movement for Self-Love

This movement can be as simple as listening to your body and enjoying an ecstatic dance session, or doing yoga poses, such as a Wheel, Camel, or Hero pose, which encourage an open heart and surrendering.

Other self-loving movements can be as simple as listening to what kind of movement your body needs. Maybe it's a deep stretch; maybe it's a massage (an opportunity to relax and receive); maybe you're full of energy and would like to try something new, a new class or activity. Perhaps you'd like to be in community and do a partnered exercise. Or maybe your inner child is in need of some play—playing basketball, soccer, tennis, pickleball, or golf; or line dancing.

Affirmations for Self-Love

I am what I am.
When I love myself, I love the Divine.
I am the love that I seek.
I am the love that permeates all things.
When I choose love, I choose the Divine within you and me.

Journal Prompts for Self-Love

- *How has Divine love showed up in my life this week?*
- *How do I show up in love even when I feel triggered and challenged?*
- *What is the most self-loving thing I can commit to?*
- *What does self-love feel like in my body, and where do I feel it? How would I describe it?*
- *What cultivates self-love in my life? Is it how I speak to myself? How I listen to my body? How I connect with my community? How can I cultivate more self-love?*
- *What fuels my Divine love?*

Creativity for Self-Love

You can't always plan these things, but set your intention to allow yourself to perceive through the lens of Divine love. Go for a walk and experience love. Write yourself a love letter. Write a love letter to the Divine. Engage in poetry or a form of Divine love that speaks through you.

Conclusion

Living in Wisdom

I'd like you to once again find a comfortable place to sit. Take a moment to settle in. Maybe ease into a few rounds of belly breathing, a gentle stretch. Revisit your affirmation.

Now think back to the first time you heard my voice in your mind as you started reading this book. How were you feeling in your body? In your mind? In your spirit? How easily were you able to shift into quiet? Into receptivity? How much of your lungs could you fill with breath? Was being still available to you? What feelings did the idea of being gentle or kind to yourself kick up? How has your mission statement for yourself anchored you? Changed with you? What have you glimpsed of yourself? Has there been maturation in your recapitulation? Evolution in your absolution?

Now arrive. Here. This is by no means the final point in your destination; it is not the ultimate of what you can achieve. But this is the part of the journey you were born for. Through your devotion and dedication to yourself throughout these pages, you are going forth with the most powerful tools you could have: Acceptance. Surrender. Choice made at the highest level. An expanded capacity to bear witness, to yourself and others. All in pursuit of purpose. Of love. Of wisdom.

We have no way of knowing how much of this journey we can accomplish in our lifetime. The burden of crossing the entire mountain range in the name of unraveling all of the trauma or suffering or

276 CONCLUSION

pain woven into your life's path does not have to sit on your shoulders. Maybe it is just a peak that you summit. Or simply leaving base camp. Remember, we are not meant to fix everything; we are all just meant to inch humanity forward as best we can, with each subsequent generation picking up where we left off and moving farther with even clearer vision because of the map and provisions that we bequeathed them.

Also remember that mastery does not mean perfection. There is no archetype of mastery to achieve. In fact, that archetype is forever innately changing because of this pure and simple fact: Your individual pursuit of mastery *becomes* the archetype. It becomes the standard. I saw this in practice while watching a young chef prepare plate after plate of the most meticulous, most devotional array of sushi and sashimi. It was truly like watching a master at play—no different than a concert pianist absorbing their entire being into a concerto or a painter in their canvas. I started talking to him about his craft, and I'll never forget what he told me: "I know that I will never be complete in pursuit of my own perfection, but every new generation of sushi chef brings something different to the art." At first, that took me by surprise—I mean, how different can traditional sushi preparations really get? But what he was describing was far more nuanced than just the rice or the fish—it was the way your hands uniquely move, the way your internal intuition guides you to select fish and make the precision knife cuts. What he had described so beautifully was what I believe to be true about healing: Your pursuit of mastery is innately your own. It is both ever evolving and ever unique purely because it is yours.

Keep that idea close as you do this work. These are my teachings and insights, but this is *your* recipe. *Your* mastery. *Your* ownership and choice to take on what perhaps had not ever been done before you. What if you could find inspiration in that idea? What if you could even find forgiveness or compassion for those who could not do what you are doing or about to do? At the very least, **know that what you're doing is enough**.

CONCLUSION   277

* * *

As you begin to take these next steps on your own—though never truly on your own and certainly never alone—I'd like to leave you with what my path has looked like since devoting myself to these very same lessons. The same lessons I assured you were battle tested and honed by the fire of pain and suffering. Because there is so much love and joy that awaits you.

I have, like you might be, been in observation of my patterns surrounding love for quite some time. In fact, for years, my affirmation had been, "My intention is to be in practice with love." I had been challenging myself to be in a deep state of observation over how I love, how I receive love, and how I move with the energy of love. What I realized is that observation had been a sneaky sort of unavailability. A holding at arm's length as I took in the information but didn't transmute it in any way. A reminder, it took *years*—plus a particularly powerful full moon release ritual and prayer ceremony—to come to that realization. The realization that how I love and how I experience love is the same, regardless of the type of love it is—romantic love, familial love, love between me and the stranger I've smiled at in line at the grocery store. And ultimately, it was the realization that I needed to graduate from my affirmation and evolve: I am *in mastery* of love. I'm not here to gather all of this information about love, I'm here to emanate love. Share love. *Create* love.

It is the softening. The arrival. When you're no longer searching, seeking, and observing and have finally embodied your wisdom. I can tell you, the view from here is beautiful. I cannot wait for you to join me.

And you will. Because as you know by now, you will reach a point when healing is no longer triage. The pieces no longer come completely apart, because they are now held together by truths so deep and so clear that no amount of darkness could negate their existence. Because with grief comes the higher consciousness and embodied wisdom.

Then, as we continue to tap into this wisdom and use it for the higher good, we become fertile soil for people around us to grow. We radiate with the kind of wisdom and love that blesses others. That becomes a beacon of what's possible and gives people the courage and inspiration to keep striving on their own unique path. A true lighthouse. The kind of cosmic influence that I know some folks on social media could only dream of having.

Allowing wisdom to bloom is our sacred service to the world. Transmuting my experiences into wisdom and sharing it with loved ones and those I teach is how *I* serve. Now, it is your destiny. Everything you have experienced up to this moment has readied the earth. Your gifts will only continue to grow. The sweet rewards will get that much sweeter. So take root here. Deepen. Then expand the potential and possibility that is your life. *Unfurl.*

Be patient with yourself.

Stay loyal to your process.

Become consistent in your practice.

Open your heart to God.

Devote time to your health.

Nourish your joy.

Trust your intuition.

Freedom will come.

It will heal.

Scan to meditate and practice with Devi

Thank You

GOD, I THANK YOU.

YES, GOD.

USE ME, LORD.

Quest Mandela, you are the light of my life, little bear. I am so grateful to have the honor of loving you!

Mom, thank you for my life and your love. I am so proud of you. You are so gifted, talented, brilliant, and beautiful. I am so proud of us!

Auntie, thank you for being in my life and being a kind and generous place to rest.

Darren, you have had the best smile since you were a little boy. Thank you for your heart and creativity. May God bless and expand our family line for all time, in every lifetime. I love you.

Deysi and Sulma, I have learned so much from you. Thank you for everything you have done for my family. Thank you for your hearts and your wisdom and your strength.

Humble Lukanga, my best friend and sacred brother, thank you for Everything you are in my life. I am honored to be your sister.

Lenard, Jess, Ret, Tati, April, Andre, Ila, Maya, Angela, Yvonne, Boogie, Lailah, Krista, Sheila, Simone, Dahi, Ajay, John Three, Ave... love you deep.

Samantha Timmons, I am endlessly grateful to you in so many ways. Thank you for all that you are! Love you.

The big four, thank you for joining me to complete our karma this lifetime. We are free.

280 **THANK YOU**

Laura, Crystal, Mikale, David, Wilbo, Candice, and all of Lifeline. *Thank you for everything and more.*

Michelle Wu, Christina Towne, and the whole Color Theory team, thank you for everything you have brought to my work. I pray success covers you.

Jared, you are magic! Thank you for your vision and your friendship. I appreciate you and the entire team at 4B Advisory so much!

Dr. Deepak Chopra, your life has changed the world and me in such profound ways. I love you and I thank you.

Carlos Segarra, this could not have happened without you! Thank you for pushing me forward and having my back.

Rachel Holtzman, the woman carved from Diamond. This journey with you has been the adventure of a lifetime. Thank you from the bottom of my heart for all you have given to this book. I am in awe of your gift. It has been an honor and true privilege to work with you.

Nana K. Twumasi, I appreciate who you are and what you bring to the world. Thank you for bringing me to Balance. Thank you to the whole team at Hachette and Balance.

Andrianna deLone and CAA, thank you.

Elizabeth Lesser, Carla Goldstein, and everyone at the Omega Institute for Holistic Studies, thank you for all you have done over the last fifty years. Love you.

Drs. Ron and Mary Hulnick, Kathy Golden, David Elliott, Karie Gonia, Vish Chatterji, Darryl Gaines...thank you for your mastery and wisdom. Love you.

Mallika Chopra, Tonia O'Connor, Dr. Sheila Patel, Jennifer Johnson, and my Chopra Global family, what we created in the pandemic was miraculous. That time together will stay in my heart forever.

The Black Effect Podcast Network, Dollie Bishop, Jacquees Peace, and all who have helped me with *Deeply Well* and *Dropping Gems*, thank you!

Maravilla, your beaches have brought me so much healing and happiness. Thank you to the entire staff for the light you have graciously shared. You feel like heaven to my heart.

Joe Kay and all of Soulection, thank you for the inspiration and the healing.

Pac, Frida, Rumi, Georgia, James, Maya, Nelson, Oprah, Fred, LeVar, Anthony, Kendrick...thank you for existing, thank you for saying yes.

Jas Waters, Wayne, Nipsey...I love you. I miss you. Thank you.

Notes

CHAPTER 8

1. https://www.ncbi.nlm.nih.gov/pmc/articles/PMC6305886/.

CHAPTER 12

1. https://www.psychologytoday.com/us/blog/understanding-grief/201710/death-and-bereavement-among-the-lakota.
2. https://www.cancercareontario.ca/sites/ccocancercare/files/assets/ACCUGriefAndLoss.pdf.
3. https://pulitzercenter.org/stories/karoshi-deep-look-japans-unforgiving-working-culture.
4. https://journals.sagepub.com/doi/10.1177/00302228231158914.
5. https://www.ncbi.nlm.nih.gov/pmc/articles/PMC6844541/; https://www.healthline.com/health/grief-physical-symptoms#heart-health.
6. https://www.medicalnewstoday.com/articles/ptsd-and-autoimmune-diseases#:~:text=Psychological%20stress%20may%20impair%20immune,overactive%20immune%20system%20over%20time.
7. https://time.com/6319549/silencing-women-sick-essay/.
8. https://journals.sagepub.com/doi/abs/10.1177/0020764018814271?journalCode=ispa.
9. https://www.healthline.com/health/grief-physical-symptoms#heart-health; https://www.ncbi.nlm.nih.gov/pmc/articles/PMC6562884/; https://www.psychologytoday.com/us/blog/fixing-families/201706/six-signs-incomplete-grief.
10. https://link.springer.com/article/10.1007/s11682-012-9179-y.
11. https://www.healthline.com/health/heart/takotsubo-cardiomyopathy.
12. https://www.ncbi.nlm.nih.gov/books/NBK507832/.

284 NOTES

13. https://onlinelibrary.wiley.com/doi/abs/10.1002/da.22929?casa_token=PYQ p
    UCGS5z4AAAAA%3Aggj-vNeWgeZS_6ORctFe7kWo2BHnYdxJYdaHEBn
    64oiGZ2wFoJrfA8tZd3lN0sUGc81L4jp_hhrwfmw.
14. https://gut.bmj.com/content/61/9/1284.
15. https://www.fastcompany.com/3045424/what-it-takes-to-change-your-brains
    -patterns-after-age-25.

CHAPTER 13

1. https://www.ncbi.nlm.nih.gov/pmc/articles/PMC8425342/#:~:text
   =Emotional%20suppression%20is%20related%20to%20elevated%20systemic
   ,regulation%20strategies%20may%20be%20associated%20with%20systemic.

CHAPTER 15

1. Tick, *Warrior's Return*, 2014, 211.

Index

A

abhyanga, 101, 205

abuse. *See also* trauma
  acceptance of, 171–172
  emotional, 127, 170
  movement/touch and, 98–99
  navigating, 34
  sexual, 59, 98, 171–172

acceptance
  affirmations for, 191
  creativity for, 192
  essential oils for, 188
  general discussion, 171–174
  journal prompts for, 191–192
  meditation for, 186–187
  movement for, 189–191
  mudras for, 187–188
  role in purpose, 21
  shattering process and, 8–9

acupuncture, 183

aesthetics, 12

affirmations
  benefits of, 85
  crafting, 91–92
  evolution of, 87–89
  for experiencing joy, 260
  for grieving, 123
  for healing and acceptance, 191
  how to use, 87–88, 92–93
  list of words for, 89–91
  versus mantras, 87
  obstacles in using, 85

overview, 84–85
  power of, 85
  practice examples, 93–96
  for releasing and finding intention, 143
  repetition of, 89, 92, 93
  for retreating, 164
  for self-care, 216
  for self-love, 273
  for setting boundaries and being in
    choice, 239
  visual reminders of, 92–93

alternate-nostril breathing (nadi shodhana
    pranayama), 74–75

amygdala, 38–39

Angelou, Maya, 236, 263

animal-assisted therapy, 181

Anjali mudra, 122–123

aromatherapy, 205–206. *See also* essential
    oils

art therapy, 181–182, 192

authentic, as qualitative word, 94, 95

authentic self, excavating, 175–177

autoimmune disease, 117–118, 130, 146

autonomic nervous system, 69

avoidance, 173–174

awareness, 21, 29–30, 31–32

ayahuasca, 185–186

Ayurveda
  active participation in, 203–204
  boundaries in, 222
  doshas, 201
  general discussion, 183

285

286   INDEX

Ayurveda (*cont.*)
    mantras, 37
    movement and touch in, 98
    neti and nasya, 208–209
    oil pulling, 208
    therapy retreat, 147–148
    tongue scraping, 207–208
    twenty-four-hour cycle in, 202–203

B
Balasana (Child's pose), 164, 189
Baldwin, James, 171
barriers
    to existing, 17–18
    to healing, 23
    to joy, 244–247
    to self-love, 266–268
beauty, path of/way of, 12
being versus knowing, xviii–xix
bereavement practices, 115–116
bergamot oil, 272
Bhagavad Gita, 52, 70
Bhutadamara mudra, 238–239
Big Joy, 247
birth chart, 201
body
    affirmations and, 85
    benefits of retreating on, 150
    breathwork and, 70–72
    including in healing, xix
    meditation and, 58–61
    movement and touch and, 98–99,
        102–103
    unreleased stress and, 130
    unresolved grief and, 117, 118–119
body clock, 202
body-scan meditation
    for experiencing joy, 253
    for grieving, 121–122
    for healing and acceptance, 187
    for releasing and finding intention, 138
    for retreating, 159–160
    seeing need for self-care, 195

    for self-care and devotion, 210
    for self-love, 270
    for setting boundaries and being in
        choice, 236–237
bodywork, 182
boundaries
    affirmations for, 239
    challenges of setting, 224–225
    creativity for, 240
    defining, 220–222
    essential oils for, 238–239
    I will versus I won't, 235–236
    journal prompts for, 239
    meditation for, 236–237
    movement for, 239
    mudras for, 237–238
    need for reciprocal relationships, 225–235
    overview, 219–220
    practices for setting, 236–240
    role modeling, 223–224
    setting in social media, 227–229
    staying flexible, 46–47
    supporting self-mastery with, 222–224
box breath, 75–76
boxing, 239
brain pathways, 11, 39–40, 89, 119
breaking process, 6–8
break-through moments, 128
breathwork
    benefits of, 70–72
    box breath, 75–76
    dirga pranayama (three-part breath), 74
    during everyday activities, 73
    in foundational meditation, 65
    before journaling, 82
    Journey Breathwork, 183–184
    before movement, 103
    nadi shodhana pranayama (alternate-
        nostril breathing), 74–75
    overview of, 72–74
    pursed-lip breathing, 76–77
    in self-care protocol, 206
    unconscious breathing versus, 69–70

INDEX 287

bridges, building, 21–22
broken heart syndrome, 118
brokenness, place of, 6–8
Buddha, 128, 131
Buddhism, 160, 163, 173, 222
building bridges, 21–22
bullet-point style for journaling, 81
burning journal entries, 81–82

C
cacao, 206
Campbell, Sheila Marie, 171
cancer, 118
cannabis, 185–186
car accident, 3–4
cardamom oil, 239
carotid atherosclerosis, 118
Cat-Cow Stretch (Marjaryasana-Bitilasana), 141–142, 190
CBT (cognitive behavioral therapy), 181
chi, 239
Child, 189
childhood trauma. *See also* original wound
    acceptance and, 171–172
    crevice work, 34–38
    emotional neglect, 36, 127
    healing from, 169–170
    navigating, 34
    Rebirthing Breathwork for, 184
    unconditional love in, 42
Child's pose (Balasana), 164, 189
Chin mudra, 211
choices, as act of creation, 13–16
Chopra, Deepak, 54, 86, 146–148, 182, 219, xvi
Chopra Global, xvi
chromotherapy, 182
chronic fatigue syndrome, 118
circadian rhythms, 205
Citta mudra, 271–272
clary sage oil, 188
cognitive behavioral therapy (CBT), 181
cold plunge, 184–185

color therapy, 182
community, resistance to joy and, 248–252
compassion, 173
compassionate touch, 182
Complex Lived Experience, 22–23
complex post-traumatic stress disorder
    (CPTSD), 22, 173
compliments, resistance to, 244–245
consciousness, 29–30, 136–137
container, creating, 53–56
containment, freedom from, 7–8
control, releasing. *See* releasing and finding
    intention
coping mechanisms, 126–129, 132–133
Corpse Pose (Savasana), 143, 190–191
CPTSD (complex post-traumatic stress
    disorder), 22, 173
creation, choices as, 13–14
creativity
    for experiencing joy, 260–261
    for grieving, 124
    for healing and acceptance, 192
    for releasing and finding intention, 144
    for retreating, 164–165
    for self-care, 216–217
    for self-love, 273–274
    for setting boundaries and being in
        choice, 240
crevice work
    affirmations and, 89
    excavating the authentic self, 175–177
    general discussion, 34–38
    journaling, 78–80
    overview, 22
    palpating for wound, 133–135
crying
    grieving, 115, 116, 120
    healing and accepting, 174
    during meditation, 61
cultural arrhythmia, 202
cultural bereavement practices, 115–116
cultural self, 175–177
curious exploration of practices, 47–49

288 INDEX

cycles in healing, 24–25
cypress oil, 163

D

daily death, 114–115, 130
daily meditation, 63–64
daily rhythm, 205
dance, 100–101, 256, 272
Dancer's Pose, 257
Dass, Ram, 116
desires, journaling, 80–81
detox, periodic, 207
devotion
    affirmations for, 216
    creativity for, 216–217
    essential oils for, 213
    journal prompts for, 216
    as key to healing, 11–13
    meditation for, 210–211
    movement for, 213–215
    mudras for, 211–212
    overview, 38, xvi
    self-care and, 198–200
dharma, 131
Dharmachakra mudra, 160–161
Dhyana mudra, 162–163, 272
dialectical behavior therapy, 181
diet, 185, 205
digestion, improving, 205
dill oil, 239
dirga pranayama (three-part breath), 74
distrust, 268
Divine energy, 4
Divine love, 264–266, 273
Divine Time-Out, 5
divorce, 4–5, 232–233, 267–268
documenting oneself, 80
dopamine, 103
dormant self, 176
doshas, 201–204
drawing boundaries, 241
D'Simone, Sah, 114
Dying the Daily Death class, 114

E

ego, 128–129
embodied state of being, 71
embodied wisdom, 168
emotional bypass, 116–117, 129
emotional healing, 110
emotional neglect, 36, 127
energy healing, 183
enneagram assessment, 201
Epsom salt baths, 136–137, 207
essential oils
    aromatherapy in self-care, 205–206
    for experiencing joy, 255
    for healing and acceptance, 188
    for releasing and finding intention,
      141
    for retreating, 163
    for self-care, 213
    for self-love, 272
    for setting boundaries and being in
      choice, 238–239
eucalyptus oil, 206
evening meditation, 63–64, 106
excavating the authentic self, 175–177
executive functioning, 71
existing, barriers to, 17–18
expertise versus mastery, 17
exploration of practices, 47–49

F

family constellation therapy, 178
fawn response, 38
fear of change, 44–45
feelings, developing, 32
feet, giving attention to, 103–104
fight response, 38
5-5-5 breathing technique, 65, 82
flexibility, 45–47
flight response, 38
flow, creating through grieving, 119–120
food, 185, 205
forest bathing, 182
forgiveness, 21–22

formula for healing, 175
Forward Fold, 213
foundational meditation, 64–66
Four Pillars of Healing, 109–110
frankincense oil, 206, 213
free will, 13
freedom after end of marriage, 5
freeze response, 38
friendships
    grieving death of friends, 3–4, 46–47,
        112–113, 152–154
    setting boundaries for
      based on reciprocity, 225–226
      inventory of helpful and hurtful,
        229–235
      in social media, 227–229

G

Ganesha mudra, 140–141
the gap, 54
generational trauma, breaking,
    169–170
geranium oil, 141, 272
goals, 30–31
God
    concept of, 14–15
    creation and, 13
    Divine love, 264–266
    loss of faith in, 112–114
    realization that we are not alone, 4
    stopping arguments with, 128–131
gratitude journaling, 80–81
grief
    affirmation for, 123
    building capacity for, 8–9
    creating flow through grieving, 119–120
    creativity for, 124
    death of friends, 3–4, 46–47, 112–113,
      152–154
    how, when, and where to grieve,
      120–121
    inevitability of, xix–xx
    journal prompts for, 123

letting pieces hit the floor, 7–8, 111–114
making peace with, 114–115
meditation for, 121–122
movement for, 123
as rite of passage, 115–116
role in purpose, 21
stagnation of, 116–119
gut, impact of grief on, 118–119
Gyan mudra, 211

H

Hāfez, 210
Hakini mudra, 161–162
Half Bow Pose, 257–258
Half Moon Pose, 259
hand positions
    Anjali mudra, 122–123
    Bhutadamara mudra, 238–239
    Chin mudra, 211
    Citta mudra, 271–272
    Dharmachakra mudra, 160–161
    Dhyana mudra, 162–163, 272
    in foundational meditation, 65
    Ganesha mudra, 140–141
    Hakini mudra, 161–162
    Jnana mudra, 211–212
    Kali mudra, 237
    Kshepana mudra, 139–140
    Lotus mudra, 270–271
    Prana mudra, 254–255
    prayer position, 66
    Prithvi mudra, 188
    Rudra mudra, 187–188
    Surya mudra, 255
    Ushas mudra, 253–254
    Uttarabodhi mudra, 138–139
    Vajra mudra, 237–238
    Vitarka mudra, 212
hands, caring for, 103–104
Hanna, Thomas, 97
happiness. See joy
Happiness mudra, 254–255
Happy Baby Pose, 256

290 INDEX

healing
  acceptance and, 8–9, 171–174
  affirmations for, 191
  barriers to, 23
  breathwork essential to, 70
  challenges of, 178–179
  creativity for, 192
  cycles in, 24–25
  essential oils for, 188
  excavating the authentic self, 175–177
  formula for, 175
  Four Pillars of Healing, 109–110
  journal prompts for, 191–192
  keys to
    creation, 13–14
    devotion, 11–13
    integrity, 16
    mastery, 16–19
    overview, 11
    purpose, 20
    wisdom, 19–20
  meditation for, 186–187
  modalities for, 179–186
  movement for, 189–191
  mudras for, 187–188
  overview, 167–170
  steps in journey, 10–11
  supporting structure for, 170–171
heart, keeping open, 5–6
heart attacks, 118
Hellinger, Bert, 178
herbal infusions, 206
Hermit Mode, 150–151
highest version, as qualitative word, 95–96
hips, giving attention to, 103
holotropic breathing, 184
horticulture therapy, 182
Howell, Tiffany, 7
Hulnick, Mary, 89
Hulnick, Ron, 89, 168
human design assessment, 201
Hussle, Nipsey, 112
hyperactivity, 38–39

hypervigilance, 39
hypoactivity, 38–39
hyssop oil, 141

I

I will versus I won't, 235–236
IBS (irritable bowel syndrome), 118, 130
immune system, 117–118
impermanence of joy, 245–246
inflammation, 130, 185, 206, 207
infrared therapy, 185
integrated state of being, 71
integrity, 16
intellectual approach to healing, xviii–xix
intention. *See also* releasing and finding
    intention
  affirmations and, 87
  finding, 135–137
  magnetism of, 30–31
  practices for finding, 138–144
  setting, 66–68
intentional touch, 182
irritable bowel syndrome (IBS), 118, 130

J

Jack, Dana, 118
jasmine oil, 272
Jnana mudra, 211–212
journaling
  about qualitative words, 91
  bullet-point style for, 81
  burning entries, 81–82
  crevice work, 78–80
  exploring past entries, 83
  foundation practice, 82–83
  as mechanism of release, 78–80
  prompts
    for experiencing joy, 260
    for grieving, 123
    for healing and acceptance, 191–192
    for releasing and finding intention,
      143
    for retreating, 164

INDEX   291

for self-care, 216
for self-love, 273
for setting boundaries and being in
choice, 239
in self-care protocol, 206
self-inquiry prompt, 82
types of, 80–81
without judgment, 80–82
Journey Breathwork, 183–184
joy
affirmations for, 260
Big Joy, 247
challenges of experiencing, 241
connecting with personal, 242–244
creativity for, 260–261
defining, 242
essential oils for, 255
inevitability of, xix–xx
journal prompts for, 260
meditation for, 253
movement for, 256–260
mudras for, 253–255
practices for experiencing, 253–261
recognizing barriers to, 244–247
resistance to community and, 248–252
role in purpose, 21
romancing the self, 252
tiny joys, 247–248
joyful discipline, as qualitative word, 94–95

K
Kahlo, Frida, 253
Kali mudra, 237
Karma Bliss, 5
keys to healing
creation, 13–14
devotion, 11–13
integrity, 16
mastery, 16–19
overview, 11
purpose, 20
wisdom, 19–20
kindness, resistance to, 244–245

knowing versus being, xviii–xix
Koharik, Jason, 7
Krishna, 265
Kshepana mudra, 139–140

L
Lamar, Kendrick, 220
lavender oil, 206, 255
Law of Pure Potentiality, 86
Law of Synchronicity, 86
letting go, 78–80
letting pieces hit the floor, 111–114
Letting-Go mudra, 139–140
Levine, Peter, 98
Life Force mudra, 254–255
life path, finding, 128
limiting beliefs, 128, 132
Lipman, Frank, 202
loneliness, 200
Lotus mudra, 270–271
Lotus position, 24
love. *See also* self-love
barriers to, 266–268
Divine, 264–266, 273
mastery of, 277
unconditional, 41–43
vulnerability in, 246–247
low eye gaze meditation, 62–63
lymphatic system, 99

M
magnesium, 207
Mandela, Nelson, 41, 137, 146
mantras, 37, 66, 87
Marjaryasana-Bitilasana (Cat-Cow Stretch),
141–142, 190
marriage
as creation, 13
end of, 4–5, 232–233, 267–268
unconditional love and, 41–43
massage, 101–104, 182, 205
mastery, 16–19, 48, 276
mastery, as qualitative word, 94, 95

292 INDEX

meditation
being in relationship with, 55–56
benefits of, 58–61
challenges of, 57, 61
crying during, 61
evening, 63–64, 106
for experiencing joy, 253
foundational, 64–66
for grieving, 121–122
for healing and acceptance, 186–187
low eye gaze, 62–63
mindful awareness in, 62
minimum amount of, 63
morning, 63–64
for releasing and finding intention, 138
resistance to, 24
for retreating, 159–160
rumination loop, breaking out of, 60
safe alternatives to, 62–63
scheduling, 63–64
for self-care, 205, 210–211
for self-love, 270
for setting boundaries and being in
choice, 236–237
setting intention, 66–68
triggering of pain in, 62–63
Menakem, Resmaa, 246–247
mental healing, 110
metamorphosis, 150
the middle way, 173
mindful awareness, 62
mindful movement, 205
mindfulness, 62
minimum amount of meditation, 63
modalities for healing, 180–186
morning meditation, 63–64
movement and touch
benefits of, 98–99, 102–103
for experiencing joy, 256–260
foundational, 103–104
for grieving, 123
for healing and acceptance, 189–191
negative feelings about, 99–100

for releasing and finding intention,
141–143
for retreating, 164
for self-care, 213–215
for self-love, 272–273
self-touch, 101–102
for setting boundaries and being in
choice, 239
somatics, 97–98
therapeutic touch, 102
mudras
Anjali, 122–123
Bhutadamara, 238–239
Chin, 211
Citta, 271–272
Dharmachakra, 160–161
Dhyana, 162–163, 272
for experiencing joy, 253–255
Ganesha, 140–141
Hakini, 161–162
for healing and acceptance, 187–188
Jnana, 211–212
Kali, 237
Kshepana, 139–140
Lotus, 270–271
overview, 65–66
Prana, 254–255
Prithvi, 188
for releasing and finding intention,
138–141
for retreating, 160–163
Rudra, 187–188
for self-care, 211–212
for self-love, 270–272
for setting boundaries and being in
choice, 237–238
Surya, 255
Ushas, 253–254
Uttarabodhi, 138–139
Vajra, 237–238
Vitarka, 212
myofascial release therapy, 182
myrrh oil, 213

INDEX 293

myrtle oil, 272
Myss, Caroline, 234–235
myth, letting unfold, 268–269

N
nadi shodhana pranayama (alternate-nostril
    breathing), 74–75
namaste position, 122–123
nasya, 208–209
natural rhythm, 202
nature
    creativity for grieving, 124
    forest bathing, 182
    horticulture therapy, 182
    retreating in, 164
Neroli oil, 255
nervous system, 38–39, 98, 103
neti, 208–209
neural pathways, 11, 39–40, 89, 119
New Year, importance of, 88
nutrition, 185, 205

O
office altar, 54
oil pulling, 208
O'Keeffe, Georgia, 167, 175
original wound. *See also* releasing and
    finding intention
    crevice work, 34–38
    defined, 36
    identifying spiritual curriculum,
        126–128
    palpating for wound, 133–135
Over the Moon Pose, 258–260
oxytocin, 103

P
Padma mudra, 270–271
pain, emotional
    acceptance of purpose, 5–6
    embracing, xvii
    letting go, 78–80
    triggered in meditation, 62–63

pain, physical
    palpating for wound, 133–135
    unreleased stress and, 130
    unresolved grief and, 118–119
palpating for wound, 133–135
panchakarma retreat, 146–148
parasympathetic nervous system, 70
Paschimottanasana (Seated Forward Bend),
    142
peace, making with grief, 114–115
people pleasing, 126–129, 132–133
peppermint oil, 206
periodic detox, 207
physical healing, 110
Pilates, 101, 205, 239
Pilates, Joseph, 101
pillars of practice, 52–53
portal days, 88
positive feedback, resistance to, 244–245
positivity, xvii
post-retreat plan, 158–159
post-traumatic stress disorder (PTSD), 22,
    118, 173
practices
    being in relationship with, 55
    creating container for, 53–56
    crevice work, 34–38
    for experiencing joy, 253–261
    exploration of, 47–49
    fear of change, 44–45
    for grieving, 121–124
    for healing and acceptance, 186–192
    impact on nervous system, 38–39
    importance of, 29
    neural pathways and, 39–40
    pillars of, 52–53
    for releasing and finding intention,
        138–144
    resistance to, 33–34
    for retreating, 159–165
    sacred spaces, 53–56
    seasonal changes, 49–50
    for self-care and devotion, 210–217

294 INDEX

practices (*cont.*)
for self-love, 269
slowness of process, 43–44
staying flexible, 45–47
prana, 239
Prana mudra, 254–255
prana shakti, 70
pranayama
dirga (three-part breath), 74
nadi shodhana (alternate-nostril
breathing), 74–75
overview of, 70
prayer position, 66, 122–123
precious, as qualitative word, 93–94, 95
Prithvi mudra, 188
psilocybin mushrooms, 185–186
psychedelics, 185–186
psychological benefits of meditation,
58
PTSD (post-traumatic stress disorder), 22,
118, 173
Pure Potentiality, Law of, 86
purpose
finding, 127, 128, 136
formula for finding, 20–22
as key to healing, 20
meaning of, 20
pursed-lip breathing, 76–77

Q
qi, 183, 202
qigong, 215, 239
qualitative words, 89–91. *See also*
affirmations

R
Radha, 265
radical gratitude, xvii
reading, 206
Rebirthing Breathwork, 184
recapitulation, 105–106
receptivity, 65, 66
reciprocal relationships, 225–235

recording journal entries, 81
releasing and finding intention
affirmations for, 143
creativity for, 144
essential oils for, 141
Find Intention, 135–137
finding life path, 128
journal prompts for, 143
meditation for, 138
movement for, 141–143
mudras for, 138–141
Palpate for the Wound, 133–135
Release, 131–133
spiritual curriculum, 126–127
steps in, 131–137
stop arguing with God, 128–131
resistance to healing practices, 24
responsibilities, turning into rituals,
209–210
retreat
affirmations for, 164
benefits of, 148–150
creativity for, 164–165
with Deepak Chopra, 146–148
doing the work along with, 151–152
essential oils for, 163
finding right experience, 154–157
finding soft space for, 152–154
Hermit Mode, 150–151
journal prompts for, 164
maximizing time during, 157–158
meditation for, 159–160
movement for, 164
mudras for, 160–163
post-retreat plan, 158–159
practices for retreating, 159–165
questions for exploring options,
155–156
trauma-informed facilitators,
155
rite of passage, grief as, 115–116
role modeling, 223–224
romancing the self, 252

INDEX 295

romantic relationships
  barriers to joy, recognizing, 246–247
  as creation, 13
  end of, 4–5, 232–233, 267–268
  people pleasing in, 132–133
  unconditional love and, 41–43
rose oil, 272
Rudra mudra, 187–188
Rumi, 3, 15, 111, 126, 159, 265, 269,
    xvii
rumination loop, breaking out of, 60
running, 141
Rye, Angela, 225

S
sacred spaces
  creating, 53–56
  journaling in, 82
  meditating on qualitative words, 91
safe space, xiv
"Sai Weng Lost His Horse" parable,
    168–169
sandalwood oil, 163
Sanskrit mantras, 37
sauna therapy, 184
Savasana (Corpse Pose), 143, 190–191
scaffolding process, 170–171
scheduling meditation, 63–64
SCN (suprachiasmatic nucleus), 203
seasonal changes, 49–50, 144
Seated Forward Bend (Paschimottanasana),
    142
self-care
  affirmations for, 216
  aversion to, 193–196
  benefits of movement on body, 102–103
  creativity for, 216–217
  devotion and, 12, 198–200
  essential oils for, 213
  journal prompts for, 216
  leveling up, 196–198
  meditation for, 210–211
  movement for, 213–215

mudras for, 211–212
options for, 205–209
resistance to, 99–100
Self-Care Road Map, 200–205
turning responsibilities into rituals,
    209–210
Self-Care, Simplified series, 121
Self-Care Road Map, 200–205
self-inquiry. *See* journaling
selflessness, 194
self-love, xvi
  affirmations for, 273
  creativity for, 273–274
  Divine love and, 264–266
  essential oils for, 272
  general discussion, 263–266
  journal prompts for, 273
  letting your myth unfold, 268–269
  meditation for, 270
  movement for, 272–273
  mudras for, 270–272
  practices for, 269
  recognizing barriers to, 266–268
self-massage, 101–104, 204
self-mastery, supporting with boundaries,
    222–224
self-silencing, 118
self-study, 19
self-touch, 101–102
Senghor, Shaka, 178–179
The Seven Spiritual Laws of Success (Chopra),
    86, 147
sexual abuse, 59, 98, 171–172
shallow breath pattern, 69
shattering process, 6–8, 111–114
shinrin-yoku, 182
Silent Generation, 173–174
sleep, 118–119, 135, xvi
slowness of process, 43–44
social media, setting boundaries in,
    227–229
soft space, 152–154, xiv
soldiers, reintegration of, 174

296 INDEX

somatics. *See also* movement and touch
 benefits of, 98–99, 102–103
 foundational practices, 103–104
 general discussion, 182
 overview, 97–98
 types of, 100–102
sound therapy, 181
space of pure potentiality, 54
spiritual awakening, xix
spiritual curriculum
 crafting, 126–127
 finding intention, 135–137
 joy and, 244
 overview, 9
 palpating for wound, 133–134
 setting boundaries, 219
spiritual healing, 110
stagnation of grief, 116–119
Steeple mudra, 139–140
steps in healing journey, 10–11
storytelling and confession, 174
stress
 box breathing for, 75–76
 grief and, 118
 relieving through meditation, 58–59
stretching, 101
Sun Salutations, 214–215, 256
Supine Bound Angle Pose (Supta Baddha
 Konasana), 142
Supine Twist (Supta Matsyendrasana),
 142
supplements, 185
Supported Legs up the Wall pose, 190, 191
supporting structure for healing, 170–171
suprachiasmatic nucleus (SCN), 203
Supta Baddha Konasana (Supine Bound
 Angle Pose), 142
Supta Matsyendrasana (Supine Twist),
 142
surrendering, 130–131
Surya mudra, 255
swimming, 141
Synchronicity, Law of, 86

T

tai chi, 101, 205, 215, 239
Takotsubo cardiomyopathy, 118
TCM (Traditional Chinese Medicine), 98,
 183, 202, 203–204, 222
tea as ritual, 206
therapeutic touch, 102
therapy modalities, 180–186
three-part breath (dirga pranayama),
 74
thyme oil, 188
Tick, Edward, 174
tiny joys, 200, 247–248
tongue scraping, 207–208
touch. *See* movement and touch
touch starvation, 102
toxic positivity, 116
Traditional Chinese Medicine (TCM), 98,
 183, 202, 203–204, 222
transcendence, 223
trauma. *See also* original wound
 acceptance and, 171–172
 autoimmune disease and, 117–118
 benefits of meditation for discussing,
 59–60
 choices limited by, 13
 crevice work, 22–23
 healing from, 169–170
 letting go, 78–80
 movement and touch for healing from,
 97, 98–99
 navigating, 34
 resistance to self-care after, 193–194
 triggers in meditation, 59–60
trauma-focused therapy, 181
trauma-informed facilitators, 155
traveling with tools, 55
triggers
 acceptance and, 8–9, 173
 in affirmations, 85
 benefits of meditation for, 59–60
 from joy, 246
 in meditation, 62–63

INDEX 297

truths, embracing, xvii–xviii
twenty-four-hour cycles, 202–203

U

unconditional love, 41–43
unconscious breathing, 69–70
Ushas mudra, 253–254
Uttarabodhi mudra, 138–139

V

Vajra mudra, 237–238
vibration, 37
Vitarka mudra, 212
voice memos for journals, 81

W

Wayne, death of, 3–4
weightlifting, 239
well-being area, 53–56
Wide-Legged Forward Fold, 213–214
wisdom, 19–20, 275–278
workplace values, boundaries in,
      221
worthiness for self-care, 193–195

Y

yoga. *See also* mudras
      breathwork, 70, 74–75
      for experiencing joy, 256–260
      foundational, 103–104
      general discussion, 182
      for grieving, 123
      for healing and acceptance, 189–191
      mantras, 37, 66, 87
      props for, 191
      for releasing and finding intention,
            141–143
      for retreating, 164
      for self-care, 205, 213–215
      for self-love, 272–273
      for setting boundaries and being in
            choice, 239, 240
      as somatic practice, 101
      vibration in, 37
Yoga Sutras of Patanjali, 70

Z

Zen area, 53–56
Zulu Nation Tribes of South Africa, 178

About the Author

Devi Brown is one of the most sought-after wellness educators and creative advisers in the country. Through her signature blend of advanced meditation, breathwork, metaphysical philosophy, spiritual psychology, and holistic trauma-informed facilitation that she has developed through her own complex lived experience and multidisciplinary education, Devi has touched the lives of countless students, including renowned artists, athletes, and executives of global corporations. She served as the chief impact officer of Chopra Global before founding her own company, Devi Brown Well-Being. She is currently the host of a leading spirituality podcast, *Deeply Well*, is the author of *Crystal Bliss*, and proudly serves on the board of directors at the Omega Institute for Holistic Studies. She lives in Los Angeles with her son.